The Ancient Witnesses

A Journey to Discover Our Sacred Roots

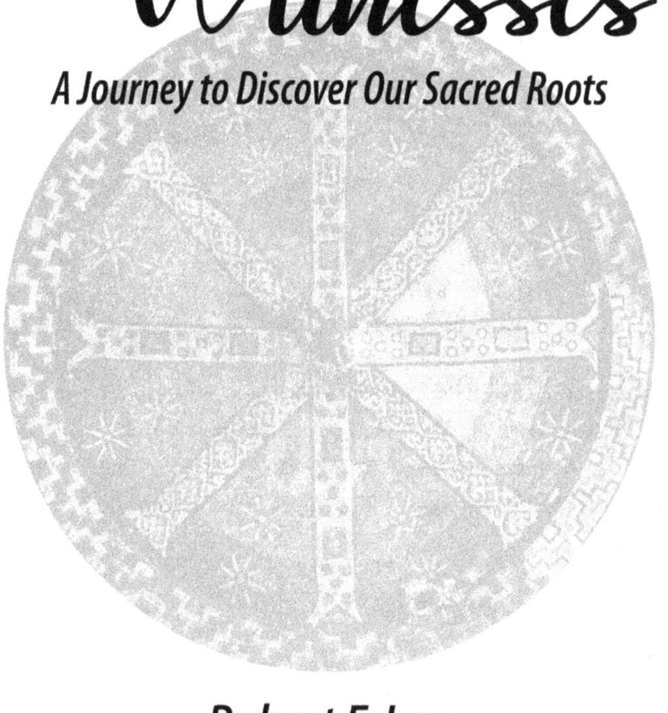

Robert F. Lay

Graphic Design and Illustrations by David Gutierrez

TUMI Press • 3701 East 13th Street North • Wichita, Kansas 67208

The Urban Ministry Institute
3701 E. 13th Street
Wichita, KS 67208

ISBN 978-1-62932-906-2

The Urban Ministry Institute is a ministry of World Impact, Inc.

For my TUMI students,
who continually supply what is
lacking in my faith

(1 Thessalonians 3:10)

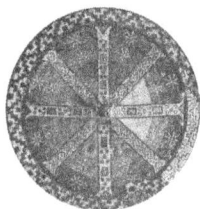

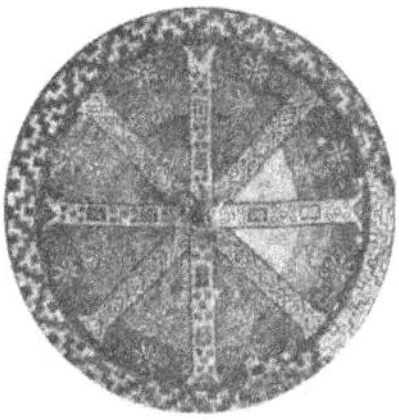

Table of Contents

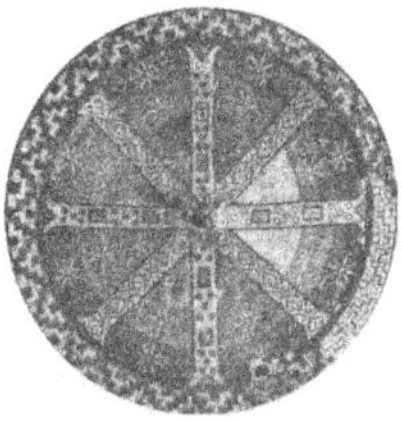

Preface & Acknowledgments

Anyone familiar with city life has encountered the perplexing variety of Christian churches found on many street corners. Interspersed with these are false churches preaching "another gospel" than the one proclaimed by Jesus Christ and the Twelve. Yet, "no one can lay a foundation other than Jesus Christ," wrote the Apostle Paul to the Corinthians. He also warned them to take care just how they built on that foundation (1 Corinthians 3:10-15). Churches not founded on "the faith that was once for all delivered to the saints" (Jude 1:3) are in danger of losing their way.

Today more than ever, urban ministers must be grounded in historic Christian orthodoxy if the Church is to withstand the flood of contemporary heresy. But given the current indifference toward the historical creeds, councils and doctrinal standards that anchored previous generations in the historic Christian faith, how will the Church maintain its orthodoxy, the standard of right belief? In a book entitled *Sacred Roots: A Primer in the Great Tradition*, the Reverend Dr. Don Davis offered both an apologetic and a blueprint for reconnecting urban pastors to Nicene orthodoxy—the foundational-doctrinal beliefs of the early Church.[1] As Davis writes, "We seek to understand (the Great Tradition) as the sacred roots of our Christian identity, and are committed to exploring ways that this tradition may renew evangelical faith and mission in the cities among the poor" (14).

The Ancient Witnesses: A Journey to Discover Our Sacred Roots is my contribution to this important mission. It aims to awaken the curiosity of urban ministers for their long-lost family of faith while introducing them to some of their foundational sermons, letters, and treatises. The book is framed by the story of several pastors-in-training who meet and dialogue with the historical Church Fathers.[2] The historical figures presented in this book are portrayed in a manner consistent with the character revealed in their respective writings. Every line spoken by an ancient witness is either a direct quotation or a simplified paraphrase and is attributed to its source. In an earlier draft, these were set apart in block quotations. Since readers tend to skip such quotations, however, I decided to weave the fathers' words more thoroughly into the narrative. Those who follow my

---

1 *Nicaean orthodoxy* refers to doctrinal beliefs affirmed at the First Ecumenical Council, known as the Council of Nicaea (pronounced *Nai-see-ah*) convened by the Emperor Constantine in AD 325 to settle doctrinal disputes in the Church, and ratified at the Second Ecumenical Council, known as the Council of Constantinople in AD 381. An "Ecumenical Council" is one that includes all the churches. See Don L. Davis, *Sacred Roots: A Primer on Retrieving the Great Tradition*. (The Urban Ministry Institute, 2010), 30, 42-45.

2 I have adopted a convention used by respected authors. To paraphrase one of them, "I propose to bring these figures together in our imaginations so that we can overhear them talking from their various points of view." In James Fowler, *Stages of Faith* (Harper San Francisco, 1981), 41.

documentation can judge for themselves how well I've represented these ancient sources.

Not everyone who contributed to the historical development of Nicene Orthodoxy came to be known as a Church Father. The concept of *Ancient Witnesses* is broad enough to include others such as Tertullian of Carthage and Origen of Alexandria who made significant contributions though their legacies are controversial. The arrangement of the book follows the theological framework—"From Before to Beyond Time"—described in Dr. Davis's *Sacred Roots*. Each chapter unpacks select quotations from the ancient witnesses in relation to the "economy" (to use a favorite term of the fathers) or theme of each time period. In Chapter 1, "A Journey to Nicaea," readers are introduced to the modern-day pastors-in-training on a tour of ancient Eastern Christianity. In Chapter 2, "Before Time," the pastors encounter the development of the doctrine of the Holy Trinity. In Chapter 3, "The Beginning of Time," they sample the fathers' views on Creation and the Fall. In Chapters 4 and 5, "The Unfolding of Time," they hear the fathers' comments on several Old Testament themes, including the Promise (Patriarchs), the Exodus and Covenant at Sinai, the Promised Land, the City, Temple, and Throne, the Exile, and the Remnant.[3] In Chapter 6, "The Fullness of Time," they listen as the fathers exegete the Gospels, and in Chapter 7 "The Last Times," Acts and the Epistles. In Chapter 8, "The Fulfillment of Time," the pastors ask the fathers questions about the afterlife and hear answers based on 1 Thessalonians and Revelation. In Chapter 9, "Beyond Time," the journey comes to close as the stage is set for a potential future adventure.

---

3 Here and elsewhere in the book, I draw on Susanne de Dietrich's, *God's Unfolding Purpose* (Philadelphia: Westminster Press, 1960).

Many of the quotations found in these pages are from the *Early Church Fathers: Ante-Nicene, Nicene & Post-Nicene Fathers*, an easily accessible set of books. In my endnotes, the standard references to historical documents (for example II.23.1 = book 2, chapter 23, section 1) are followed by those for the *Early Church Fathers*, for example, ANF 3,141 = *Ante-Nicene Fathers* volume 3, page 141. NPNF 1.5, 365 = *Nicene & Post-Nicene Fathers*, Series 1, volume 5, page 365, and NPNF 2.11, 53 = *Nicene & Post-Nicene Fathers,* Series 2, volume 11, page 53. Additional sources are cited in the notes and the bibliography. Scripture quotations are from the English Standard Version unless otherwise noted. The ancients did not cite the Bible by chapter and verse as we do, but these are footnoted for the reader's convenience.

The story of *The Ancient Witnesses* takes place in modern day Iznik, Turkey, known historically as Nicaea (pronounced Nai-see-ah). According to the ancient Church historian Eusebius (*Life of Constantine*, III.10), the Nicene Council met (AD 325) at the Summer Palace of Emperor Constantine. The location of the palace was lost to history after it was destroyed. To aid my imagination in describing the chamber where the events of *The Ancient Witnesses* take place, I studied photographs and architectural diagrams from an ancient Nicaean church. My description of the "Athenaeum" as well as the book's illustrations are based on these historical images.[4]

Also helpful were photos from the "Walls of Nicaea" website posted by Roberto Piperno (at *http://romeartlover.*

4 The source is a book published by the German art historian Theodor Schmit entitled *Die Koimesis-Kirche von Nikaia, das Bauwerk und die Mosaiken mit 35 Tafeln* (which translates, *The Dormition Church in Nicaea, the Building and the Mosaics, with 35 plates* (photos and diagrams), Berlin: Walter de Gruyter, 1927.

tripod.com/Nicea.html) and used here by his kind permission.

Many libraries provided the necessary resources for my research, especially the Getty Research Institute Library of Los Angeles, the Hoose Library of Philosophy at the University of Southern California, the Charles E. Young Research Library at the University of California at Los Angeles, the David Allen Hubbard Library at Fuller Theological Seminary in Pasadena, and the Masters Seminary Library in Sun Valley, California.

As already noted, *Ancient Witnesses* was inspired by the vision outlined in *Sacred Roots*. I am also indebted to its author, Don Davis, for his strategic suggestions and encouragement throughout this project. From time to time, I met with a group of gifted young theologian-authors (the "L.A. Inklings") with whom I shared drafts and benefited greatly from their feedback. The founder of this group, Dr. Hank Voss, went the extra mile by reading and providing detailed feedback on each draft; this book bears his stamp.

Late in my academic career, I resigned my faculty position at Taylor University (Upland, Indiana) to join the staff of World Impact. Teaching and ministering alongside students enrolled in The Urban Ministry Institute (*www.tumi.org*) has provided the setting and inspiration for this book.

Los Angeles, Fall 2018.

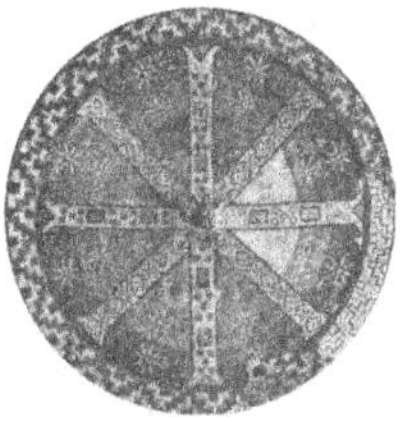

Prologue: A Heavenly Library

"I've always imagined that Paradise will be a kind of library," said Cesar, quoting his favorite author.[1]

"Heaven's library has every book ever written!" declared Preacher.

"How will you read them," asked Joseph, "you don't know all those languages."

"They'll all be in Spanish," said Cesar, "the heavenly language."

"No way," I objected, "Revelation says every tribe and tongue and nation will be represented in heaven, and so will their books."

"In that case, Ari, you're gonna need a lot of translators" said Preacher.

"No," I replied, "in heaven I will know *all* the languages."

1 Jorge Luis Borges

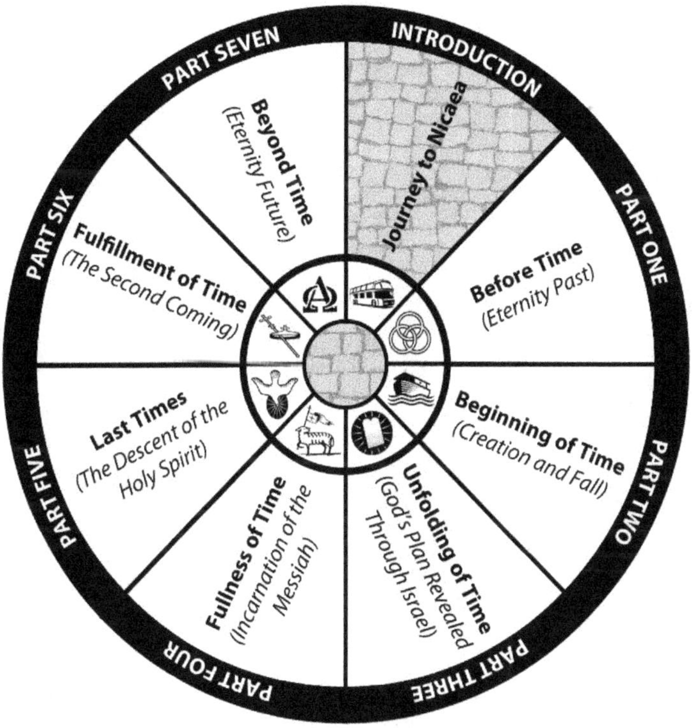

INTRODUCTION
Journey to Nicaea
PART ONE
Before Time
(Eternity Past)
PART TWO
Beginning of Time
(Creation and Fall)
PART THREE
Unfolding of Time
(God's Plan Revealed Through Israel)
PART FOUR
Fullness of Time
(Incarnation of the Messiah)
PART FIVE
Last Times
(The Descent of the Holy Spirit)
PART SIX
Fulfillment of Time
(The Second Coming)
PART SEVEN
Beyond Time
(Eternity Future)

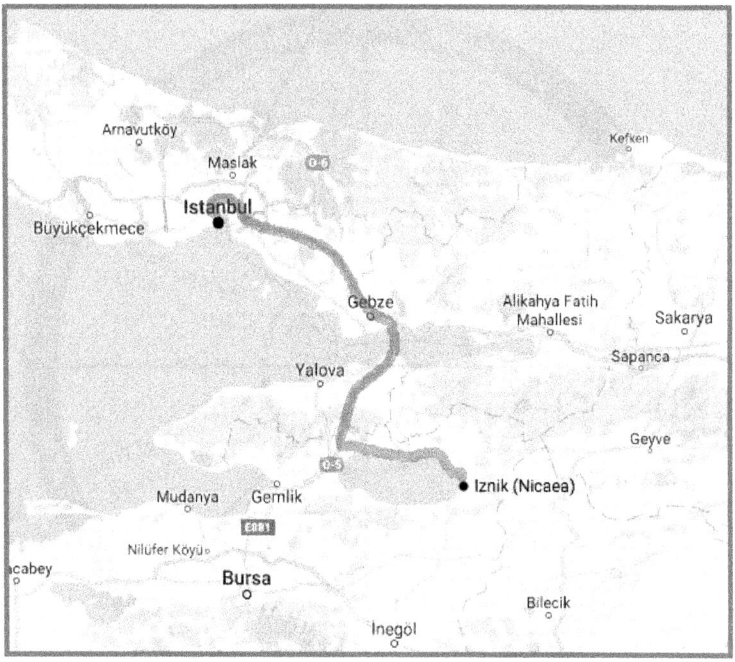

Fig. 1 The route from Istanbul to Iznik (Nicaea) is a distance of approximately 90 miles or 2 hours by bus.

Chapter 1: A Journey to Nicaea

"Ar-ay," Preacher called to me from a seat in the back of the bus, "you gonna read, the whole trip?"

We'd only been traveling an hour or so, but the warmth of the bus and the steady rattle of windows had lulled me to sleep. I had been reading my copy of Eusebius' *Church History*, but now the book was just shielding my eyes from the glare of the sunrise.

"I need to finish this before we get to Iznik," I replied, stretching and yawning.

"Where?" asked Preacher, moving up to my seat.

"Nicaea," I corrected myself, calling our destination by its ancient name. Earlier that morning our bus had left Istanbul heading east toward the city famous for the historic Christian Council it had hosted in AD 325. There, my fellow students and I would complete our study-abroad course in *Ancient Christianity*.

"What will we *see* in Nai-*see*-ah, brothers?" asked Preacher, teasing our friends in the row ahead of us.

"Let me guess," replied Joseph, "everything but you studying?" Cesar, next to him, laughed.

Our bus carried a dozen of us who had enrolled in the course, along with our guide and instructor, Father Greg, a Greek Orthodox Priest. None of knew Father Greg very well. He did not teach on campus but only led study tours. He was an older man, not very tall, slightly overweight and balding. He wore a clerical collar and white shirt that made him seem unapproachable. But he had a kind face, and he reminded me of the actor who plays Father Brown in the TV series by that name.

I had met my fellow classmates in line at the registrar's office where we discovered we had something in common: each of us lacked a Church history course credit required for a pastor's certificate. Among several appealing options, including a *History of Missions* and *Heroes of the Reformation*, the *Ancient Christianity* course was far less interesting. But the study tour would cram the needed credits into just a few weeks, and we would visit locations where ancient Church history actually happened. Halfway to Nicaea, Father Greg told us to introduce ourselves in small groups.

"Everybody knows Ar-ay," said Preacher, slapping my knee.

"How do you spell that?" asked Joseph, suspecting Preacher's pronunciation was off.

"A-r-i," I said, "it's Ari."

"What kinda name is that?" asked Preacher.

"Ari is short for Ariel," I explained, "it's Hebrew, and it means lion of God."

"So, you're Jewish? asked Cesar.

"I'm a fulfilled Jew," I replied.

"What does that mean?" asked Preacher.

"That's a Jew who's found the Messiah," said Cesar, smiling.

"Exactly," I agreed.

I shared that I had grown up in a Jewish family in west Los Angeles and had become a follower of Christ at a Harvest revival at the Hollywood Bowl.

"After sharing my new faith with my family, they basically disowned me," I explained.

"That's harsh!" said Preacher.

"Yeah," I replied, "my dad didn't throw me out of the house, but he warned me never to mention Jesus in his presence."

The bus driver announced that we'd be stopping for fuel soon, so I cut my story short.

"On my nineteen birthday, I moved out and joined a mission organization founded to evangelize Jewish people in and around Hollywood. That was awkward for my family since we had relatives in the area, so I decided to open a branch of the mission in another part of the country. They sent me to Atlanta where, at first, I attended pastors' gatherings and led Seder services to raise awareness of our Jewish heritage. Then I enrolled in seminary where I met you guys."

Preacher agreed to share next, but didn't know where to begin.

"Why do they call you Preacher?" asked Joseph.

"They called me that on the yard," he said, admitting he had done time in prison. I had never known anyone who spent time in prison so I did not know what to say.

"It wasn't so bad," Preacher explained, after an awkward silence, "it gave me time to think about where my life was headed, and a chaplain helped me read the

Bible. Once I knew what the Lord had done for me, I just had to preach. So, they called me Preacher!"

"What's your favorite period of Church history?" I asked.

"I wish I'd lived during the Azusa Street revival!" he said.

Preacher, who was a pastor-in-training, explained that his denomination—the Church of God in Christ—expected all God's people to be filled with the Spirit and to exercise spiritual gifts.

"What's your church?" Preacher asked Joseph.

"We're Baptists," said Joseph.

"Southern Baptist?" asked Cesar.

"National Baptist Convention of America," said Joseph, "what else do you want to know?"

"Were you named for Joseph in the Bible?" asked Preacher.

"I don't know," he admitted, "I never asked."

When the bus stopped for refueling, we got off and waited in line for the only bathroom for miles around. Afterwards, I walked around back of the station to look out at the countryside. My friends were there, and Cesar had just begun sharing about his life.

Cesar was one of the smartest guys I'd ever met, and he had a wonderful way with words: as he spoke, you could almost see the places he was describing, including the beautiful mountains, rivers, and people of Guatemala. Cesar had grown up in Guatemala City—a hub of drug trafficking and violence in Central America. His father was a medical doctor whose brothers had been recruited into a drug cartel. By the time Cesar was in high school he had to stand up to drug traffickers in his neighborhood, which put his life and family at risk. His decision to prepare for ministry by attending a seminary in the U.S. eased the pressures on his family and probably saved his life.

After Cesar shared his story we boarded the bus again and continued getting to know one another. As our bus carried us deep into the Turkish countryside we saw evidence of the earthquake which had devastated the country just two years before.[1] There were collapsed bridges and demolished buildings, but also some new construction underway.

Constantine's Palace

"How's the book?" asked Preacher, pointing to my copy of Eusebius' *Church History*, after we'd run out of things to talk about.

"Haven't you started reading it yet?" I asked, since it was required for our class.

"What's it about?" he asked, ignoring my question.

"It's about the early Church," I replied.

Preacher waved his hand for me to continue.

"It tells the story of Christianity from the Nazarene to the Nicene Council' I added, reading from the book jacket.

"That happened in Nicaea, right?"

"That's why they call it the Nicene Council, Preacher" said Cesar, rolling his eyes.

1 The Izmit earthquake, registering at 7.6 on the Richter Scale, struck Izmit in central Turkey on August 17, 1999, and was one of the most severe earthquakes in recorded history.

"The book says they met at Constantine's summer palace," I added.

"We gonna see that?" asked Preacher.

"The palace? No, it's lost," I explained.

"How do you lose a palace?" asked Preacher.

"Maybe in the earthquake," said Cesar.

"I think it's been missing a lot longer than that," I said.

As our bus approached Nicaea late that afternoon, Father Greg pointed out many historical sites as we passed them on the road. At the city limits, our bus threaded the *Istanbul Kapisi* gate built by ancient Romans. Soon after, the city center came into view with ancient churches and mosques and historical ruins visible in every direction. When we arrived at our hotel, Father Greg reminded us to finish our book reviews and told us to get a good night's sleep. I unpacked quickly and set up my laptop to work. Before I could begin, Joseph was at my door.

"Ready for an adventure?" he asked.

"I have to finish my book report," I replied.

"Take a walk with us first," he coaxed. I could see Preacher and Cesar, waiting at the end of the hall.

"Where are you going?" I asked.

"To find Constantine's palace!"

"It's lost," I repeated, "nobody knows where it's at!"

"That's why we're going to look for it," Joseph laughed, "it's an adventure!"

I didn't feel much like working at that moment, so I closed my laptop and went with them, hoping I would not regret my decision.

"Where are you going to look?" I asked when we caught up to the others.

Cesar handed me a map—Historical Sites of Nicaea—he'd picked up in the motel lobby.

"According to this," he said, "the ruins of Constantine's summer palace may have been flooded by the lake."

The street we were walking on led to Lake Iznik on the western edge of town. There in the distance was an ancient stone wall which, from our viewpoint, appeared to hold back the water. The evening was cool and peaceful, and the wall slowly rose before us as we approached it. It was almost dark when we reached the wall. Cesar read aloud from the map in the fading light:

The fortified city walls provided a barrier against attack in medieval times, guarding the city's access to water and supplies when under siege.

"We should probably head back now," I suggested. Cesar, pretending not to hear me, began climbing a heap of rocks piled against the wall.

"Where are you going?" I called.

"We haven't found the palace yet," he called back. We watched as he scaled the rubble, and then used cracks in the wall to climb the rest of the way up. On top, the wall was apparently flat. Cesar stood up and looked out, comparing the map to whatever lay beyond the wall. Joseph, Preacher and I stretched out on the grass to wait. When we looked up again, Cesar was gone. We got up and moved back from the wall for a better view, but Cesar was nowhere in sight.

"Maybe he climbed down the other side," said Joseph.

"Into the lake?" asked Preacher.

"We don't really know what's over there," Joseph replied. With that, he began climbing the wall where Cesar had climbed up. Preacher soon followed. I moved back in time to see them walking atop the wall in opposite directions, calling out for Cesar. Soon they were out of sight, and even the sound of their voices faded.

Feeling restless, I decided to climb up before it was too dark to see anything. Following their moves, I made my way up the rubble pausing to scope out potential footholds in the wall. Luckily, the cracks were wider than

Fig. 2 Remains of the 4th century Byzantine wall constructed with thin brick and courses of marble. Iznik, Turkey. By courtesy of Roberto Piperno.

they appeared from below. Wedging my hands and feet between rocks, I ascended the wall by a series of small steps until I was able to lift a leg over and lie down on top of the wall. It wasn't as flat as I'd hoped. I looked over the edge and down into the dark, calm waters, lapping below. Then I looked out onto the lake, which was black as pitch but ringed by a tiny string of lights on the distant shore. Finally, my gaze turned back inside the wall, where Nicaea looked like a beautiful garden decorated with ancient ruins. The lights of our motel shone in the distance. After a few moments I saw Joseph and Cesar coming my way, walking along the ground. Obviously, they'd found a place to climb down. Preacher was also making his way toward me, still atop the wall. I needed to climb down before it was too dark to see. First, however, I stood up and shouted to my friends to show that I, too, had scaled the walls of Nicaea. That's when I heard a soft popping noise under my feet. The rubble beneath me gave way like a trap door, and I was sliding down the far side of the wall! I grabbed for anything to hold onto, pulling a small avalanche of rubble after me and feeling the impact of the huge stone blocks on my body as I slid over each one. At the bottom of the wall, my feet splashed into the cold water of the lake—a shock to my body, though the water was only waist-deep. Now on the other side of the wall, I was cut off from my friends and in darkness.

The Rescue

My eyes adapted to an eerie glow hovering over the lake as I took stock of my situation. Aside from a few scrapes, I was not injured. The cold water numbed my stinging shins and left me breathless. The wall I had slid down, I could now see, was rounded like a silo. I wondered if this could be one of the towers of Constantine's palace.

Clinging to the tower wall, I inched my way along its base, testing every step to avoid deeper water. This brought me to where the tower met the wall on one side. From here the wall stretched on as far as I could see; it was no use to go any farther. Looking up, I saw that the wall was damp and smooth with nothing to hold on to.

Looking back at the tower, though, I saw a pile of dirt and stones where I had splashed down into the lake. Above that, I saw something that made me shout aloud. It was a narrow port or gun slot, cut into the tower. Wading back over as quickly as I could, I pulled myself up and peered in. Nothing was visible through the port, but I felt warm air escaping from the tower and heard sounds, like the sound of men singing.

"Help!" I yelled, smacking the stone beside the port repeatedly with one hand while holding on with the other. Losing my grip, I slipped back into the lake. Climbing up again, I called into the port until my hands gave way and I slipped back down. After a while I gave up. Resting my forehead against the rock wall, I had to fight the thought that I might never be found. I prayed. Several minutes passed; it began to rain. Suddenly, I felt the touch of a human hand on my shoulder. I turned quickly to see a man standing next to me in the water. Instinctively, I looked out onto the lake: Where had he come from? There was no boat, so he must have waded through the water from somewhere else.

"Who are you?" I asked. He said nothing, but bowing at the waist he touched his clasped hands to his forehead in a gesture of servitude. The look in his eyes revealed his empathy for my predicament. He wore a hooded robe and had sack slung over one shoulder. Why is he dressed in that costume, I wondered, is he a tour guide? The man motioned for me to follow him, and began sloshing his way through the water along the wall. I wanted to follow but was exhausted and unsteady on my feet. He came back to help: with his back to me, he placed my hands on his shoulders and the two of us waded slowly through the water along the wall. By now, wind was blowing the rain into our faces.

We came to a recess in the wall just above the water line. This must be where my rescuer had come from, I reasoned. He pulled on a weather-beaten board and a hatch in the wall opened. A light flickered from inside, and he used his clasped hands as a step to boost me through the hatch and into a tunnel. Pulling himself up after me, he closed the hatch as the wind and rain beat against it. Dipping wet and shaking from the cold, I collapsed on the hard floor of the little haven which was lit by the stump of a torch wedged into a crack in the wall.

"Where are we?" I asked, when I had caught my breath. He made no reply, but reached into his sack and pulled out a small loaf of bread and a full wineskin. He broke off a piece of bread and offered it to me along with the wineskin. I tried the bread, which was stale and tasteless, and I choked on the crumbs. Without thinking, I took the wineskin from him and drank down a gulp. Whatever it was, it was delicious and it warmed my throat and stomach.

"What is this place?" I asked, when my throat had cleared. He answered, but not in any words I could understand; I shook my head. Then he pulled a thick scrap of paper from his bag and began drawing something on it with a piece of charcoal. Whatever he was drawing, he took his time. Exhausted from my ordeal, I leaned back against the wall, closed my eyes and fell asleep, thinking about Joseph's invitation, "Ready for an adventure?"

When I awoke, my rescuer was gone. Only the stump of a torch, now extinguished, and the scrap of paper—his drawing—remained. Whether I had slept for a few minutes or an hour, I could not say. Faint light seeped in around the hatch, illumining the way into the tunnel. I held the paper up to the light, hoping it was a map to lead me back to my friends. It was not a map, at least not one I could read. The choice left to me was simple but agonizing: I could venture into the tunnel, hopefully to find my rescuer; or, I could exit by the hatch and take my chances out on the lake again. It did not take me long to decide. I stuffed the paper into my pocket, took a deep breath and began to make my way into the tunnel.

The passageway was low and narrow, and it snaked sharply to the left a few feet in. I crept slowly around the corner, aware of my breathing at every moment, fighting the feeling that the tunnel might close in on me. I stopped when the light behind me—the light seeping in around the hatch—was cut off from view. I waited in the darkness for a while. There was no room to turn around, and to back out of the tunnel would have been difficult. When my eyes adjusted, I could see a faint glow coming from farther in the tunnel. I moved slowly toward it until the source of the light came directly into view. At that moment I struck my head against the top of the passageway.

Bending over I rubbed my head. What had happened came clear as I recovered: I had seen something that shocked me, like the time a pair of racoon eyes reflected the beam of my flashlight during an overnight campout. The image that met my eyes caused me to flinch and hit my head. Even with my eyes closed that image still burned brightly in my mind. It was a pattern of tiny light and dark squares, like a child's lite bright toy, making a wheel with spokes formed by two overlapping crosses turned at an angle to one another. Against the darkness of the tunnel, the wheel and crosses looked like a clock face divided into sections.

Opening my eyes cautiously, I met the light source again, forcing myself to look at it without turning away. The sensation—that the thing was looking at me—eventually passed, and I realized I was gazing at a hologram—an image floating on a beam or column of light. I moved toward the image and, as I did, it receded until only a vertical shaft of pure light about the size of a man remained. On hands and knees, I crawled the final few feet to the light shaft, which appeared to be projected through an opening either above or below the passageway. Into the light I placed first my hand and then my arm; nothing happened. Next, I leaned my face into the light with my eyes closed. Instantly I felt lightheaded, and a low vibration pulsed in my ears. I backed out and rested for a while. I tried again, this time keeping my eyes open, but was blinded by the image of the wheel and crosses. Looking through the image, which took practice, I could see solid rock blocking my way forward. Looking up into the light shaft, however, I could see a connecting passageway above me. Being in the light shaft was like being under water: I held my breath for as long as I was in it.

After several failed attempts, I managed to climb into the upper passageway. Moving down a new branch of tunnel, I paused and looked back: how I had climbed up I could not exactly recall. Shaking off the feeling that I'd missed something, I moved quickly on though the corridor which, before long, ended at another hatch. There was no handle, so I kicked the hatch as hard as I could. It swung open inside the walls of Nicaea, and as I stepped though, I saw Preacher at a distance. As soon as he saw me, he turned to call the others. At that moment, the full impact of my ordeal hit me and I felt my knees buckle beneath me.

I must have passed out. I could hear my friends' voices around me. I was lying on my back with my head resting on something soft. When I opened my eyes, I could see Cesar peering into the hatch. He was asking Preacher about what exactly he had seen when I emerged from inside the wall. From their conversation, I could tell none of them had seen anything unusual, and that I alone had found my way into the wall. After a while, I was able to sit up and share the details of my adventure, including the strange image that had blinded me, and about the man who had rescued me.

"Who was he, and where is he now?" asked Cesar.

"I don't know," I answered, "when I woke up he was gone."

"Did you ask him about Constantine's Palace?" he asked.

"He didn't speak English," I explained. Then I remembered the drawing he left me, and pulled it from my pocket.

"But he drew this," I said, handing the folded paper to Cesar.

"What is it?" asked Preacher, crowding in to see.

"It's not a map," I said, "that's all I know."

The two of them examined the drawing without saying a word, then passed it to Joseph who looked it over carefully.

"Is this the image you saw in the cave, Ari" asked Joseph, handing the paper back to me. Here in the light the drawing looked more or less like the wheel and crosses that had stunned my eyes. I nodded; Cesar climbed into the open hatch and began making his way down the corridor.

"This must be the passage to the Emperor's Palace!" we heard him call out.

"Wait," Joseph called back into the tunnel, "you don't know where it comes out!"

It was quiet for a moment, then Cesar reappeared at the hatch.

"Ari knows!" he said, grinning at me.

The others watched for my reaction to Cesar's challenge. Though I had passed through the wall, I had not discovered anything like a palace. But I was feeling stronger, so as Cesar climbed out, I got up and peered into the hatch trying to recall the twists and turns of my route.

"Don't even think about going back in there" warned Joseph, "we need to get you back to the hotel to rest!" I wondered if Joseph was feeling guilty for convincing me to come on the walk, since I had fallen. Cesar announced that he was going to explore the tunnel with or without us, and Preacher suggested we at least find the man who rescued me and try to communicate with him by drawing.

"It's not far to the other side," I begged Joseph, "besides, I want you to see the image for yourself."

Our Late Night Adventure

It was now completely dark, with only a few widely-spaced street lights showing the way to our hotel in the distance. We stood there silently for a while, until Preacher broke the stillness.

"Forward, men!" he said, pulling a cell phone from his hip pocket and using it to light the way. Cesar and I followed close behind, and Joseph, reluctantly, came in after us. As soon as Preacher encountered the dazzling image of the wheel and crosses, he froze in his tracks.

Cesar took the lead briefly, then also stopped, his expression like a deer caught in high-beam headlights. Explaining that the image was harmless, I led the rest of the way to the light shaft. Peering down into the opening, I was surprised to see the wheel and crosses floating over what appeared to be a deep cavern.

"It must be an illusion," I said, fighting a surge of motion sickness. Joseph again insisted we return to the motel, and Preacher seemed ready to agree with him.

"Alright," I said, "but first let me prove something to myself." I felt sure that what I was seeing was an illusion and that my legs could reach the lower tunnel. I asked Preacher to lower me through the opening, but not to let go of my hand.

"Don't do it," said Joseph to Preacher, who nodded in agreement.

"That's right," said Cesar, "lower me!"

After much arguing, Joseph reluctantly agreed for Preacher to lower Cesar, who was smaller than me, into the light shaft, with the understanding that he was to pull him up at the first sign of trouble. If all went well, I suggested, then Joseph would lower Preacher, still holding to Cesar's hand, into the passage. After that, I would follow Joseph, and like a human chain we would stay connected no matter what happened. I warned everyone to keep their eyes open. One by one we entered the light shaft. As before, I held my breath, my focus narrowing to Joseph's hand as I held on.

Next thing I knew, we were walking single file, like circus elephants holding trunk to tail, only with our hands, down a wide tunnel I did not recognize. Cesar, out in front, paused to look back at the light shaft we'd just passed through. I also looked back, and the peculiar sensation of having missed something returned. Walking on, Cesar led us further in, with none of us asking whether we should keep going or even where we were going. At some point our conversation took up where it left off before we'd passed through the light shaft.

"Where are we going?" Joseph whispered loudly to Cesar.

"This is the way to the palace, right Ari?" asked Cesar.

"I have no idea," I whispered back, "I didn't come this way."

Letting go of one another's hands, we lost our forward momentum and came to a stop. Further along, the passage ended at a small door set within a stone arch.

"Let's go back," said Joseph, "we don't belong here."

"Aren't you curious about what's behind that door?" asked Cesar.

"We're *tres*passing," he replied, accenting the word as if to stress its truth.

This struck me as funny since Joseph was the one who persuaded me to come on the adventure in the first place.

"Come on!" said Preacher, reaching for the door as we held our breath. He pulled on it but it did not open.

"Let me have a look," said Cesar, who carefully examined the door and found that it rested on a track made to slide into the wall. After blowing dirt and pebbles out of the track, he slid the door open with surprising ease, revealing a narrow crawlspace. He moved quickly into this passage on his hands and knees, crawling no more than a few feet before calling back,

"Come look at this!"

Preacher followed Cesar without hesitation. I crawled in after the two of them, and Joseph came in after me, muttering something I couldn't quite hear.

The Reading Room

The passageway opened into a great hall that stretched into the distance. It was so still and quiet, none of us dared to speak a word as we took in our surroundings. Diffused light filtered through an atrium high above our heads, illuminating particles of dust that floated on the air. A familiar odor—the smell of old books—filled the hall. As our eyes adjusted to the light, the outlines of furnishings slowly took shape. Both sides of the hall were lined with book shelves groaning under the weight of thousands of old volumes bound in light and dark-skinned parchment. Some were enormous folios, lying flat on the lower shelves. Other volumes were arranged upright as in a typical library, on shelves reaching about as high as any of us could reach. Above that, myriads of smaller books filled little niches.

Cesar moved quickly over to the books, and as he did there was a soft crunching noise beneath his feet. I stooped down to find that what sounded like dried leaves was in fact torn manuscript pages scattered like puzzle pieces all over the floor.

"Check this out," said Preacher, opening a cabinet to reveal hundreds of nested scrolls.

"Are those old maps?" I asked. Preacher unrolled one and spread it out on a narrow table.

"It's covered with writing," he said, "it's no map."

"They're books," said Cesar, "ancient books."

"We shouldn't be touching *anything*," said Joseph, distressed.

"But if this is the palace library," said Cesar, "then we've found Constantine's palace!"

"It might be a museum," said Joseph, "in which case *we* are *tres*passing."

"Unless..." said Cesar.

"What?" asked Preacher.

"What if this is the lost library of Alexandria!" he said, his voice trembling with excitement.

"You saw that on the History Channel," said Preacher, "it burned down."

"You're right," agreed Cesar, "and what a tragedy—that library had all the literature of the ancient world."

"What are all these books?" I asked.

"I'm not sure yet," said Cesar, but some are written in Greek."

"Lemme see that," said Joseph, suddenly becoming interested.

"He was the best Greek student in our class," said Preacher.

Joseph read the title page from the book Cesar had pulled off the shelf.

"This is not simple Koine Greek," he said, referring to the ancient language of the New Testament. "It's later, and more difficult to read."

"What about the title," asked Cesar, "can you read that?"

"*Didache tone dodeka Apostalone*," read Joseph.

"*Teaching of the Twelve Apostles*," said Cesar and Joseph, translating in unison.

"How about this one?" I asked, pulling another volume from the shelf.

"*Apologia protei huper Christianon*—it's something like, *First Apology to the Christians*," said Joseph.

"Can you read it to us?" I asked. Joseph shook his head.

"They taught us to read the Greek New Testament, not the Church Fathers," he said.

"Are all these volumes by the fathers?" I asked.

"I wouldn't doubt it," said Joseph, "there were hundreds of them and they wrote a lot."

Cesar suddenly looked miserable. He sat down at one of the tables and began to leaf through the *Teaching of the Twelve Apostles* page by page.

"The world of the early Church is in my hands," he said, "and I can't read about it." Dejected, he put his head down on the table as we continued exploring the library. A few moments later we heard him reciting,

"There are two ways, one of life and one of death, and there is a great difference between these two ways."

Still face down on the table, there was an eerie glow like a halo around Cesar's head.

"Dang," said Preacher.

Joseph grabbed Cesar by shoulders and lifted his head off the table.

"Is he alive?" asked Preacher.

Cesar rubbed his eyes as if waking up from a nap.

"Why did you stop me?" he asked.

"You scared the life out of us, that's why," said Joseph.

"What happened to you?" I asked.

"I was just listening to the book," he explained, though he could see by our expressions we did not understand.

"Try it yourself," he said, "put your head down here, next to the book."

Joseph and I looked at each other: if Cesar was hallucinating, we needed to get him to a doctor quickly. We looked the table over, but there seemed to be nothing unusual about it. None of us dared to try out Cesar's discovery.

"That's fine," said Cesar, "bring *me* another book."

Joseph handed him Justin Martyr's *First Apology*. Cesar open the book and placed it face down on the table, then he rested his forehead on the table next to it. In a moment the eerie glow reappeared, and Cesar began reciting the book, word for word. After a while, Cesar lifted his head on his own. Preacher sat down at the table and tried out the "reader" next; then Joseph, and finally me.

Soon we were all bringing books from the shelves to the table to read, or rather to have read to us. It's hard to describe what this experience was like. Cesar called it virtual reality, and with a little practice I too began to see images and to sense impressions which followed the reading. For example, while reading the *Martrydom of Polycarp*, I could feel the heat and see the flames which, miraculously, did not harm Polycarp. Feeling more drawn into the scene with each page, I lifted my head to stop the reading before Polycarp's persecutors found another way to put him to death. I next began reading an epic parable called *The Shepherd of Hermas*. This was a fascinating but strange tale which left me feeling unsettled from its opening scene, and I soon stopped.

My problem, I realized, was that I remembered very little of what I had learned about these authors and their times from my reading of Eusebius' *Church History*. Since my copy was back at the hotel, I waited for Joseph to lift his head and asked him to help me find the book on the shelf. He also found me a copy of another book by Justin Martyr, and I soon settled into a long and interesting read.

Meeting Justin Martyr

The two volumes introduced me to Justin Martyr, who lived a hundred years after the resurrection of Jesus. Justin, whose Latin name means *justice*, was a Samaritan, having been born to the people rejected by the Jews (see Luke 9:51-56 and John 4:9). Growing up a Samaritan did not keep Justin from developing a passion to learn about God. However, it did make it impossible for him to learn from the Jewish rabbis, who would chase him away from their synagogues. Justin's own family members probably shunned their son's constant questions about the family's Samaritan beliefs and customs. Justin had to teach himself to read the philosophical texts which he studied in secret.

When Justin was old enough, he set out on his own journey in search of truth. This led him to Athens—the intellectual center of the ancient world—and to his following several philosophers as a disciple. When none of these teachers could offer Justin a knowledge of God deep enough to satisfy his curiosity, he began to doubt he would ever find the true path. Then one day he met an old man on a beach who introduced him to Jesus the Messiah. Justin shared his quest for truth and the man pointed him to the Bible. In the teachings of Jesus, Justin testified, he found peace and power, contentment and a new sense of calling as a philosopher.

In time, Justin became famous among Gentile Christians as a great *apologist*, able to explain and defend the Christian faith against its critics and heretics. He traveled and taught widely, visiting Rome during an era of severe persecution and the spread of many false teachings. The Apostle Paul had appealed for justice to the Emperor Nero a century earlier (Acts 25:10-11), and Justin authored his *Apology* as an appeal to Caesar Antoninus Pius, the emperor of his times, to intervene on behalf of persecuted Christians.

To be known as a follower of Christ in Justin's time was dangerous: even a false accusation was enough to get you killed. Many believers kept their faith secret, and most churches met in secret. It's not that Christians were afraid to confess Christ, but they could not take a chance on revealing the identities of children and other family members. Also, many rumors were spread about Christians being blood thirsty ("they drink the blood of Christ!") and cannibals ("they eat the body of Christ!"). Just as the Jews were hated by Romans in the early centuries after Christ, the Christians were more so. They were the targets of violence and oppression with none to defend them in society. In publishing his *Apology* and later his *Dialogue with Trypho*, Justin was a voice crying out for justice on behalf of Christians, and for challenging false teachers within the Church. His writings and public debates made him a target, and his open witness to Christ cost him his life when he was publicly executed, just a few years after Polycarp.

After a while, I sat up. My forehead, I realized, had been resting between the *History* and the *Dialogue*, which had given me something like a parallel reading. Putting Justin's *Dialogue* back on the shelf felt like more than simply returning a book to its place. Justin Martyr was now a familiar presence with us in the library.

Irenaeus of Lyon and his Against All Heresies

Next, I chose the first book in a five-volume set entitled *Against the Heresies*. Unlike Justin's *Apology*, this book opened with many strange ideas that were difficult to understand. After listening to a few pages of it, I reopened Eusebius' *History* to learn more about the author, Irenaeus of Lyon.

Unlike Justin, Irenaeus had been born into a Christian family. His home town was Smyrna, in ancient Greece, a city famous as one of the seven cities named in the book of Revelation, and as the birth place of both Homer, the classical Greek poet, and Polycarp the martyr. Hearing this made me wish I had listened to more of Polycarp's story. In fact, at the very time Polycarp was martyred, Irenaeus left his home and family to fulfill the Great Commission, traveling to Rome and eventually beyond the Alps to the northern frontier of the Roman Empire.[2] During his visit to Rome, Irenaeus encountered the teaching of two infamous heretics, Marcion and Valentinius. In *Against the Heresies*, Irenaeus described their teachings in minute detail, disproving them from the Scriptures. Irenaeus described the heresies as *Gnosis* or *Knowledge Falsely So-Called*, saying they were "the very abyss of madness and blasphemy against Christ." Ironically, though Gnosis (knowledge) was supposed to be secret and available only to the chosen few, the language of these documents suggested they were

2 That is to Lugdunum, Gaul, which is modern day Lyon, France.

meant for a wide audience.[3] These heresies were in the form of *myths*—bizarre stories whose symbols could be interpreted in many different ways. To borrow the Apostle Paul's words, the Gnostics were devoted to "myths and endless genealogies."[4]

Many of the stories were about the gods and creation. I understood now why Irenaeus was the ideal critic for these books: he was born, as I mentioned, in the birth place of Homer and was thoroughly schooled in Greek literature and its myths. In other words, he had a mind for this stuff. We think of the doctrine of the Trinity as hard to comprehend but the Gnostic myths were convoluted on purpose: they were cosmic dramas whose episodes varied from teacher to teacher. Taking the place of the Trinity was the so-called *Pleroma*, or fullness, a pantheon of *Aeons*—eternal ones—spawned by a "Father Aeon prior to all," and producing more aeons through interrelations with one another. The last of these, *Sophia* (Wisdom), fell from her place in the Pleroma through her overpowering desire to know the Father.

"According to these myths," explained Irenaeus, "Sophia's tears were the source of all the seas, rivers, and springs. From her smile came the light, and from her confusion and frustration came the hills, the rocks, and the trees."

The point of the Gnostic myths seemed to be that God was completely unknowable, and that the creation was evil—the result of a mistake.

---

3 The original book of heresies was written in Coptic, a basic, everyday language spoken and read by the people—especially monks—of Irenaeus's time.

4 1 Timothy 1:4. It is not known if the doctrine Paul opposed was the same Gnosticism described by Irenaeus.

Being introduced to Irenaeus helped me to realize how little I knew about the ancient world. Rome and other cities of the empire were bustling centers of activity where philosophies and religions and cultures mixed freely. Men like Justin and Irenaeus were cosmopolitan citizens at home in a diverse and complex world.

Tertullian of Carthage

I was next introduced to a proud man from Carthage—an important center of ancient Christianity in northern Africa. Carthage had been a small colony which, after being conquered by the Romans, grew into a magnificent city of more than a quarter-million people. More than this, Carthage was a city of privilege in the empire. As the center of political power and influence in Roman North Africa, it had been granted special building projects and athletic games by Rome. The city also had more political and religious freedoms than other imperial cities. This meant that there were far fewer Roman soldiers stationed within the city, and a great diversity of cultures, including violent Berbers.

The proud culture of Carthage had fostered a church that was fiercely independent in its outlook. After Tertullian's day, a schismatic sect known as the Donatists[5] rose up and become a major thorn in the flesh of the North African Bishops, including Augustine of Hippo. In Rome the Church of Carthage was always seen as a problem, like the Corinthians were for the Apostle Paul.

Tertullian converted to Christianity as an adult. He was a master apologist, able to answer any question and

---

5 Their leader, Bishop Donatus of Carthage, expelled from the church any Christians who avoided persecution by hiding or failing to confess their faith in Christ.

out-debate any heretic or intellectual. For this reason, he was much admired and in-demand as a *controversialist* [6] in the Church: he had an amazing gift for words and for debating. In a memorable line, he wrote that the heretic Praxeus had "crucified the Father and chased away the Holy Spirit"—a reference to modalism.[7] But Tertullian lacked patience with Church leaders, especially bishops who were unable to match wits with him. He called some of them fools, and quickly fell out of favor with those who formerly called on him to serve the Church with his gifts. He would have died all alone but was invited to join a divisive group known as the Montanists. They also condemned the high Church leaders, and isolated themselves far from Rome in a remote place where they considered themselves to be the only true Church.

I felt kinship and sympathy for this ancient believer who, single handedly, had defeated notorious heretics, invented Trinitarian language (speaking of the divine "Persons" of the Trinity), and was known in our day as the Father of Christian theology in the Latin language. His attitude toward Roman Church leaders and his association with the Montanists stained his otherwise brilliant record, keeping him off the roles, so to speak, of the fathers and doctors of the Church.

Origen of Alexandria

He was born in the legendary city named for Alexander the Great, who conqueror the then known world and became the ambassador of Greek culture. Origen's parents

---

6 Christian leaders who would debate unbelievers in public before an audience.

7 The view that God appeared in different modes of being (see chapter 2).

were Christian, and his father—who trained his son thoroughly in Greek and Biblical studies—was martyred during the persecution under the Roman Emperor Septimus Severus.[8] The family's possessions were taken over by the empire, so Origen opened an elementary school to support his mother and six younger brothers. Origen's gift for teaching became widely known, and the Bishop of Alexandria appointed him as his lead catechist, or teacher, for new believers in the Church.

In time, Origen became famous both as a brilliant thinker and deeply spiritual man, causing his bishop to be suspicious and envious. Origen traveled widely in order to teach and to debate with heretics. Bishops in other cities heaped praise and honors on Origen. When one of them—the Bishop of Caesarea—ordained Origen as a priest, the Bishop of Alexandria angrily declared Origen's ordination invalid, and banned him from his home church. Origen remained in Caesarea to teach, study, and publish his writings. When persecution again broke out, this time under the Emperor Decius, Origen was imprisoned and tortured. As the most famous Christian of his day, his persecutors wanted him to deny Christ, but he did not. Origen was eventually freed, but died from the trauma of his torture a short time later at the age of 69.

Origen's character is best conveyed by the idea of fearless passion for the truth. He was the first Christian scholar to collect and compare manuscripts of the Bible. He authored brilliant commentaries on every book of scripture, and was quoted by admirers and enemies alike. His ground-breaking theology set the agenda for the doctrine of the Trinity for centuries. But his legacy was

---

8 Roman Emperor from AD 193 to 211.

stained by jealousy and misunderstanding, and his many contributions to the Church are hardly recognized.

Meeting Ephrem the Syrian

The more I read, the more vivid the images of my reading became. Was I reading or dreaming all of this? It was difficult to say.

Now, the library held many texts in Greek and Latin, reflecting the ancient divisions of the Church into east and west. Scattered here and there, however, were volumes authored by a third major family of Christian witnesses. These were written primarily in Aramaic and Syriac, both of which are written from right to left like Hebrew. These texts were composed by the fathers from ancient Mesopotamia (Iraq), Aramea (Syria), and Persia (Iran), Phoenicia (Lebanon), and Asia Minor (Turkey).

I pulled one of the Syriac books from the shelf and flipped through page after page of the exotic, backwards writing, or so it looked to me. When I heard a noise behind me, I turned to find its author—Ephrem of Syria—standing behind me. He was a short man with a large head and a face as peaceful as a still pond. His robe was beautifully embroidered and he wore a white turban or head scarf. He had a broad forehead, a large flat nose and laughing eyes—just imagine Santa Claus with a closely-cropped beard.[9]

"So many profound works," I said, pointing at the shelves. Ephrem just waved his hand as if to say, "It's nothing."

---

9 These imaginative details and those of Ephrem as a singing child prodigy are my impression of the Church Father but not based on reported facts.

"I'm reading one of your books!" I said, eager to talk to him.

"What *are* books?" he replied to no one in particular.

I could not think of what to say to that. I stared at the open book with its exotic handwriting. Then, I answered,

"It's where the words are!"

He looked at me in a way I'll never forget: it was the same look, I believe, that Jesus gave the rich young ruler in Mark's Gospel, where it says, "Jesus looked at him and loved him."[10] In any case, Ephrem touched his finger to his forehead and then patted his chest and said,

"The words are in here, brother, or they are nowhere at all."

I smiled; he was right, of course. Then I remembered that ancient culture was oral as opposed to written or literate.

"Besides," he continued, "which of these books can sing?"

Sing? I thought to myself, *who expects a book to sing?* Then it hit me: the words in the book I had been looking at—Ephrem's own book—were arranged in strophes like poetry, they were songs, hymns.

"Books can't sing," I agreed, "but they can teach you what to sing, because they're hymns, your hymns!"

"The *Midrasha*?" he asked, furrowing his brow.

"I don't know," I replied, "what does that mean?"

Midrasha, Ephrem explained, were special songs composed in order to teach. Then he told me about his church school in Nisibis (ancient Turkey), his home city, where the teachers would sing their lessons to their

---

10 Mark 10:21 NIV.

students, who would echo them to learn the lesson. Then, in a voice as clear as a trumpet, Ephrem sang out,

In the midst of the Church is a fountain
Those who thirst for eternal life come and drink
Thirsty ears drink up and learn and, in return,
they dispense
They drink their fill of the Scriptures and become
fountains of praise![11]

The beautiful lyrics pictured the Church's teaching as a life-giving fountain whose waters spawned worshiping streams.

Often, particularly when he had something profound to say, Ephrem would break out in song. From what he told me of his childhood, he must have been a musical prodigy. For example, he astonished his parents by singing in reaction to childhood experiences like a skinned knee, or being wronged by his brother, or seeing a man brutally punished for stealing sheep. While other children would laugh or cry, spontaneous songs would spring from Ephrem's lips, telling of the smell of warm bread baked by his mother, or the sight of the full moon on a cold night, or the terrible sound of Roman soldiers terrorizing his village.

Ephrem's community recognized his gift as from God. Bishop Jacob of Nisibis baptized Ephrem and took him along when he attended the famous Council of Nicaea. After that experience, Ephrem began to sing about the Garden of Eden, the fall of Adam and Eve, the majesty of God, and eventually even composed songs about

---

11 Maier, Carmen E. 2012. *Poetry as exegesis: Ephrem the Syrian's method of scriptural interpretation especially as seen in his Hymns on paradise and Hymns on unleavened bread.* Ph.D Dissertation, Princeton Theological Seminary.

the Nicene Creed. As we talked, Ephrem pulled one of his *Midrasha* or hymn books from the shelf to explain a passage in *Hymns of Paradise* where he describes the Serpent as if it were a dog!

"I thought you didn't like books," I said.

"The written *Midrasha*—has its place," he admitted. Then he sang a little song that described his writings as "footprints left behind by an author no longer present." I wish I could remember all of the words.

Reading Reflections

At this point I closed the book by Ephrem the Syrian in order to ponder the wondrous experience of "reading" in this place. The four of us were, of course, from a modern, literate society where reading is most often a silent and solitary act.[12] In elementary school we had "silent reading time." In this library, however, reading was an auditory experience—you literally heard the words being read aloud. More than that, with a little practice, the books on the shelves became living characters, and the more you "read" them the better you knew them. I had heard the names of Justin Martyr, Irenaeus, Tertullian and Origen before, but here they were becoming familiar friends.

As my fellow students lifted their heads, we shared our impressions of the ancient fathers we had met.

"They're like children," said Preacher.

"If that's true, then they're very smart children!" replied Joseph.

"They seemed naïve to me," I agreed, "but now I'm thinking that they just think differently than we do."

---

12 Ancient cultures were "oral" in that they prized the spoken word above writing, and read aloud.

"What are you saying?" asked Joseph.

"I'm not sure how to explain it," I replied.

"We're from modernity," said Cesar, "of course we think differently!"

"In what way?" asked Joseph.

"For us," explained Cesar, "ideas are invisible things our heads—neural impulses that register in the brain but are otherwise unreal."

"Sounds unreal to me," said Preacher, making a pun.

"For the ancients," Cesar continued, "words and ideas *were* real; they had a tangible reality they no longer have for us."

"But we can think objectively about our ideas," said Joseph, "they couldn't."

"Maybe not," said Cesar, "but have you thought about what it means to be objective?"

"Not really," admitted Joseph.

"It means we hold everything at arm's length and make no commitment to it," he explained. "To these men, we're merely spectators, but they could never be spectators. Once they see the truth they must act on it!"

"More reading will help us see their viewpoint, right?" I asked.

"The 'reader' enables us to understand their language," said Cesar, "but that doesn't mean we understand *them*."

The Athenaeum

Cesar's comment reminded me of something our professor might say, and if anyone could shed light on our discovery it was Father Greg. The others agreed we should get him involved. As we were arguing about who should return to look for him, there was a noise at the far end of the room. Then a door opened, and a man entered the hall and walked quickly toward us. As he emerged from the shadows I recognized him as my rescuer!

"I expected five of you," he said, "where is the other man?"

This was confusing since the man who had rescued me spoke in a way I did not understand. The four of us looked at one another, with no idea who the lost man might be.

"You told him about us?" asked Cesar.

"No," I said, "there was no time."

"How did you know Ari was not alone?" he asked the man.

"Ari?" said the man, "so, you are Ariel?"

"Dang," said Preacher, "he knows your name."

Just to make sure, I asked the man if he was the one who had rescued me, which he confirmed with a broad smile. Then I asked about what had happened after I fell asleep. He explained that he had been expecting the arrival of five men in a boat from a place he called *Kios*. Having found me in the lake, he feared our boat had sunk and the others were drowned. While I slept, he waded into lake again to look for them, and when he returned I had gone.

"But we are not from Kios," I said.

"I know," he said, "you are from beyond Kios." I agreed, not sure what else to say.[13]

---

13 Kios is an ancient port city on the coast of the Sea of Marmara, whose modern name is Gemlik. Ancient travelers to Nicaea might indeed arrive at the Port of Kios, travel overland to the western shore of Lake Izkin and then take a boat across to Nicaea.

"Welcome to the Athenaeum," he said, turning to the others.

"Athenaeum?" asked Joseph, "what is that?" My guide looked puzzled.

"Are you not here to use the library?" he asked.

"Oh, yes!" said Cesar, "we *are* here to use the library!"

"Then follow me," he said, as he headed toward the far end of the hall.

The Crux

Our guide led us out of the quiet hall into a circular arena at the center of a large auditorium filled with people. The dull roar of hundreds of conversations surrounded us. The furnishings here reminded me of a chapel but also a courtroom. There were choir stalls, fancy high back chairs and a table filled with old books, all arranged around a lectern at the center.[14] Our guide was busy with some sort of preparations.

"What is this place?" I asked him.

"This is where the witnesses testify," he replied.

"Witnesses?" I asked.

He pointed beyond the low wall enclosing the arena to a multitude who sat with their backs to us.

"This is the strangest auditorium I've ever seen," said Joseph.

"He called it an Athenaeum," said Cesar, but where's the stage?"

"I think we're on it," said Joseph.

---

14 Medieval monks who recited and sang the Psalms during worship were seated in choir stalls.

"Then why are they all facing the other way?" asked Cesar.

The Athenaeum surrounded us like an auditorium filled with people seated in several sections. But there were no risers or bleachers; everyone sat on the same level, and the focus was outward. Something about the layout seemed familiar. Taking the drawing made by our guide from my pocket, I could now see that it was the floor plan for this place. Seven of the pie-shaped sections were filled with the ancient witnesses; the eighth section was the hall of books.

"What *up?*" said Preacher, looking at crowd.

Each of the sections were filled with people arrayed in robes, tunics, togas, and priestly vestments. Some of these ancient-looking garments appeared to be made of animal skin, roughly stitched together. Others were woven of fine linen, ornate and beautiful, with silk appliques. A few men were clad in armor—one held a shield, another had a sword strapped to his side. Several others carried shepherds' staffs in their hands. Everyone was talking and no one seemed to notice us.

"Exactly what kind of library is this?" Joseph asked our guide.

"The Athenaeum is a living library," he explained, "the authors themselves explain their works."

"Dang!" said Preacher, "you mean we get to check out the authors and not just the books?" Our guide smiled, and Cesar looked as if he'd been transported to heaven. Once more I thought of Father Greg, who would love this place and could probably explain what we were seeing. When I told our guide there was someone else I wanted to bring to the Athenaeum, he seemed greatly relieved. I promised to return soon.

I found my way back to the hatch that opened into Nicaea and was surprised to find it still dark outside. Looking at my watch, I noticed it had stopped soon after the time we first entered the passage. As I walked toward the hotel, I knew I would need a good excuse to convince Father Greg to come with me. I thought of telling him we had discovered Constantine's summer palace, but our guide called it the Athenaeum. As it happened I didn't need to say anything. Father Greg was in the hotel lobby waiting for the four of us to return.

"Where have you been?" he asked, "and where are the others?"

"I'll show you," I said. We left the hotel and walked quickly toward the wall.

When we arrived, I climbed into the passageway but Father Greg would not follow. So, I told him everything that had happened beginning with my accident. It was when I described the image of the wheel and crosses that he seemed convinced we'd discovered something truly important.

"It may be Constantine's crest," he said.

"What's that?" I asked.

"It's a symbol based on the Emperor's heavenly vision," he explained. Father Greg now willingly followed me into the passageway. We had not gone far when, as before, the bright image shot out of the darkness at us. Instantly he shielded his eyes. I looked directly at the image as I had learned to do, and coached him to do the same. Once his eyes grew accustomed to the image he confirmed that it was an ancient symbol.

We moved slowly through the passage way, and I began to wonder if bringing Father Greg along was really a good idea. On the one hand, without his knowledge we could not prove we had made a truly miraculous discovery. On the other hand, he would know if what we were seeing was fake. With these doubts in my mind, we arrived at the small door leading into the book-filled hall. My doubts were relieved as soon as Father Greg began to examine the old books and especially when I demonstrated the reader. I also shared our guide's description of the living library, and as soon as I could I led him into the Athenaeum. The others welcomed us, and Father Greg was visibly relieved now that all his missing students were accounted for. He introduced himself to our guide.

"I am Father Gregory," he said.

"You are vigilant!" [15] our guide replied, bowing to him. Father Greg looked surprised, and the two of them talked for a while before our guide returned to his station.

"He's the one who rescued me from the lake," I told Father Greg.

"He was speaking ancient Greek," said Father Greg, "how could you understand him?"

"We understand everything here in the Athenaeum," I replied, "but don't ask me how."

Father Greg, amazed, just shook his head. Then he began exploring the Athenaeum, going section to section talking with some of the ancient men whom our guide called witnesses.

"What do you think?" I asked him, when he returned.

---

15 The name Gregory is formed from the Greek word that means watchful or vigilant.

"I've never heard or seen anything like it," he replied, "these men speak ancient Greek, but I also heard Latin, Aramaic, and Syriac being spoken!"

"You know all those languages?" I asked.

"I've studied them for years," he said, "but I've never heard anyone speaking them fluently until now." There were tears in Father Greg's eyes.

From time to time our guide went out to various sections within the Athenaeum, and would return with one or more of the ancient witnesses. Before long, the choir stalls and chairs within our arena were filled. Our guide showed the five of us to a bench where we were to sit, and began sifting through the old books on the table next to his lectern.

"What's happens now?" asked Joseph.

"That's up to Mentor," said Father Greg.

"Who's that?" asked Cesar.

"They call your guide Mentor," he replied.

"Mentor?" asked Preacher, "is that like a librarian?"

"He's going to help us access the library's holdings," explained the priest.

"How does that work?" I asked.

Father Greg paused to consider how he could best describe what he'd learned about the Athenaeum.

"All the books in this library convey scenes from one story," said Father Greg.

"What story?" asked Cesar.

"God's story," said the priest, "the Creation, the Fall—everything that's happened and that will happen until Christ returns again!"

"Dang!" said Preacher, with a look of awe on his face.

"Precisely," said Father Greg.

"Do we get to check out the books?" asked Cesar, anxiously.

"It's better than that, Cesar," I said, reminding him about what Mentor said, "we get to hear from the authors themselves!"

"Are we going to hear from all of them?" asked Joseph, pointing to the hundreds of witnesses seated throughout the Athenaeum.

"I believe we are to hear select witnesses from each section," said Father Greg.

"Do you know why there are seven sections?" I asked

"If I understood Mentor correctly," said Father Greg, "each section represents one of chapter of the Story."

"Do we know what the chapters are?" asked Joseph.

"Each chapter represents a *dispensation*," said the priest, "in other words, a distinct time period mentioned in Scripture."

"Like, the End Times?" asked Preacher.

"Precisely," said Father Greg, "but that chapter, obviously, comes later on."

"What's first?" I asked

"The *Time before Time*," he replied.

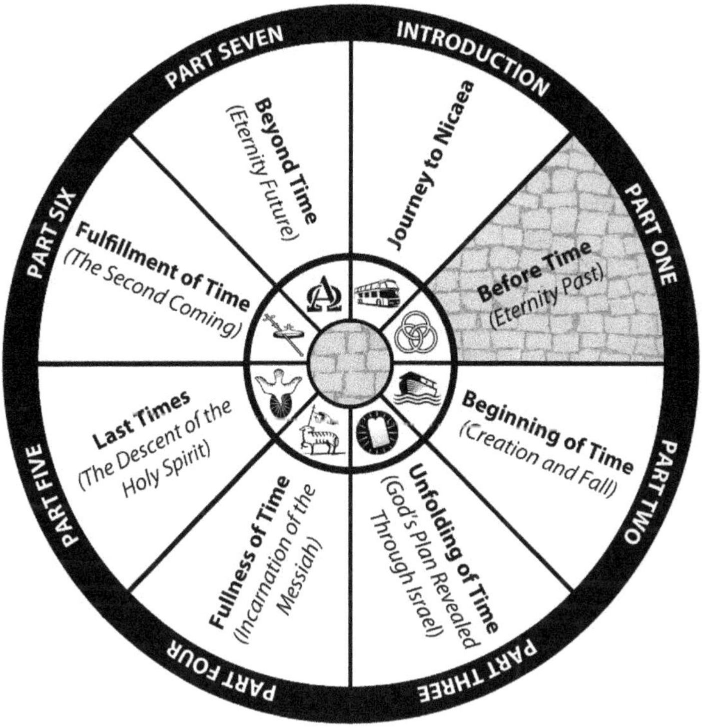
INTRODUCTION
Journey to Nicaea
PART ONE
Before Time
(Eternity Past)
PART TWO
Beginning of Time
(Creation and Fall)
PART THREE
Unfolding of Time
(God's Plan Revealed Through Israel)
PART FOUR
Fullness of Time
(Incarnation of the Messiah)
PART FIVE
Last Times
(The Descent of the Holy Spirit)
PART SIX
Fulfillment of Time
(The Second Coming)
PART SEVEN
Beyond Time
(Eternity Future)

Chapter 2: The Time Before Time

As we waited for the first chapter to begin, I pressed Father Greg to tell me what he really thought about our discovery.

"There are at least two ways to look at everything, Ari," he said.

"You don't believe we've gone back in time?" I asked.

"I do believe in miracles," he said, "but we must consider other possibilities."

"Like what?" I asked.

"This might be a historical reenactment," he said.

"A what?" asked Preacher, overhearing.

"A historical play, Edward. People travel from all over the world to visit Nicaea, so these men might be local actors who are paid to enact an early Church council—like Nicaea."

"Is that what Mentor said," asked Cesar.

"No," admitted Father Greg, "Mentor is either a good actor or he truly believes he is the keeper of this library."

The Attributes of God

A hush had fallen over the Athenaeum. The five of us sat next to one another on our bench, facing an odd three-cornered lectern at which Mentor now stood. The seats in our arena were filled with ancient witnesses, and Mentor announced to all that the first chapter—*The Time Before Time*—would introduce us to the Triune God, Father, Son, and Holy Spirit.

"Consider the eternal attributes of our Creator," Mentor began, "our God is *omnipotent*: He is all-powerful; our God is *omniscient*: He is all-knowing; our God is *omnipresent*: He is everywhere present.

"Wait," said Preacher aside to us, "I thought this was about the time before time."

"He's introducing the attributes of God," explained Father Greg, "because God alone existed in eternity past."

"I get it," said Preacher.

"Our God is also *immutable,*" said Mentor, "although humans are *mutable*, that is changeable, God is *immutable*, unchangeable. To recognize God as immutable is to understand that he is, first of all, invariable."

Mentor introduced a witness he called Quinti Septimi Florentis Tertulliani.

"It's Tertullian!" whispered Father Greg, "the Church Father who first used the term "persons" to describe the Holy Trinity."

I had "met" Tertullian in the book hall, but Father Greg was seeing him for the first time. Tertullian was a tall, dark-skinned man who smelled of tobacco and

Fig. 3 Three-sided lectern (pictured center) located inside the Dormition Church of Nicaea before it was destroyed in the Greco-Turkish War of 1919-1922. By courtesy of Walter De Gruvter.

seemed to be in a foul mood.[1] Commenting on the immutability of God, Tertullian rapped in Latin!

> "Our God is perfectly free," he began, "and this
> is divine integrity,
> For what God is God always will be
> In Him no change shall we ever see.
>
> Not so for the moon, the stars and the sun
> They change every night in the courses they run
> Our God without loss and never with gain
> Remains Himself and is ever the same."[2]

As Tertullian sat down I saw a look of disbelief on my friends' faces—except for Preacher, who was delighted by Tertullian's poetic rap.

"As our brother Tertullian suggests," replied Mentor, "while the heavenly spheres vary in their phases, God's glory never changes; God's character—His love, truth, justice, and mercy—never varies with circumstances.

"Human life involves continual change from birth to death," Mentor continued, "and we mortals tend to think of change as good because so much about ourselves and our world needs changing. But God does not change in any way."

"Augustine, Bishop of Hippo," Mentor next announced, "please enlighten us further."

Augustine rose from a throne-like chair in the arena.

---

1 These imaginative details are my impression of Tertullian but not based on reported facts about the ancient witness.

2 A poetic paraphrase of Tertullian, *Ad Nationes* (*To the Heathen*) II.6 (ANF 3, 134-135).

"He's one of the four great doctors of the Western Church!" whispered Father Greg. "He wrote the *Confessions* and *The City of God* and many great theological works!"[3]

"I can only elaborate on our brother's concise message," Augustine began, "for God to change would entail losing some aspect of his perfection. If God gains something new, then what he was before was lacking. Anything new to emerge in God's substance would mean He cannot truly be called eternal. Thus, God's essence, by which he is, has absolutely nothing changeable about its eternity or its truth or its will; there truth is eternal and love is eternal."[4]

"So, in other words," Mentor clarified, "God's attributes such as His truth, His will, His love, are identical to God himself, and are therefore also eternal?" Augustine nodded once, in agreement, and sat down.

"Just as God is *invariable*," Mentor continued, "He is also *unalterable*. No one and nothing can bring about any change in God's eternal nature. Our heavenly Father, in other words, is *impassible*: unlike us humans, he is not vulnerable to suffering or injury, and he is not swayed by events or emotions. This is not to say

---

3 The Four Doctors of the Church were so named because of their great learning and impact. For the Western, Latin-speaking churches, these were Ambrose, Jerome, Augustine, and Gregory the Great. The Eastern, Greek-speaking churches identified Athanasius, Gregory of Nazianzus, Basil the Great, and John Chysostom as their selections. For more, see Christopher Hall, *Reading Scripture with the Church Fathers* (Downer's Grove, IL: InterVarsity Press, 1998), chapters 4 and 5.

4 *Confessions* XI.10 (NPNF 1.1, 167) and *The Trinity* IV, Preface/ Prologue (NPNF I.3, 69). See Hal M. Helms, translator, *The Confessions of St. Augustine* (Orleans, MA: Paraclete Press, 1986), 239, and Edmond Hill, translator, *The Trinity* (Brooklyn: New City Press, 1991), 153.

our God is uncompassionate toward his creation, but that his eternal purpose and perspective can never be redirected or altered in any way by an outside force. Friends, consider the words of Malachi. Speaking for God, the prophet says *For I the Lord do not change; therefore you, O children of Jacob, are not consumed*" (Malachi 3:6).

"Amen!" said the ancient witnesses in unison. Mentor continued,

"It is one thing to acknowledge the attributes of God but quite another to know God personally. Was it not to Moses that God revealed his eternal nature personally by disclosing his covenant name, the LORD?" The witnesses nodded in agreement.

"In Exodus, for example, we read of Moses' response to God when he was commissioned to guide the Israelites out of Egypt."

Mentor read from a large Bible opened on the lectern.

> *Then Moses said to God, "If I come to the people of Israel and say to them, 'The God of your fathers has sent me to you,' and they ask me, 'What is his name?' what shall I say to them?' God said to Moses, 'I am who I am.'" And he said, "Say this to the people of Israel, 'I am has sent me to you'" (Exodus 3:13–14).*

"His name 'I AM' comes from the Hebrew verb meaning "to be," said one of the witnesses.

"Thank you, brother Jerome," replied Mentor, "even God's name reveals his nature as the source of all life."

How Can God Be One and Three?

Mentor now announced the first question to be put to the witnesses—*How can God be one and yet also three?*[5] He told the witnesses to prepare, and also gave us time to talk among ourselves.

"How can God be one and three—that was *the* central question at the Nicene Council," said Father Greg.

"Why'd they need a council for that?" asked Preacher.

"The Nicene Council invented the Trinity," said Cesar confidently, "didn't you know?"

"You did *not* learn that in my class!" said Father Greg, shocked.

"No," Cesar admitted, "I heard that on a YouTube video."

"I thought the Church had always believed in the Holy Trinity," I said.

"That's correct," said Father Greg, "and the Nicene Council did *not* invent the Holy Trinity."

"What was the Council for?" asked Preacher.

"Politics," said Cesar, the Fathers had to decide who would be in charge of the Church."

"Not true," said Father Greg, shaking his head.

"Cesar," I interrupted, "you can't learn Church history from the internet—there were no politics at the Nicaea Council!"

"I wouldn't say that," Father Greg disagreed.

"So the Nicene Council was political?" asked Joseph.

---

5 Says Karl Barth, "In every Christian confession…the deepest question is this, how can God be one and yet also three." See his *Church Dogmatics: The Doctrine of the Word of God I.1*, 302.

"Not in the way you're thinking," replied Father Greg, "but there were opposing parties or factions."

"Who?" asked Joseph and I, at the same time.

"The *Monarchists* emphasized God's oneness," he explained.

"Monarchy?" said Preacher, "that sounds like a king."

"Precisely," said Father Greg, "God the Father is King—the One God."

"But Jesus and the Holy Spirit are fully God too," said Joseph.

"Of course," the priest agreed, "and that point was emphasized by those who taught a view called the *Economic Trinity*."

Preacher wagged his head as if our talk was so much nonsense.

"God *is* the great three-in-one," he said, "what else do you need to know?"

"One God, but three *whats,* Edward?" asked Father Greg.

"Three *whats*? Father, Son, and Holy Spirit, that's what. You're a priest and you don't know that?"

"Edward," said Father Greg patiently, "the Father is God, right?

"Tell me something I don't know!" said Preacher.

"But the Son and the Holy Spirit *also* are God, right?

"What's your point, Rabbi?"

The three of us rolled our eyes at Preacher, and Father Greg continued,

"If all three are God, then what do you say when somebody accuses you of worshiping three gods?"

Preacher said nothing, then Father Greg tried a different approach.

"You do remember, Edward, how Jesus commanded his disciples to baptize in name of the Father, and the Son, and the Holy Spirit?"

"That's the Great Commission," said Preacher.

"Precisely," said Father Greg, "but the first disciples were Jews, right?" he asked.

Preacher agreed.

"And being Jews" he continued, "they believed that *the Lord our God the Lord is One*, as we read in Deuteronomy 6:4. But as Christians they also worshipped Jesus and the Holy Spirit too. The problem was, how could they worship the Father *and* the Son *and* the Holy Spirit, while saying that God is one?

"What's the answer?" asked Preacher.

"Well," he continued, "the Church Fathers gave many answers."

"Like what?" replied Preacher, curious.

"Like, that Jesus and the Holy Spirit were the Word and Wisdom of God—his two hands."

"Hmm," Preacher scratched his head, "I like that."

"Yes, although it doesn't tell us very much," Father Greg admitted, "but, perhaps, the ancient witnesses can help us?"

Overhearing our conversation, one of the witnesses saluted.[6]

"Ignatius of Antioch," announced Mentor.

"He's one of the Apostolic Fathers," whispered Father Greg.[7]

Ignatius was a small man with a humble manner. He had coppery-brown skin and a sparse, unkempt beard. His robe was emblazoned with a blood-red cross. He stood, and as he spoke, his voice rang like a trumpet.

"Seeing the whole congregation of you in faith and love," Ignatius began, "I exhort you to study to do all things in harmony with God, for as long as your bishop presides here in the place of God..." He held out his hand to Mentor.

"and your presbyters in the place of the assembly of the apostles," he indicated his fellow ancient witnesses,

"along with you deacons who are most dear to me, being entrusted with the ministry of Jesus Christ." With this last statement he indicated us pastors, and then was silent.

"What's the matter with the old dude?" asked Preacher.

"Quiet, Preacher," Joseph hushed, "he's testifying."

"Those were his opening remarks, "whispered Father Greg, "he's waiting for the moderator to ask the question."

---

6 To be recognized to speak, an ancient witness would not raise his hand as is our modern custom, but would offer a modified Roman salute: touching his right hand to his chest, he would then extend his right arm.

7 The Apostolic Fathers were the first generation of Church leaders after the death of the twelve Apostles.

"*How can God be one and three?*" Mentor asked Ignatius, after a brief silence.

"Do not let anyone pass your way with corrupted doctrine," Ignatius replied, "and do not allow them to plant it among you. Cover your ears to avoid the things being planted by them, because you are stones of a temple prepared beforehand for the building of God the Father, hoisted up to the heights by the crane of Jesus Christ, which is the cross, using as a rope the Holy Spirit. For your faith is what lifts you, and love is the way that leads up to God."[8]

Ignatius sat down.

"He gave us a picture of the Trinity," said Joseph, "One God with three roles: God the Father was building His Church, with the help of a crane—the Cross of Christ—and a rope—the Holy Spirit."

"Dang!" said Preacher, "that's some theology!"

"It doesn't tell us much more than that God had two hands," Cesar objected.

At this, another witness—whom Mentor called Hippolytus—spoke up.

"What do the Scriptures say about the Word?" he asked Mentor, who promptly read the opening words of John's Gospel.

In the beginning was the Word,
and the Word was with God,
and the Word was God.

Hippolytus stood up from his place at one of the choir stalls.

8 Ignatius of Antioch, Letter to the Ephesians, 9.1 (Holmes 191; ANF 1, 53).

"If the Word was *with* God, and also *was* God," said Hippolytus, "does this speak of two Gods? No indeed, One God and two Persons."

"But there are three persons in the Trinity," Preacher Objected.

"Truly," agreed Hippolytus, "there is a third *economy*—the grace of the Holy Spirit."

"*Economy*?" said Preacher, "I thought we were talking about the Holy Spirit."

"*Economy* is the term some of the early fathers used to describe the manifestation of the Trinity," explained Father Greg.

"Now I'm really confused," said Preacher.

"God is One," repeated Hippolytus, "it is the Father who commands, and the Son who obeys, and the Holy Spirit who gives the understanding. We cannot even think of One God without believing in Father and Son and Holy Spirit."

"I believe that too," said Cesar, "but it stills sounds like there are three Gods."

"But the *economy of harmony* points to one God," said Hippolytus.

Preacher and Cesar both looked puzzled, so I tried to clear things up.

What Has Been Believed Everywhere, Always, and By All

"The witnesses believe in the Holy Trinity," I said, "they just used different words to describe it, isn't that right?" I asked Father Greg.

"Keep in mind that the doctrine of the Holy Trinity took time to develop," he replied, without answering my question.

"But I thought you said the Church had always believed in the Holy Trinity," I objected.

"Of course," he agreed, "but it took the fathers time to comprehend and to explain what *all Christians everywhere had always believed.*"[9]

"In other words," said Joseph, "they didn't have words for everything they believed in?"

"Precisely," agreed Father Greg.

"So did the Nicene Council invent the word *Trinity*?" asked Cesar.

Father Greg took a deep breath, rubbed his eyes and went over to speak with Mentor who, in turn, spoke to the witnesses; two of them saluted at once.

"There," said Father Greg, "these two witnesses not only wrote about the Trinity, but also used the actual term in their writings."[10]

"And they attended the Nicene Council?" asked Cesar.

"These fathers lived a hundred years or more before Council met!" replied Father Greg.

"So much for YouTube," I teased Cesar, "the Nicene Council did *not* invent the Trinity and did not even coin the term *Trinity*."

---

9 Known as the Vincentian Canon, the statement, "What has been believed everywhere, always, and by all" (Latin: *quod ubique, quod semper, quod ab omnibus creditum est*), was formulated by Vincent of Lérins (c. AD 450s) to settle questions of orthodox (right) belief.

10 These were Theophilus and Origen.

"That is correct," said Father Greg, "but the Ante-Nicene Fathers—those who lived prior to the Nicene Council—taught a doctrine of the *economic Trinity*, which means the one God was manifested in different ways at different times."

"But we know that God never changes," objected Preacher.

"That is also correct," said Father Greg, "and that is why, in time, the doctrine of the *economic Trinity* was revised."

"What was wrong with it?" asked Joseph.

"It sounded too much like *Modalism*, which is a heresy" said Father Greg.

"What kinda heresy?" asked Preacher, frowning.

"Some believed that God took the form of Father in the Old Testament days," replied Father Greg, "then he became the Only Begotten Son at the time of Jesus's earthly ministry, and finally, with the birth of the Church at Pentecost, God took the form of the Holy Spirit."

"But our God…."

"I know, Edward, our God never changes, and the Nicene Creed teaches that the Son and the Holy Spirit are eternal, just as the Father is eternal."

"So how can God be one and three?" asked Preacher.

"Ultimately," said Father Greg, "it's a mystery."

"That's just what my Sunday School teacher used to say," said Preacher, disappointed.

"Shall we continue?" asked Mentor.

"Yes, indeed!" said Father Greg.

"Justin Martyr," announced Mentor.

"He was one of the first great apologists of the early Church," said Father Greg.

Justin Martyr wore a philosopher's tunic. He was a young man with a full beard and bare chested. The sash of his robe, draped over one shoulder, was marked with a blood-red cross. As he came to the lectern, Mentor repeated his question.

"*How can God be one and three?*"

Clearing his voice, Justin Martyr began,

"We confess the true God, the Father of righteousness and temperance and the other virtues, who is free from all impurity—both Him and the Son who came forth from Him and the prophetic Spirit, we worship and adore, knowing them in reason and truth, and declaring without grudging to everyone who wishes to learn as we have been taught."[11]

"I wish to learn!" I said aloud, blushing as my words echoed throughout the arena. Justin Martyr continued,

"Christ, being both Lord and God, the Son of God, appeared to Moses in the glory of the burning bush, and in the judgment of Sodom, and even in the naming of Joshua.[12] He was the power of God sent to all these, appearing in whatever form the Father pleased. Indeed, they call him *the Logos* because he carries a message from the Father to men. As the light from the sun radiates from the sun itself, Christ's power radiates from the Father's power and cannot be separated. Nor is the Father's power thereby reduced, for after starting many

11 Justin Martyr, *First Apology*, chapter 6 (ANF 1, 164).

12 The Hebrew name, Joshua, means "Yahweh saves," whose Greek translation is Jesus.

fires from a single fire, we see that the original fire is undiminished."[13]

The Logos of God

Justin Martyr paused to give us time to ponder his words.

"Did he answer the question?" asked Preacher.

"Of course!" said Cesar, "the Father is like the sun, Jesus is the sun rays, and the Holy Spirit is its warmth."

"That's cool!" said Preacher.

"No, that's hot!" replied Cesar, teasing.

"He also said the Son of God was sent in whatever form the Father chose," I added, "but that sounds a little like *Modalism*."

"Ask the Apologist to say more about *the Logos*," said Father Greg.

"The what?" asked Preacher.

"The Word," explained Father Greg, "in Greek, *logos* is the Word."

"So, Jesus is *the Logos*?" I asked.

"Precisely," said Father Greg.

I wasn't sure what to ask, but Justin Martyr had overheard Father Greg and replied,

"We admire the philosophers for their knowledge of *the Logos*—the reason—in all men, yet they understood *the Logos* only in part, and were unaware that Christ, who appeared for our sakes, became a whole rational being—*Logos*—body, reason, and soul. Our doctrines, then, are

---

13 Paraphrase based on Justin Martyr, *First Apology*, especially chapter 63(ANF 1, 184) and *Dialogue with Trypho*, chapters 113 and 132 (ANF 1, 255 and 266).

greater than their teachings. For they did not know the whole of the Word—the *Logos*—which is Christ."[14]

"Who cares about philosophers?" said Preacher, "weren't they the pagans?"

"I believe our heavenly Father cares about them," Justin Martyr replied. Preacher was quiet, and Justin Martyr explained at length that the Greek philosophers believed that God was so far beyond the material world that only a series of *emanations* or "waves from God" eventually led to creation. This was not the biblical view, he explained, but resulted from their belief that created matter was evil.

"*Logos theology* was an important step in the development of our doctrine of the Trinity," added Father Greg. "It attempted to balance the *Monarchy*—One God—with the *Economy*—three Persons.

"What would Turtle say about that?" asked Preacher, who was looking bored.

"Turtle?" asked Father Greg.

"Him," said Preacher, pointing to Tertullian. Mentor called on Tertullian, who stood and recited.

---

14 See Justin Martyr, *First Apology* 32.8 (ANF 1,173); *Second Apology*, 8.1 (ANF 1, 191). See also J.N.D. Kelly, *Early Christian Doctrines*, Rev. Edition (Harper San Francisco, 1978), 96-97. In choosing *logos*, John probably had in mind the Old Testament word, *dabar*. *Dabar* is biblical Hebrew for *word*, *a message*, or *a matter*, as in the verse, "After these things the word (*dabar*) of the Lord came to Abraham" (Gen.15:1). In this sense, John identified Jesus as the word of God: Jesus was God's message. For ancient philosophers, however, the *logos* was the very first emanation or wave from God, and the "DNA of creation." Justin Martyr, himself a philosopher, used the familiar vocabulary to witness to the philosophers. Just as the Apostle Paul had declared "the unknown God" to the philosophers of Athens (Acts 17:23), Justin Martyr identified the *logos* of God as none other than Jesus. For more on the philosophical use of logos, see J.N.D. Kelly, pages 9-11.

"From the roots to the fruit join the parts that make the tree,

As the Father with the Son and the Spirit make three,

But the Three of them are One, in the bosom they begun

They're *Economy* and *Monarchy* for all eternity."[15]

"Dang!" said Preacher, delighted with Tertullian's recitation.

"Wait," said Joseph, "does that really explain how God can be one and yet three also?"

"The tree is not severed from the roots," answered Tertullian, "for while the root and the tree are distinctly two things, they are joined. Just as a fountain and the river that flows from it are two forms but indivisible. In like manner the Trinity, flowing down from the Father, through intertwined and connected steps, does not disturb the *Monarchy* even as it guards the state of the *Economy*."

Justin Martyr, having been interrupted, now continued his explanation of *the Logos*, whom he described as the "thought" or the "mind" of the Father, and the blueprint or plan in the mind of God. Jesus was the Father's *Logos* or blueprint for His creation. *The Logos* had been in the bosom of the Father from the very beginning, as Tertullian had recited, where it could be called the *Integral Word* of God. But, through the *Incarnation*, the Word became the *expressed or spoken Word of God*, revealing the Father. Justin drew on other ideas from the philosophers to prove that Jesus Christ was *the Logos* in whom they believed, though they did not know him. Just as the Apostle Paul had declared

15 Adapted from Tertullian, Against Praxeas, 7 & 8, ANF 3, 602-603.

"the unknown God" to the philosophers of Athens (Acts 17:23), Justin Martyr identified *the Logos* of God as none other than Jesus!

What Was God Doing Before Creation?

After Justin Martyr took his seat, Mentor announced it was time to move on to the next chapter, *The Beginning of Time*.

"But I have another question!" said Preacher.

"Very well," said Mentor, "what is it?"

"What was God doing before he made heaven and earth?" asked Preacher.

"I'll tell you what He was doing," called out one of the ancient witnesses, "He was preparing hell for people who ask questions like that!"

Scornful laughter erupted from some of the other witnesses, and Mentor reminded them to be recognized before speaking. Augustine saluted,

"Mentor, may I answer the young man's question?"

Mentor invited the Bishop of Hippo to the lectern.

"May I know your name, young man?" asked Augustine, smiling warmly.

"My name is Edward, sir, but they call me Preacher."

"An excellent name! And where do you hail from, Preacher?"

Preacher hesitated.

"Do they know about Atlanta?" he said aside to us.

"The pastors are from beyond Kios," said Mentor.

"Very well," he replied, "and we are from Hippo Regius..."

"Excuse me?" said Preacher.

"I'll explain later," said Father Greg.

"In Hippo Regius," Augustine continued, "there are foolish people who say, 'Before God created heaven and earth, he was unoccupied. When God *did* create, then a new thing came about—a new intention in God—and therefore God is not eternally the same."

"But Jesus Christ is the same yesterday, today, and forever," replied Preacher.

"An excellent reply to those fools!" declared Augustine.

"Thanks," said Preacher, "but what do you say to them?"

"I explain that while all creatures change, God's *will* is not a creature: it existed before God created anything, and nothing at all would be created unless God first willed it."

"That's a good answer," said Preacher, "what do they say to that?"

"They say, 'If God eternally wanted a creation, then why is creation itself not eternal?"

"Whoa!" said Preacher, that's a tough one.

"Truly it is!" agreed Augustine, laughing, "But that just shows they do not understand You, O Lord."

Preacher turned around to see who Augustine was talking to.

"If they suppose God was resting for long ages before he created anything," Augustine continued, "they err because he had not yet created time! Do you understand me, my young friend?"

"Not really," Preacher admitted.

"It's quite simple," said Augustine, "they wonder what the Almighty was doing then, before creation, but before creation there was no 'then' because there was no time!"

"I get that," said Preacher, "there wadn't no *then* then!"

Augustine, smiling, sat down.

"That's Saint Augustine!" whispered Father Greg, enraptured. Then, blushing, he corrected himself.

"I mean, that actor is wonderful."

"You are great, O Lord, and highly to be praised!" shouted Augustine from his seat.

The Mystery of Iniquity

Mentor called on Joseph, who had raised his hand.

"I have a question also," he said.

"Me too," I added.

"Very well," agreed Mentor, "if your questions concern the time before time."

We hesitated, unsure; then Joseph asked,

"When did evil enter the world?"

And I said,

"I want to know why God created man with a free will knowing he would disobey?"

"God is not the author of rebellion," replied Mentor, "nor did he create Satan as he *now* is—a murderer and the father of lies.[16] He was an angel created without sin who chose to oppose God's authority. By his example and influence, he led other angels in rebellion against the

16 John 8.44.

Almighty.[17] These became the principalities and powers opposed to God's eternal purposes, and their presence is the mystery of iniquity." Mentor read from the lectern Bible,

> *For the mystery of iniquity is already at work. Only he who now restrains it will do so until he is out of the way.*[18]

"I've always wondered what that verse means," said Joseph, so Mentor continued,

"This *mystery of iniquity*, or *of lawlessness*, is Satan's plan and purpose which sprang into action at his rebellion, soon after his creation as an angel. Few biblical passages describe the entrance of evil into God's good creation. There is a brief description in Ephesians[19] of Christ's triumph at his resurrection over rebellious forces in the cosmos.

> *When Christ ascended on high he led a host of captives....*

"These hints concerning the mystery of iniquity are drawn from longer reflections on evil found in the Hebrew Scriptures,[20] especially the Prophet Isaiah. Isaiah

---

17 Rev.12:7-12.

18 From 2 Thess. 2:7 NKJV. We understand the meaning of this phrase by examining passages that speak of "the mystery of Christ" (Eph.3.4) as His eternal purposes (Eph.1.9), namely, His plan of salvation (Rom.11:25; 16:25; 1 Cor.15:51). In those passages, *mystery* speaks of God's eternal purposes which were hidden but now have been made known, with special reference to the *fulfillment* of that purpose." F.F. Bruce, *1 and 2 Thessalonians*. Word Biblical Commentary, Vol. 45 (Dallas: Word, 1998), 170, emphasis in original.

19 Namely, in Eph. 3.8

20 That is, the Old Testament.

spoke against the rebellious King of Babylon who exalted himself as a sovereign Lord over God's people, Israel. As we read about this king's prideful presumption, however, we perceive the rebellious spirit of Satan who inspired the King's disobedience." Again, Mentor read,

> *How you are fallen from heaven, O Day Star,*
> *son of Dawn!*
> *How you are cut down to the ground, you who laid*
> *the nations low!*
> *You said in your heart, 'I will ascend to heaven;*
> *above the stars of God*
> *I will set my throne on high; I will sit on the mount*
> *of assembly in the far reaches of the north;*
> *I will ascend above the heights of the clouds;*
> *I will make myself like the Most High.'*
> *But you are brought down to Sheol, to the far reaches*
> *of the pit.*[21]

"Now, if this passage shows us the pride that led to Satan's rebellion and fall, then we can see the consequence of his rebellion in Revelation." Turning the pages of the lectern Bible, Mentor read,

> *Now war arose in heaven, Michael and his angels fighting against the dragon. And the dragon and his angels fought back, but he was defeated, and there was no longer any place for them in heaven. And the great dragon was thrown down, that ancient serpent, who is called the devil and Satan, the deceiver of the whole world—he was thrown down to the earth, and his angels were thrown down with him.*[22]

---

21 Isa. 14:12-15.

22 Rev. 12:7-9

"Both passages," Mentor concluded, "tell of the cosmic or heavenly rebellion against the 'Most High,' and both describe the rebel Satan's defeat. In another passage, when the disciples returned from their mission of preaching and casting out demons, Jesus declared 'I saw Satan fall like lightening from heaven.'[23] When exactly did Satan begin to rebel, and when was he expelled from heaven? It must have been before he appeared as the serpent in the Garden of Eden."

Augustine saluted again and was called on by Mentor.

"As I have explained in my work, *The Literal Meaning of Genesis*, I believe that Satan's fall came soon after he was created, since as we read in the Gospel of John, our Lord Jesus Christ described Satan as "a murderer from the beginning."[24]

By now, Joseph's question—When did evil enter the world?—had been addressed. Mentor had not forgotten my question, but changed it to include the angels. He phrased it like this, "Why had God given his creatures—humans and angels—free will, knowing some would rebel?"

Origen of Alexandria was called on to testify. He was very old, and rose with great difficulty as if in pain, but his voice was strong and clear.

"In His ineffable word and wisdom," Origen began, "God, the Father of all things, determined that his creatures should be free to exercise their own will.

---

23 Luke 10:18.

24 See John 8.44, and Augustine, *The Literal Meaning of Genesis* XI.16.21 (not in NPNF) in Edmond Hill, *On Genesis* (New York: New City Press, 2002), 440.

Otherwise, they would be shaped by an external will into something they were never intended to be.[25]

"Whatever His reasons," Origen continued, "while a great and distinguished order of celestial beings—the good angels—is arrayed in the glory of their offices, the same is true of the Enemy's forces who, occupying evil ranks, became principalities, powers, rulers of the darkness of the world, spirits of wickedness, malignant spirits, or unclean demons. These were not created evil, but they have become so by choice and by their progress in wickedness."[26]

As we pondered his words, Origen sat back down.

Thanking each of the Fathers for their contributions to the first session, Mentor announced a break, after which we all sang an ancient doxology. Some of the witnesses kept their seats while others returned to various sections of the Athenaeum.

"I need to get back and prepare for class!" said Father Greg, remembering the time. He went to thank Mentor, and I wondered if we would have to leave the Athenaeum also.

"Are you leaving now?" asked Joseph, when Father Greg returned.

"Not just yet," he said.

"What changed your mind?" asked Cesar.

"Mentor asked me if I had a better place to prepare to teach about the Church Fathers," said the priest, "and I had to admit I do not."

---

25 Origen, *On First Principles* II.1.2, paraphrased. (ANF 4, 268).

26 Origen, *On First Principles* I.8.4. (ANF 4, 266).

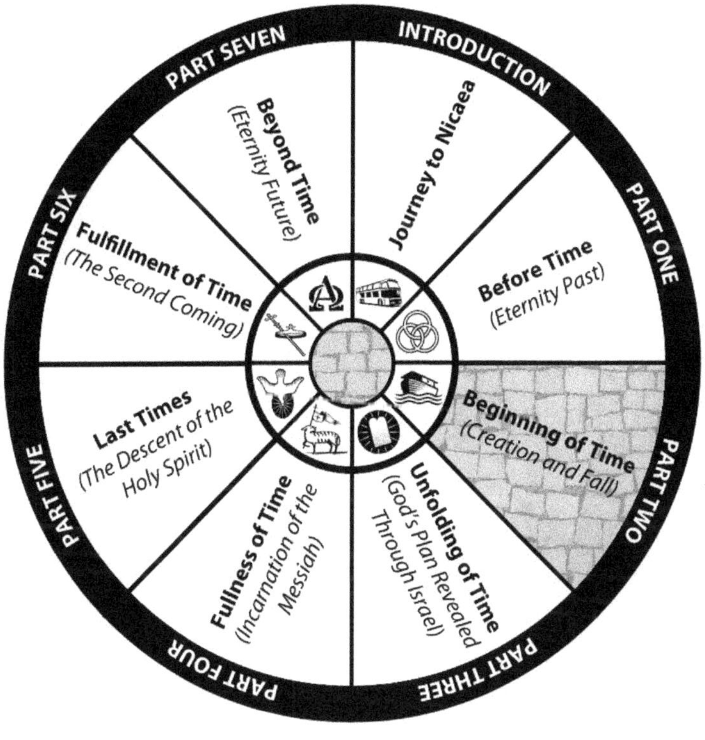
INTRODUCTION
Journey to Nicaea
PART ONE
Before Time
(Eternity Past)
PART TWO
Beginning of Time
(Creation and Fall)
PART THREE
Unfolding of Time
(God's Plan Revealed Through Israel)
PART FOUR
Fullness of Time
(Incarnation of the Messiah)
PART FIVE
Last Times
(The Descent of the Holy Spirit)
PART SIX
Fulfillment of Time
(The Second Coming)
PART SEVEN
Beyond Time
(Eternity Future)

Chapter 3: The Beginning of Time

During the break I strolled around our arena, leaving by one of four small gates—these were positioned at 3 o'clock, 6 o'clock, 9 o'clock, and 12:00—leading to the surrounding sections where hundreds of ancient witnesses awaited the call to testify. Mentor, I learned, called this place "the Crux," which makes sense since it was where the overlapping crosses converged at the center. I asked him about the seating arrangement within the Crux. He pointed out two sets of choir stalls—one for the pre-Nicene and the other for Nicene and post-Nicene witnesses[1]—arranged on either side of the threefold lectern, and three high back chairs near the 12:00 o'clock gate. These, he explained, were for the Church Historians.[2]

1 Pre-Nicene (more commonly called Ante-Nicene) witnesses were those who lived and wrote before the Nicene Council met in AD 325. Nicene and Post-Nicene were those who live and wrote during or after the Council.

2 For Eusebius of Caesarea, Socrates of Constantinople, and Evagrius of Antioch, the three ancient Church historians.

In the Beginning

It was time for the next session to begin. As soon as the theme of Creation was announced, several ancient witnesses formed a line at the threefold lectern. Mentor began by recapping the previous session.

"Brothers, the first episode concluded with a vision of our Triune God surrounded by an angelic host reflecting His glory. Meanwhile a dark host—principalities and powers—arrayed itself against the sons of light, casting a shadow across the bright creation. Against this backdrop the first man was created and placed in the garden to care for it. Now let us explore the Book of Beginnings, with which our great canon of Scriptures opens."

He read slowly and with feeling,

> *In the beginning, God created the heavens and the earth. The earth was without form and void, and darkness was over the face of the deep. And the Spirit of God was hovering over the face of the waters. And God said, "Let there be light," and there was light. And God saw that the light was good, and God separated the light from darkness.*[3]

"As you know, brothers," Mentor continued, "our Gnostic opponents—those who profess a wisdom falsely so-called—claimed that the Almighty created the cosmos

---

3 Gen. 1:1–4 (ESV).

from eternally existing matter.[4] Let us recall the Church's teaching in response to that heresy."

Mentor called on the first speaker, who stood and said,

"The authors of Scripture taught us with one consent that God made all things *ex nihilo,*[5] for nothing was coequal to God. Before all things, God had his own Word within, and his Wisdom as a helper in the things that were created by him."[6]

"Thank you brother Theophilus," said Mentor, "and who else will testify to this doctrine?" Several witnesses saluted.[7] Mentor called on Tertullian.

"As Theophilus testifies, if any material was necessary to God in the creation of the world, then God had a far nobler and more suitable material—His own Wisdom."[8]

---

4 These included various Gnostic philosophers of the 2nd century AD who taught that a "demiurge"—a god-like creature who was "powerful but not all powerful, and not always good"—was responsible for organizing chaotic, uncreated matter (their understanding of Genesis 1:2) into the world we now see (Irène Fernandez, "Creation: Historical and Systematic Theology" in Jean-Yves Lacoste (ed.), *Encyclopedia of Christian Theology*, Vol.1 380-381).

5 Latin for "out of nothing."

6 *Theophilus to Autolycus*, II.10. (ANF 2, 97-98). The Ante-Nicene Father says "coeval with God" meaning "coequal;" "nothing is coequal with God" means nothing existed before God's act of creating.

7 To be recognized to speak, an ancient witness would not raise his hand as is our modern custom, but would offer a modified Roman salute: touching his right hand to his chest, he would then extend his right arm. In answer to Mentor's question, several men saluted, namely Clement of Alexandria, Athenagoras, Irenaeus, and Tertullian.

8 Tertullian, *Against Hermogenes*, 18.1 (ANF 3, 487).

"Agreed, said Mentor, "and how is this confirmed?"

"Consider the words of Solomon," Tertullian replied, and he began reciting from the book of Proverbs:

> *The Lord possessed me at the beginning of his work, the first of his acts of old. Ages ago I was set up, at the first, before the beginning of the earth. When there were no depths I was brought forth...then I was beside him, like a master workman, and I was daily his delight, rejoicing before him always, rejoicing in his inhabited world and delighting in the children of man.*[9]

"*Created me!* The Lord *created me* at the beginning of his work!" shouted a voice from somewhere in the Athenaeum.[10] His outburst was quickly drowned out by the shouts of other witnesses,

"*Possessed* by him," Tertullian repeated.

"He was *begotten* by him," said Justin Martyr.

"*Firstborn* of him," said Origen.[11]

"What's happening?" asked Joseph.

"They disagree on the translation of that verse in Proverbs," said Father Greg, who explained that the phrase *the Lord possessed me* had been translated various

---

9 Prov. 8:22–24a, 30-31. J. Robert Wright notes that "in the book of Proverbs, this verse (8:22) received the greatest volume of comments from the writers of the early Church...." In *Proverbs, Ecclesiastes, Song of Solomon*, Ancient Christian Commentary on Scripture, vol. IX (Downers Grove: InterVarsity Press, 2005), 60.

10 The claim that Christ had been created by God as the "firstborn of creation" was advanced by Arius and others who were judged to be heretics by the Nicene Council.

11 See J. Robert Wright, *Proverbs, Ecclesiastes, Song of Solomon*, Ancient Christian Commentary on Scripture IX (60-61).

ways, including *the Lord created me*" by a few ancient witnesses.

"What does your Bible say, Joseph?" I asked. He quickly turned to the passage and read aloud,

"The Lord *possessed* me at the beginning of His work."[12]

From the Pre-Nicene choir, an elderly father, Athenagorus, saluted and was called on.

"As Mentor has already shown," he began, "we acknowledge one God, uncreated, eternal, invisible, impassible, incomprehensible, illimitable, who is apprehended by understanding and reason alone, who is encompassed by light, and beauty, and spirit, and power ineffable, by whom the universe has been created through His Logos, and set in order, and is maintained."[13]

The witness's words were eloquent, and I listened carefully for his explanation of the Son's relationship to the Father.

"Let no one think that this talk of God having a Son is ridiculous," Athenagorus continued, "for we have not come to our views on either God the Father or his Son as do the poets, who create myths in which they present the gods as no better than men. On the contrary, the Son of God is the Logos of the Father—He is *in* the Father and the Father is *in* the Son. But if in your great wisdom you would like to know what *Son* means, I will tell you in a few brief words: it means that he is the *first begotten* of the Father. This term is used not because he was created

12 The Authorized, or King James, Version.

13 Athenagorus, *A Plea for the Christians*, X (ANF 2, 133).

by the Father, for the Father had the Logos in Himself from the very beginning."[14]

Following Athenagorus, several more witnesses spoke on the passage in Proverbs

Mentor directed those still waiting their turns to speak on the opening words of Genesis.

"I wish to comment on *and the Spirit of God was hovering over the face of the waters*," said Ephrem of Syria, whom I had met in the reading room. Mentor nodded his approval and the witness commented.

"The spirit *hovered* in order for us to learn that the work of creation was the unified work of the Spirit with the Father and the Son," explained Ephrem. "The Father spoke, the Son created, and the Spirit hovered, demonstrating its unity with the other persons. All creation was brought to perfection and accomplished by the Trinity."[15]

Ambrose of Milan next rose and added,

"The Spirit fittingly moved over the earth, destined to bear fruit because by the aid of the Spirit it held the seeds of new birth, which were to sprout according to the

---

14 Athenagorus, same as above, but see also J. Robert Wright, *Proverbs, Ecclesiastes, Song of Solomon*, Ancient Christian Commentary on Scripture, vol. IX, 61; and William R. Schoedel (ed), *Athenagorus, Legatio and De Resurrectione* (Oxford, 1972), 20-21.

15 Ephrem the Syrian, *Commentary on Genesis* 1 (quotation from Andrew Louth. Ancient Christian Commentary on Scripture. *Genesis 1-2*, 6), emphasis added. Some works of Ephrem are in NPNF 2.13, but not his *Commentary on Genesis*.

words of the prophet: *Send forth thy spirit and they shall be created and you shall renew the face of the earth.*"[16]

We discussed the insights of these two Post-Nicene witnesses among ourselves.

"I know that all of the Trinity was involved in creation," said Joseph, "but how did he get the new birth out of the spirit hovering over the water?"

"Intertextuality," said Father Greg.

"What's that?" asked Cesar.

"It's like cross referencing" the priest explained, "one verse sheds light on another. Ambrose quoted the psalms—*send forth thy spirit*—to explain why the Holy Spirit was hovering over creation."

The line of ancient witnesses waiting to testify on the opening verses of Genesis never seemed to run out: those who offered testimony were replaced by others as soon as they took their seats. Many of these witnesses carried large commentaries on the six days of creation.[17] At some point Mentor intervened to change the subject,

"Brothers, our Book of Beginnings opened with the creation of the heavens and earth, but it climaxes with the creation of humanity. Each day's creation speech began with words such as "let there be…", or "let the earth bring forth." But the final creation command—"Let *us* make man in *our* image, and after *our* likeness"—sets our ancestors apart, suggesting that our God was in dialogue with others as He created humankind. With

---

16 Ps. 104:30, and Ambrose, *Hexameron* 1.8 (Louth, Ancient Christian Commentary on Scripture, 5). Some works of Ambrose are in NPNF 2.10, but not his *Hexameron*.

17 These were known as *Hexameron*, a Greek term that combines the word six (*hexa*) with days (*eimeron*).

whom was our God speaking?" Mentor called on three Pre-Nicene witnesses to the lectern.

Barnabas: God was speaking to His Son, "Let Us make man after Our image, and after Our likeness..."[18]

Justin Martyr: In saying "Let us make," God conversed with someone who was numerically distinct from Himself and a rational Being....Later God said, "Behold Adam has become as one of us, to know good and evil." In saying, "as one of us" Moses has declared there are a certain number of persons associated with one another... at least two."[19]

Irenaeus of Lyons: "With Him were always present the Word and Wisdom, the Son and the Spirit, by whom and in whom freely and spontaneously He made all things, to whom also He speaks, saying, "Let us make man after Our image and likeness."[20]

Apostolic Authority

Mentor thanked the three Pre-Nicene witnesses who, he explained, were the first to recognize the dialogue between the members of the Holy Trinity concerning humanity's creation.

"Drawing on their testimony," he continued, "our later witnesses have agreed that Genesis reveals the Trinity in collaboration at the creation—a conclusion which is at the heart of the Story of God as well as the doctrine of humanity. To open our discussion on the

---

18 *Epistle of Barnabas*, vi. (ANF 1, 140).

19 Justin Martyr, *Dialogue with Trypho* LXII (ANF 2, 128).

20 Irenaeus, *Against Heresies*, IV.XX.1 (ANF 1:487-8).

nature of humankind, I have invited Brother Irenaeus because of his special role in the battle against heresy."[21]

"I must first point out," Irenaeus began, "that anyone who wants to know the truth should focus upon the tradition of the Apostles which has spread throughout the entire world." As he said this, a certain look came over Mentor's face suggesting he'd heard the speech before.

"Those of us gathered here in this Assembly," Irenaeus continued, "can recall those whom the Apostles appointed as overseers in the churches; and we know their successors too, down to our own times. The Apostles took care to appoint those who were blameless, expecting them to take their place of leading and to serve faithfully, knowing this would be a great blessing to the Church if they would persevere, but a disaster if they should ever fall away. In this way, the life-giving faith which passed from the Apostles to us has been handed down in truth."[22]

After mentioning the Apostles Peter and Paul, Irenaeus listed the names of those they appointed bishops of Rome, beginning with Linus, who was appointed by Peter, Anacletus, whom Linus appointed, and so on with Clement, Evaristius, Alexander, and Sixtus, whose name means he was sixth in the line from Peter. Now, I had been taught that the doctrine of apostolic succession—that there was an unbroken line from Peter to the present-day Pope in Rome—was false. Yet here was a Church Father, apparently laying the foundation for such a doctrine. I decided to ask Father Greg what he thought about the idea.

---

21 Irenaeus of Lyon authored the massive *Against Heresies* (Latin title *Adversus Haereses*) in the late Second Century AD.

22 Irenaeus, *Against Heresies*, III.III.1 (ANF 1:415).

"In the Greek Orthodox Church," he whispered, "every bishop is considered a successor of Peter, not just those named by Irenaeus. Besides," said Father Greg, "Irenaeus is not arguing for the primacy of the Roman Catholic Church but for the reliability of the apostolic doctrine."

Irenaeus went on naming Bishops until he came to the legendary Christian martyr Polycarp.

"Polycarp was instructed by the Apostles and spoke with many who had seen Christ face to face, and was appointed bishop of the Church in Smyrna by apostles in Asia. I myself met him in my early youth, for he lived a very long time; and as a very old man, gloriously and most nobly suffering martyrdom, departed this life, having always taught the things which he had learned from the Apostles, and which the Church has handed down, and which alone are true. To these things all the Asian Churches testify, as do also those men who have succeeded Polycarp down to the present time. He was a man of much greater weight, and a more steadfast witness of truth, than Valentinus and Marcion and the rest of the heretics."[23]

The Creation of Humankind

Now that Irenaeus had made his case for the authenticity of the Apostle's doctrine, Mentor returned to the subject of the creation of humanity.

"Brothers," said Mentor, "thanks to Christ's holy Apostles we know that our God created the man and woman good. However, before the *Story of God* was

23 Irenaeus, *Against Heresies*, III.III.4 (ANF 1:416).

rightly told,[24] many believed that our world of physical matter, humans included, was the creation of an evil *demi-god*. The Gnostic heretics taught that the immaterial soul[25] alone had value, and that the spiritual man was one who denied his flesh entirely and who strove to free his immaterial soul from the prison of his body. Our brother's task," Mentor indicated Irenaeus, "was to teach a biblical view of man that could defeat the gnostic spirituality of our day."

"We note first of all," began Irenaeus, "that contrary to Gnostic teaching, the flesh is God's handiwork, possessing the image of God in its formation.[26] The heretics therefore blaspheme God whenever they teach that the flesh—which truly is God's workmanship—cannot be saved.[27] Next, we point out that, in addition to the immaterial soul, man has a second immaterial faculty—a spirit, which is the special endowment of God to all believers. For as we read in the Apostle's first letter to the Thessalonians (5:23)," he recited...

> *Now may the God of peace himself sanctify you completely, and may your whole spirit and soul and body be kept blameless at the coming of our Lord Jesus Christ.*

There was a stir among the seated witnesses suggesting a disagreement on this view—that humans are comprised of a body, a soul, and a spirit. Irenaeus quickly added,

---

24 Also known as the Great Tradition, these were the teachings and practices from the first five centuries of the early Church.

25 "Immaterial (without material) soul" means the soul is entirely distinct from the material body.

26 Irenaeus, *Against Heresies,* V.VI.1-2. (ANF 1, 531-532).

27 Irenaeus, *Against Heresies* IV. Preface. 4. (ANF 1, 463 paraphrased).

"The truly spiritual man is not a pure, un-embodied soul as our Gnostics opponents teach. Rather, when the spirit, blended with the soul, is united to God's handiwork, the body, then man is made spiritual and perfect because of the outpouring of the Spirit: and this is *he* who was made in the image *and* likeness of God.[28]

"Honored teacher," asked Mentor, "are you making a distinction between *the image* of God and *the likeness* of God?

"Truly," said Irenaeus, "based on the passage I have read."

"Are you are saying," Mentor continued, "that man was created both a body and a soul *in the image* of God, but that the redeemed man, perfected by God's Spirit, is created "in the image *and* likeness of God?"

"Just as you say," affirmed Irenaeus.

"Then how we are to understand the words of Genesis, *Let us make man in our image, after our likeness*?"[29] asked Mentor.

"That passage speaks of man's eternal destiny in Christ," Irenaeus explained, "God created man in His own image *and* provided a way for him to be conformed to his likeness—that is, to his Son—after the Fall."[30]

"Someone may ask," said Mentor, "does this teaching elevate the spirit above the body?"

---

28 Irenaeus, *Against Heresies* V.VI.1. (ANF 1, 532), emphasis added.

29 Genesis 1:26.

30 An interpretation of what Irenaeus says in V.VI.1 (ANF 1, 532), not a quotation.

"Not at all," Irenaeus replied, "for the body is the temple of God.[31] And God made man a free agent from the beginning, possessing his own power, even as he does his own soul, to obey the demands of God voluntarily, not by compulsion."[32]

"So, then, the soul is the seat of decision making?" asked Mentor.

"Yes," he replied, I affirm the essential rationality of the soul."

"Thank you, honored Irenaeus." The witness returned to his place in the pre-Nicene choir stalls as Mentor summarized,

"On the question of the nature of man, whether he is composed of body, soul, and spirit; or body and soul; or body and spirit, our witnesses have not reached consensus." As Mentor said this we could hear Irenaeus reciting the Thessalonian passage again, "*...may your entire body, soul, and spirit be kept blameless...*"

"In any case," Mentor continued, "as we explore the creation of humankind in the image of God, we are reminded that rationality—intelligence—is an essential part of that image."

Mentor now called on Justin Martyr.

"In the beginning," said the great apologist, "God made the human race with the power of thought and of choosing the truth and doing right, so that all men are without excuse before God; for they have been born rational and contemplative."[33]

---

31 Irenaeus, *Against Heresies* V.VI.1. (ANF 1, 532), emphasis added.

32 Irenaeus, *Against Heresies*, IV.XXXVII.1. (ANF 1, 518).

33 Justin Martyr, *First Apology*, XXVIII. (ANF 1, 172).

"The terms of this view is quite clear," said Mentor, "including the power of thought, choosing truth, and doing right. Man is born rational—he can reason within himself—and contemplative—he can reflect on the accuracy of his thinking and his beliefs. In sum, he can think for himself and he is free to choose the good."

"There is something more," said Justin Martyr. Mentor nodded.

"In my day," added the apologist," pagans believed that humans could only do evil because they had been created by an evil god. I wrote my *Apology* to defend the intelligence and morality of my fellow believers who were being wrongly persecuted."[34]

"And from that work, we have all benefited" said Mentor. The witnesses answered with a resounding "amen."

The Origin of Sin

"We have examined the creation and constitution of humankind," said Mentor. "Now we must consider the origin of human sin in the light of the mystery of iniquity already described, and the response of our earthly parents."

"Earthly parents?" Preacher asked Father Greg.

"He means Adam and Eve," said the priest quietly, "we're going to hear about the Fall of Man in Genesis 3."

Mentor now invited two familiar witnesses back to the lectern to testify, and a third we had not met. Ambrose of Milan, gave a brief opening statement:

34 Justin Martyr wrote the Roman Emperor to offer "an unexceptional account of their (the Christian) life and doctrine" (*First Apology*, III. ANF 1, 163).

"The blessed couple inhabiting the Garden of God enflamed the Devil with envy. For he loathed their favored status and detested the idea that a creature formed from the dirt should be elected to Paradise!"[35]

I had never considered the idea that Satan was jealous of Adam and Eve and their special relationship with God.

"Why didn't they just kill that nasty snake?" asked Preacher, loudly enough for everyone to hear.

The three witnesses looked at one another. The one we had not met, a Syrian witness—Severian of Gabal—replied,

"Please, do not picture the serpent as repulsive, at least not in the beginning. I believe that his ugliness resulted from the curse. After all, why would our mother Eve listen to a repulsive creature? Remember: Adam named every creature and all were created to serve him. Now then, imagine a dog with his master and you are not far from seeing how the serpent might have served Adam prior to the fall. His nearness to humanity, as pets are near to their masters, made the serpent a suitable servant to man but, sadly, a useful tool for the devil."[36]

"Indeed," added Ephrem, "Scripture says the serpent was 'craftier than any other beast of the field,' but that

---

35 Paraphrase of Ambrose, *Liber de Paradiso*, XII. PL 14.318. Compare John Savage, Saint Ambrose, *Hexameron, Paradies, and Cain and Abel* in the Fathers of the Church, vol. 42, pages 332-333.

36 Severian of Gabala, *On the Creation of the World* 6.2. Severian's writings are not published in NPNF. The translation is based on *Patrologia Graeca* 56:485-486. See also Louth, Ancient Christian Commentary on Scripture: *Genesis 1-11*, 74-75.

does not mean he was smarter than Adam or that he was evil before being used by Satan."[37]

"You are saying that God created the serpent good?" asked Mentor, joining the discussion.

"Every creature God created was created good!" replied Severian, "that the serpent was craftier than other beasts may suggest only that he was better suited to befriend the man and woman."

"The serpent stayed close by them," said Ephrem, "except in the midst of the Garden, where he could not enter."[38]

"Why could the serpent not enter the garden?" asked Mentor.

"I believe no creatures except the man and woman were permitted in the inner region of Paradise, where the man and woman communed with God," replied Ephrem. "We sing about this in our *Hymns of Paradise*. Would you like to hear?" asked Ephrem.

"Yes, please," said Mentor.

Ephrem went to one of the passageways and called to some witnesses seated in the second section. Several hooded figures came into the Crux and stood around the lectern. Led by Ephrem they began to sing:

As for that part of the Garden, my beloved,
Which is situated so gloriously at the summit of
that height...
Perhaps that blessed tree, the Tree of Life is,

37 Based on Ephrem of Syria, *Commentary on Genesis*, Section II.15 (not in NPNF) in Sebastian Brock, *Hymns on Paradise, Saint Ephrem the Syrian* (Crestwood, NY: St. Vladimir's Seminary Press, 1990), pages 206-210.

38 Same as previous note.

By its rays the sun of Paradise.

In the very midst He planted the Tree of Knowledge,
Endowing it with awe, hedging it in with dread,
So that it might straightway serve as a boundary to
The inner region of Paradise.

The serpent could not enter Paradise,
For neither animal nor bird was permitted to approach
the inner region of Paradise,
And Adam had to go out to meet them;
So the serpent cunningly learned through questioning
Eve
the nature of Paradise,
what it was and how it was ordered.

When the accursed one learned how
The glory of that inner Tabernacle
as if in a sanctuary was hidden from them,
And that the Tree of Knowledge clothed with a
commandment
Served as the veil for the sanctuary,
He realized that its fruit was the key of justice
That would open the eyes of the bold
—and cause them great remorse.[39]

As their singing ended, the hymn's final stanza echoed throughout the chamber. Everyone appeared deep in thought, and for a while no one spoke.

How can I describe the beauty of the Syrian hymn? The hooded singing figures were in fact women with

---

39 Paraphrase of Sebastian Brock, *Hymns on Paradise, Saint Ephrem the Syrian* (Crestwood, NY: St. Vladimir's Seminary Press, 1990), Hymn 3, pages 90-92.

angelic voices. They sung in a heavenly language unlike anything we'd yet heard.[40] It was as if this language was invented expressly for singing. The melody and the lyrics were of one piece that lifted us to the summit of the garden, then made us to feel the awesome sanctity of the holy place within the garden, and finally evoked a powerful sense of remorse at the Fall.

"I never heard of a dog in the garden of Eden!" teased Preacher, about the first Syrian's comment.

"He didn't say the serpent *was* a dog," corrected Joseph, "he said that before the fall the serpent was like a pet to the man and woman."

"Yeah, but he said the serpent couldn't even get into the garden, so how'd he tempt Eve?"

"I wondered about that myself," said Joseph.

"Scripture doesn't say the serpent was with Eve when she ate the fruit," said Cesar,

Joseph pulled his Bible from his pocket and began reading the passage silently.

"Maybe Adam went outside the garden to name all the animals," I said.

"Adam was in the garden 'til he got kicked out," said Preacher, "how could he name the animals if they wadn't in the garden?"

"Scripture says God put the man in the garden to tend it," Father Greg agreed, "but it does not say he was forbidden to leave the garden."

"If he left the garden, how could he get past the guardian angels?" demanded Preacher.

---

40 Syriac, the language of Ephrem of Syria.

"You mean the Cherubim with a sword," said Joseph, "but that didn't happen until after the Fall. And Cesar's right, Genesis 3 does not say the serpent was with Eve at the tree."

"Whatever," said Preacher.

"What the Syrian Fathers teach makes sense from a sacramental point of view," explained Father Greg.

"A sacramental point of view?" asked Joseph.

"Yes, a view that relates these things to the act of worship. In other words, as you read the opening chapters of Genesis look for anything related to worship or liturgy."

Joseph skimmed the opening pages of his Bible.

"I'm not really sure what to look for," he admitted.

"What do you think of when you think of worship?" asked Father Greg, borrowing Joseph's Bible to look for himself.

"Hmm, guitars I guess, and people singing or clapping," said Joseph.

"Anything else?" asked the priest.

"We dance during worship at my church," added Cesar.

"What about the Eucharist?" asked the priest.

"The what?" asked Preacher, rejoining the discussion.

"That's the Catholic term for the Lord's Supper," said Cesar.

"It's the biblical term," the priest corrected, "it means thanksgiving. Would you agree, the Lord's Supper is an act of worship?"

"Yeah, but there's no Lord's Supper in Genesis," said Preacher.

"Maybe not," said Father Greg, "but there are sacramental elements are there."

"Like what?" asked Joseph.

"There's a river," said the priest, "does that remind you of anything?

"Well, it's not the Jordan River," I said, "but it reminds me of baptism."

"Excellent" said Father Greg,

"There's gold and precious stones there too," said Cesar, "like offerings."

"There are sacrifices mentioned in chapter 4," Joseph added.

"Listen to this," I said, reading over Father Greg's shoulder, "Therefore a man shall leave his father and his mother and hold fast to his wife, and they shall become one flesh,[41] —it's a wedding!"

"Precisely," agreed Father Greg, "sacrifice, worship, even a wedding, here in the opening chapters of Genesis. Then, in Exodus we read about the tabernacle with its holy place and holy of holies, built according to God's design; and in Leviticus we read about what happens when someone offers strange fire on the altar…"

"So what?" Preacher interrupted.

"It's an interpretation, Edward," said Father Greg. "The Syrian witnesses view the garden as a temple or sanctuary, and the forbidden fruit as a type of veil preventing Adam and Eve from eating from the tree of life."

"That's not how I pictured it," said Preacher, shaking his head.

---

41 Genesis 2:24 (ESV).

"It's not how I pictured the scene either," agreed Father Greg, "but it makes sense, doesn't it?"[42]

Two Paradises and Two Falls

After our discussion Mentor thanked the three Fathers and offered this summary of their insights as we listened.

"Two paradises have been *narrated* for us: a heavenly paradise of pure light and an earthly paradise of life—the first paradise for angelic beings, the second for humankind. Satan was envious of the earthly couple's favored status before God—their "election to Eden" as our brother Ambrose described. Then, as our Syrian brothers taught, Satan asked subtle questions of our mother, Eve, through the voice of the serpent. This is how he discovered that the Almighty had placed a veil over the most holy place of the Garden to prevent the man and woman from eating fruit from the tree of life. The Serpent, jealous as he was of Adam and Eve, infected our mother with the same envy that caused him to be expelled from heaven. Thus, the fallen angel convinced

---

42 Ephrem imagines the Garden of Eden very differently than today's readers (those who bother to imagine the scene at all). Eden is not just a pretty park but truly is the garden of God where the man and woman commune with God as if in a sanctuary. Like the Tabernacle described in Exodus, as one moves from the outer court though a series of chambers into the most holy place—the Holy of Holies—one draws near to the very presence of God. Genesis 3:22 indicates that Adam and Eve had not eaten from the Tree of Life. And according to Ephrem's hymn, the Tree of the Knowledge of Good and Evil prevented them from doing so—it served the same function as the veil of the Tabernacle later served, to prevent unauthorized entrance into the most holy place with the consequence of death. It makes sense, given this view of the garden, that the serpent was not present when Eve ate the forbidden fruit.

her to violate the most holy place of the garden by eating the fruit of knowledge."[43]

In my mind's eye I pictured the angels of heaven feeding on God's light just as the man and woman enjoyed the fruit of paradise. In disobeying God's command to not eat of the tree of the knowledge of good and evil, the man and woman turned away from the light just as the rebellious angels had done. The tragedy of this "double Fall" echoed in my thoughts as Ephrem's magnificent hymn echoed in my memory.

"We thank our God in Christ Jesus," Mentor continued, "because after the tragedy of the Fall, Good News is announced: the curse pronounced upon the serpent includes these words," Mentor read from the lectern Bible,

> *I will put enmity between you and the woman, and between your offspring and her offspring; he shall bruise your head, and you shall bruise his heel.*[44]

"The woman's offspring is Christ," added Joseph, "God promised to make Him triumph over the serpent!" Mentor nodded, and called on Justin Martyr who had saluted.

"Some may ask," said the apologist, "why didn't God simply forbid there to be a serpent, instead of saying 'I will put enmity between him and the woman, and between his seed and her seed?'"[45]

---

43 This interpretation follows a pattern seen by some in 2 Chron. 26:16-21.

44 Gen. 3:15.

45 Justin Martyr, *Dialogue with Trypho the Jew*, 102 (ANF 1, 250).

Preacher beamed proudly, having asked the question himself.

"Of course, God could have simply denied the serpent existence," Justin Martyr continued, "yet since He knew that it would be good, He created angels and men free to do that which is righteous; and He appointed periods of time during which He knew it would be good for them to have the exercise of free-will."[46]

"The passage announces Good News," added Mentor, "since our God promised to make hatred the enduring mark of the relationship between the woman's offspring, Christ, and Satan. This means that the reign of evil will not last forever, because a time will come when the Savior of the world, born to one of Eve's descendants, will be the one to bruise the serpent's head!"[47]

The seated witnesses shouted "amen!"

"Christ has summed up all things," added Irenaeus, "waging war against our enemy and crushing him who had at the beginning led us away as captives in Adam, trampling on Satan's head, just as you read in Genesis, 'And I will put enmity between you and the woman, and between your seed and her seed.'"[48]

Jonah and the Big Fish

As Mentor concluded *The Time Before Time*, announcing the upcoming theme—*The Unfolding of Time*, Preacher

---

46 Same as previous note.

47 Mentor's statement is based Susanne de Dietrich, *God's Unfolding Purpose*, 37.

48 Irenaeus, *Against Heresies* V.21.1 (ANF 1,548).

went to speak with one of the ancient witnesses. Joseph and I followed along to listen in.

"Father Eary-us" said Preacher, mispronouncing Irenaeus's name, "I have a question."

Irenaeus nodded.

"My granny was a real saint," began Preacher, "she raised me and my brother and led us to the Lord. She worked two jobs to help us kids through school. But last year on her way home from the bus stop she was stabbed to death—it was in the newspaper."

Irenaeus listened attentively, with a look of compassion.

"Maybe you don't know the answer to this," said Preacher, "but if God is a loving God..." He paused as his voice trembled, and Irenaeus placed a hand on Preacher's shoulder.

"If death brings on mortality," replied Irenaeus, "then how much more will life, when it arrives, will make us alive again!" Preacher listened closely.

"Isaiah the Prophet says that God has wiped away every tear from every face," Irenaeus continued, "our former life is over because it was not given by the Spirit but by the breath."[49]

Preacher looked puzzled, and the ancient witness took a different approach.

"You have heard of Jonah?" asked Irenaeus.

"Jonah was swallowed by the whale," said Preacher, somewhat sadly.

49 Irenaeus, *Against Heresies* V.12.1 (ANF 1, 537).

"Think about this, young man," said Irenaeus, "in his patience, God permitted Jonah to be swallowed by the great fish."

"But that was Jonah's punishment!" Preacher objected.

"No, my brother, it was his salvation, don't you see?" said Irenaeus. "God appointed the great fish not to destroy Jonah; but so that when vomited up, he would glorify the God who had lavished on him such an undeserved deliverance. And through God's word, Jonah was commanded to bring the Ninevites to repentance, so they would be converted to the Lord who would deliver them from death also. The Ninevites were awestruck at the sign of Jonah, and each of them repented from his evil way![50]" Preacher began to smile.

"So it was from the very beginning," Irenaeus concluded, "God allowed man to be swallowed up by the great whale who was the author of sin—Satan—not so the man would be destroyed, but so the plan of salvation would be accomplished by the Word, and be evident in the sign of Jonah."[51]

Preacher thanked Irenaeus, and we returned to our bench.

"What did you think of his answer, Preacher?" asked Joseph.

"It was okay I guess" said Preacher, "but I still don't know why my granny had to die.

"I think Irenaeus was giving you a challenge," I said.

---

50 Paraphrase of Irenaeus, *Against Heresies* III.20.1 (ANF 1, 449). The sign of Jonah is mentioned in Luke 11:29.

51 Paraphrase of Irenaeus, *Against Heresies* III.20.1 (ANF 1.449-450).

"What'd you mean?" asked Preacher.

"Let's say you were Jonah," I suggested, "and that you were swallowed by the whale when your grandmother was murdered."

"Okay," said Preacher, "now what?"

"Exactly," I agreed, "now what will you do?"

Preacher, confused, looked at Joseph who shrugged.

"What did Jonah do after he was swallowed by the whale, Preacher?" I asked.

Preacher grinned.

"Jonah prayed, the whale puked, and Jonah preached!" he said, quoting one of his own sermon titles, "I guess that means I got find those guys who killed my granny and preach to 'em."

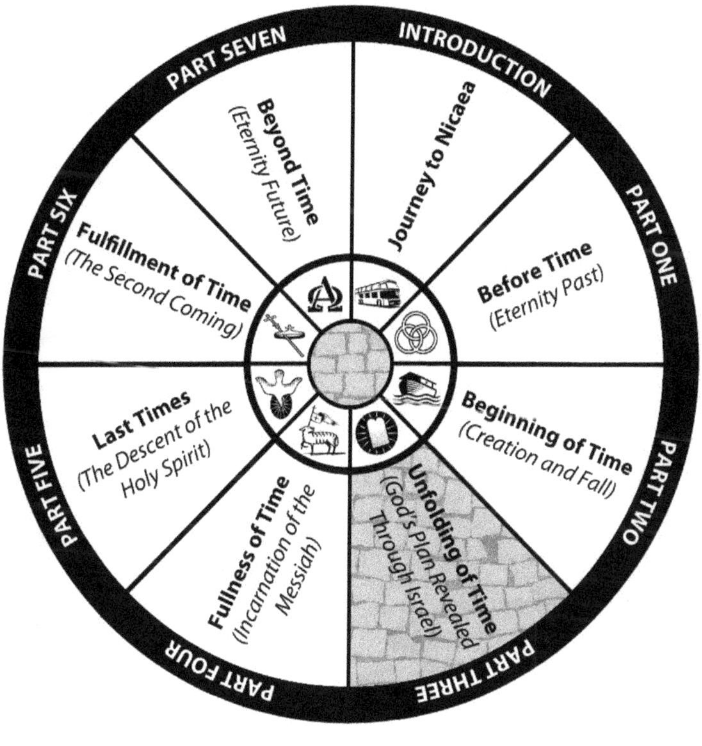

INTRODUCTION
Journey to Nicaea
PART ONE
Before Time
(Eternity Past)
PART TWO
Beginning of Time
(Creation and Fall)
PART THREE
Unfolding of Time
(God's Plan Revealed Through Israel)
PART FOUR
Fullness of Time
(Incarnation of the Messiah)
PART FIVE
Last Times
(The Descent of the Holy Spirit)
PART SIX
Fulfillment of Time
(The Second Coming)
PART SEVEN
Beyond Time
(Eternity Future)

Chapter 4: The Unfolding of Time, Part 1

The five of us and Mentor were alone in the Crux when it was time for the next session to begin.

"When do the witnesses return?" asked Cesar.

"During this session you will meet them in the reading room," replied Mentor.

We looked at one another, wondering if our time in the Crux was over. Mentor noticed our concern.

"There are many episodes in the *Unfolding of Time*," he explained.[1] "The witnesses must narrate these in their respective settings so that you may fully grasp them."

---

1 While "the unfolding of time" is not an expression found in the Bible, it effectively names the period after the fall of humankind and up to the advent of the Savior, with his inauguration of God's kingdom. It begins, accordingly, with the call of Abraham in Genesis 12 and continues through the end of the Old Testament and the beginning of the New, where its conclusion is marked by these words in Mark's Gospel, "Now after John was arrested, Jesus came into Galilee, proclaiming the gospel of God, and saying, *The time is fulfilled, and the kingdom of God is at hand*; repent and believe in the gospel" (Mark 1:14–15 ESV, emphasis added). Following the outline provided by Suzanne de Dietrich in *God's Unfolding Purpose*, chapters 4 and 5 explore the interaction of God with his people leading up to the incarnation. In sum, it tells the story of Israel as the chosen people of God.

We all knew how life-like reading in the reading room could be, and Mentor let us know we would be returning to the Crux.

Now he tested us on the previous session.

"When was the first announcement of the Good News?" he asked.

Father Greg smiled but did not reply.

"Matthew's Gospel is first," answered Joseph.

"But Mark's Gospel was earlier," I countered, recalling what I had learned at our seminary.

"Which of them is right," Mentor? asked Cesar.

"Listen carefully to the question," he replied, "and draw your answer from the Hebrew Scriptures."

That was the clue I needed, recalling Genesis 3:15.

"When was the message of the gospel first announced?" Mentor repeated.

"When the Lord cursed the Serpent," I answered.

"Truly," said Mentor, "and in the announcement of eternal enmity between the Serpent and the woman, between his offspring and her offspring."

"Yes!" I said, high-fiving Joseph.

"God's plan," Mentor continued, "was to send a Champion to remedy the rebellion ignited by the fallen angel."

"So, Satan started a fire that Jesus came to put out!" declared Preacher.

"Truly," agreed Mentor, "the Champion will be a future descendant of Eve who will come forth from Abraham, of whom you shall soon hear."

"I love the story of Abraham!" said Preacher.

"Many episodes flow from his story," said Mentor, "from Abraham's call to the return of a faithful remnant from exile."

"Can you tell us exactly what episodes we'll be seeing?" asked Cesar.

Mentor named the following, which I recorded in my journal.

1. The Promise and the Patriarchs
2. The Exodus and the Covenant at Sinai
3. The Promised Land
4. The City, the Temple, and the Throne
5. The Exile
6. The Remnant

"You have but a brief time to explore each episode," said Mentor, "so be watchful."

"What exactly are we watching for?" asked Joseph.

"The Good News about the seed of the woman," replied Mentor.

"Do we go to the reading room now?" asked Cesar.

"You are not yet prepared," replied Mentor. He invited Cesar up to the lectern to the read aloud from the lectern Bible. Cesar stood next to Mentor, gazing at the large letters of the Greek Bible. After a moment, he began reading confidently.

Now the lord said to Abram, "Go from your country and your kindred and your father's house to the land that I

> *will show you. And I will make of you a great nation, and I will bless you and make your name great, so that you will be a blessing. I will bless those who bless you, and him who dishonors you I will curse, and in you all the families of the earth shall be blessed.*[2]

Mentor held up his hand as a signal for Cesar to pause the reading.

"Abram obeys the voice of God and makes his way to Canaan," Mentor summarized, then prompted Cesar to continue his reading.

> *Then the Lord appeared to Abram and said, "To your seed I will give this land." So he built there an altar to the Lord, who had appeared to him.*

"If we compare Abram with Noah, for God also made a promise to Noah's seed," [3] explained Mentor, "we see that His promise to Abram's seed includes a personal blessing, 'I will bless you and make your name great…', and the promise of land. Thus, we read of the Lord's intention to create a new nation from Abram's seed. 'I will make of you a great nation'" he says, "and 'to your seed I will give this land.'"

"While the Hebrews sojourned in Canaan," Mentor continued, "they had no homeland and were not a people.[4] Now, God adopts them, promising to make them his own."[5]

---

2 Gen. 12:2-3,7.

3 See Gen. 9.

4 See Deut. 26:5 and Hos. 1:9-10.

5 Exod. 6:7.

"The adoption of Israel is crucial for salvation history," added Father Greg.

"Why is that?" asked Cesar.

"This is where the people of God have their beginning," explained Father Greg.

"The Jews *were* God's chosen people until they disobeyed," said Cesar, "now it's us—the Church, and we're Gentiles."

"Wait," said Joseph, "according to Paul 'there is neither Jew nor Greek, for you are all one in Christ Jesus.'"[6]

"He also says, 'If you are Christ's then you are Abraham's offspring,'" I added.

"Please draw your answers from the Hebrew Scriptures," Mentor insisted.

"Ha!" said Cesar, "your answers are disqualified."

"But Christ is not mentioned by name in the Old Testament," said Joseph.

"Very well," said Mentor, "you may begin with the Apostle's teaching."

"If you are Christ's then you are Abraham's seed!'" repeated Joseph.

"What is the historical interpretation of that teaching?" asked Mentor.[7]

"Excuse me?" asked Joseph.

"Why did the Apostle write his epistle?" Mentor clarified.

"To correct the 'foolish Galatians,'" answered Joseph.

---

6 See Gal. 3:28-29.

7 Ancient Biblical exegesis included four levels of interpretation, the first of which—historical—sought a literal understanding of the words.

"Why does he call them foolish?" asked Mentor.

"They were falling back into their old ways—trying to earn their salvation by the Law."

"Anything more?" asked Mentor.

Cesar borrowed Joseph's Bible, turned to Galatians and began skimming chapter 3.

"There's a lot here about faith and the law…" said Cesar, "but basically Paul is saying that the Scriptures foretold that the Gentiles would be justified by their faith in God." Cesar then read this verse, aloud:

The Scripture, foreseeing that God would justify the Gentiles by faith, preached the gospel to Abraham beforehand, saying, "In you all the nations shall be blessed."[8]

"Paul is quoting the Old Testament here," concluded Cesar, "so, Genesis 3:15 is not the only verse that foretells the Gospel."

"Truly," said Mentor, "and it is through the promise of God to Abram that we become the children of Abraham, not through the flesh or lineage of Abraham. Now you are ready to listen to the witnesses as they narrate the Scriptures."

The Promise and the Patriarchs

Mentor led us out of the Crux and into the reading room.

"We have chosen these for you," he explained, pointing to several open books on the table. "Please return to the Crux after your lessons to testify to what you have seen."

"Can you tell us about the historical setting of these lessons?" asked Cesar.

8 Gal. 3:8, quoting Gen. 12:3.

"Several witnesses testify to *The Unfolding of Time*," explained Mentor. "To begin, our brother Justin Martyr testifies to a Jew in Rome; Bishop Ambrose of Milan instructs his catechumens in Milan; and Bishop Irenaeus teaches hearers on the frontier."[9]

Mentor reminded us to be watchful for the seed or offspring of the woman. As he turned to leave, the five of us took our places at the reading table. I put my head down on the table and waited, but hearing a voice, I sat up again. I found myself seated on a bench in a beautiful park. The air was fresh as early morning, and there was a gardener working nearby. I was vaguely aware of Father Greg and my fellow students nearby as well, but they were like shadows compared to the brilliant scene before us.

A young man walked by, it was Justin Martyr from the Athenaeum. An old man called out to him and the two began a dialogue.

Trypho the Jew: *Greetings, O philosopher!*[10]

Justin Martyr: *What's worth knowing, Sir?*

Trypho: *Well, as a disciple of Corinthus the Socratic, I was taught never to disrespect a man wearing the philosopher's robe, but to show kindness and to engage him in discussion for the edification of myself or for both our sakes!*

Justin: *And who are you, most excellent man?*

---

9 *Catechumen* is the ancient term for anyone being instructed in the Christian faith; *hearers* refers to beginners in the *catechesis* process.

10 A paraphrased version of portions of Justin's *Dialogue of Trypho, A Jew* chapter 1 (ANF 1, 194).

Trypho: *Trypho is my name. I am a Hebrew of the circumcision, and having escaped from the recent war, I am spending my time in Greece, mainly at Corinth.*

Justin: *Why look to philosophy? As a Jew, you have your own lawgiver and prophets.*

Trypho: *Why not consider philosophy? Don't the philosophers turn every discussion to God? And, indeed, isn't the duty of philosophy to investigate God?*

Justin: *I agree, but few philosophers know if there is one god or many, or whether they care for humanity or not. Most of them claim that if God cares for the universe and its creatures, still he cares nothing for you and I—if he did we would have no need to pray. Those who believe such things have no fear of God, but say and do whatever they want—fearing no punishment and expecting no benefit from God. Others, who believe the soul to be immortal and immaterial, see it as unaffected by the evil they do in the flesh, and suppose that it needs nothing from God.*

Trypho: *Tell me, then, what is your belief and how do you conceive of God?*

Justin answered Trypho's question by defining philosophy as *one truth*, which had been corrupted when it was divided into many schools of thought. Next, he shared how he himself had become a Christian through a dialogue with a certain old man. Trypho responded by claiming his own people's privileged status as Jews.

"*Who really are God's chosen people?* replied Justin, *for we Christians too are chosen people, and the Church is the nation promised to Abraham by God, when he told him that he would make him a father of many nations.*[11] *Christians are no tribe of barbarians but a holy people, for how else could we understand the Scriptures and discern God's plan?*[12] *You, Trypho, call yourself a son of Abraham, and rightly so. Yet, what is Abraham but a son of Noah—and we are all sons of Noah! Other nations have their ancestors, too, and there have been many great nations—Arabians, Egyptians, Idumeans*[13]*—but which is the nation God promised to Abraham? And what grace did Christ bestow on Abraham, setting him apart from Noah?*

Justin Martyr, I observed, interpreted events from the lives of Noah and Abraham in the light of the larger Story of God, as Mentor had modeled for us. Moreover, his question to Trypho—*what grace did Christ bestow on Abraham?*—testified to the presence of the Second Person of the Trinity throughout holy history. Justin Martyr answered his own question as follows.

It was Christ who called Abraham and commanded him to leave the land wherein he dwelt. And with that same voice he has also called all of us, and we have abandoned our former way of life in which we used to practice evils common to all the other inhabitants of the world. And we shall inherit the Holy Land together with Abraham, receiving our inheritance for all eternity, because by our similar faith we have become children of Abraham. For just as Abraham believed the voice of God, and was thereby

---

11 Justin's *Dialogue with Trypho, A Jew*, chapter 119, based on the translation of Thomas B. Falls, in *St. Justin Martyr, Dialogue with Trypho*. Washington, D.C.: The Catholic University of America Press. (ANF 1, 258-259).

12 By "the Scriptures" Justin Martyr refers, of course, to the Old Testament or Hebrew/Jewish Scriptures.

13 Esau's descendants, Gen. 36:9.

justified, we likewise have believed the voice of God, spoken to us by the prophets and the Apostles of Christ, and have renounced all worldly things even to death.

Justin Martyr's telling of the story not only revealed Christ's presence, but also applied the principles he found there. As I recorded these things in my journal, I noticed Father Greg and my fellow students walking toward an old stone chapel on the far side of the park. By the time I got there, they had already gone in.

The entrance to the chapel was covered by beautiful flowering vines. I could hear preaching coming from inside, so I entered through a side door and found myself in an office or library stacked high with scrolls and codices.[14] There was a small book open on a table entitled *On Abraham* and I began reading it, though it was not in English.

Reading Latin, for that was the book's language, was an interesting experience. Unlike Tertullian's chopped phrases, this author wrote long sentences with the main verb left to the end, as if to keep the reader in suspense. After reading a few lines, I realized that the speaker was preaching was on the same topic, so I laid the book aside and went to find a seat in the chapel.

There was only one seat and it was occupied by the Bishop. A hundred or more catechumens—men and women—stood listening to him as he taught. The Bishop's face was strong and wise, and his speech was eloquent. He was Bishop Ambrose whom we'd heard

---

14 A codex (plural: *codices*) is the ancient book form that preceded modern printed and bound volumes.

testify in the Crux.[15] Reading from the Bible, the Bishop commented on the story of Abraham.

"When he was tested," began Ambrose, "Abraham proved courageous;

When he was stirred up he proved faithful;

and when he was called he proved righteous;"[16]

I began taking notes in my journal.

"But why is it," asked Ambrose, "that Moses recalled the lives of the patriarchs in such detail for us? What did he mean for us to learn from the example of Abraham?"

An old man among the hearers offered an answer to the Bishop's question,

"Whatever happened bodily to Abraham is fulfilled spiritually in us," said the old man. "And since God commanded Abraham to *leave your country, your kinfolk, and your father's house*, we believe that all these things are fulfilled in us as we participate in the sacrament of baptism."[17]

Everyone listened respectfully to the man, who continued,

"Our land is our body! We go forth from our land if we abandon our fleshly habits to follow in the footsteps of Christ. We leave our kinfolk behind when through

---

15 See page 103.

16 Based on Ambrose of Milan, *On Abraham* 2.3.9. Compare Saint Ambrose of Milan, *On Abraham*, translated by Theodosia Thompkinson (Etna, California: Samford University Press, 2000), 50ff. The text is found in *Patrologia Latina* 14, 442: *Tentatur ut fortis, incitatur ut fidelis, provocatur ut Justus.*

17 Caesarius of Arles, Sermon 81 in *Father of the Church* series, volume 47, pages 3-6.

the grace of baptism we are emptied of all sins and vices. *Leave your father's house*… this must be understood spiritually since the devil was our father before the grace of Christ."

Ambrose thanked the old man for his insights, some of which reminded me of Justin Martyr's teaching.

"How did Abraham know that God was speaking to him?" the Bishop now asked his hearers. No one offered an answer, so Ambrose continued his teaching.

"Before he was called, Abraham was unable to see God. This was because the Chaldeans, Abraham's ancestors, looked to nature—the earth and the stars—for their gods. Indeed, they called the stars 'gods,' inasmuch as they believed that they exercised dominion from above."[18]

"As long as Abraham's mind was perverted by the errors of the Chaldeans," Ambrose continued, "he did not see God—for his people looked for God in things which are seen, not in things which are unseen. Now, we know that things which are seen are temporal, while unseen things are eternal.[19] God is not temporal, so He is not seen. Therefore, a mind which follows the teachings of the Chaldeans does not see God. Hence, Abraham did not see God at first."[20]

"When Abraham entered a new place," Ambrose concluded, "not a country but the true religion suited to humility, for this is the meaning of Canaan, then he began to see God and to recognize Him as God, by

---

18 Ambrose, *On Abraham* 2.3.9. My paraphrase is based on the translation of Theodosia Thompkinson, *On Abraham*. Etna, CA: Center for Traditionalist Orthodox Studies, 2000.

19 See 2 Cor. 4:18.

20 See previous note.

Whose invisible grace he perceived all things to be ruled and governed. Therefore, Scripture teaches that Abraham, leaving behind the observation of the stars, saw God."[21]

"To see God is to know God!" I wrote in my journal. According to Bishop Ambrose, Abraham slowly grew to perceive God's invisible grace which rules and governs everything. In the first place, however, the Bishop had asked how Abraham even knew he had heard the voice of God. His answer came from his understanding of the historical context. Specifically, the practice of astrology by Abram's ancestors[22] prevented Abram from hearing God's voice. Later on, however, his act of obedience in leaving his homeland enabled him to know God. In other words, Abraham could not perceive God so long as he was under the influence of Chaldean culture, but that changed when the Patriarch obeyed God's call. Ambrose compared the Chaldeans and their false religion, astrology, with Canaan—the Promised land—as a place of humility, meaning true religion.

For Ambrose, Abraham's growth in grace was a process of discovery guided by God. I continued making notes in my journal until I saw my friends leaving by the front door. Going out by way of the library, I noticed more books by Ambrose and stopped to look them over. There was *On Isaac, or the Soul,* a book about Rebekah, Isaac's wife, and her journey of conversion and growth in faith. Two other books—*Jacob and the Blessed Life*, and *On the Patriarch Joseph*—were about how these two patriarchs survived times of trial through the application

21 See previous note.

22 This, perhaps, is hinted at in in Gen. 11:27-28,

of Christian principles.[23] I was eager to read more, and decided to carry them back with to the Crux, thinking that I could always return them later.

My friends were nowhere in sight when I left, but the gardener whom I had seen earlier was working next to the chapel. Looking up, he nodded toward a path that led into a grassy pasture. I followed it down into a ravine where I found a rustic shelter built into the side of a hill. A sign over the gate said *ovile ovium*—the Sheepfold. I entered the gate, but the shelter was filled with people. Through a crack in the wall I could see a Christian teacher surrounded by hearers, all huddled together on a dirt floor.

The teacher was Irenaeus, whom I recognized from the Crux. He was teaching about the coming "dominion of the righteous over the creation," based on a Bible passage that one of his hearers read with some difficulty:[24]

> *For the earnest expectation of the creature waiteth for the manifestation of the sons of God. For the creature was made subject to vanity, not willingly, but by reason of him who hath subjected the same in hope, because the creature itself also shall be delivered from the bondage of corruption into the glorious liberty of the children of God.*[25]

---

23 This summation is based on Marcia Colish, *Ambrose's Patriarchs*. Notre Dame, Indiana: University of Notre Dame Press (2005).

24 Irenaeus, *Against Heresies*, V. XXXII. Here, Irenaeus reports his view of the millennium—the thousand-year reign of Christ hinted at in Rev. 20:4-6. For an analysis of the ancient Church's perspective see Charles E. Hill, *Regnum Caelorum: Patterns of Millennial Thought in Early Christianity, 2nd ed*. Grand Rapids, MI.: Eerdmans, 2001.

25 Rom. 8:19–21, quoted from the King James Version which, like the Latin version used by Irenaeus, speaks of the *creature* awaiting redemption instead of the *creation*, as most modern translations have it.

This prophecy, as Irenaeus called the passage, explained the delay in the fulfillment of God's promises, and foretold future blessings. Through their faith in Christ, he explained, believers would become co-heirs of the promises of God.

"Although God promised Abraham the inheritance of the land," explained Irenaeus, "he did not receive it during the time of his sojourn there. Yet, together with his seed—those who fear God and believe in Him—he shall receive it at the resurrection of the just."[26]

"For it is necessary," Irenaeus continued, "for the righteous first to receive the promise of the inheritance which God promised to the fathers, and later to reign in it, when they rise again to behold God in this creation which is renovated, after which the judgment takes place."[27]

"It is only right," he concluded, "that in that same creation in which they toiled or were afflicted, being proven by their suffering, they should receive the reward of their suffering; and that in the creation in which they were slain because of their love of God, in that they should be raised again; and that in the creation in which they endured slavery—there they should reign. For God is rich in all things, and all things are His. It is fitting, therefore, that the creation itself, being restored to its original condition, should be ruled by the righteous with none to oppose them."[28]

Irenaeus's hearers were silent, and I wondered if they were permitted to ask questions. Perhaps they did not

---

26 Irenaeus, *Against Heresies*, V.XXXII (ANF 1, 561).

27 See previous note.

28 See previous note.

know enough to ask questions. I moved to the door and, over the heads of the packed-in hearers, I asked,

"Will Abraham reign over the Promised Land when Christ returns?"

"Yes, my son" replied Irenaeus to me, "and you too will reign over those enemies who have oppressed you in this life, for Christ returns to restore the creation under the dominion of the righteous, then the prophecy will be fulfilled—the creature will experience the glorious liberty of the sons of God!"[29] To the group, Irenaeus then added,

"God's promise to Abraham should give you hope and the strength to endure hardship, as it kept him strong throughout his long life, during which he patiently awaited his inheritance in spite of the fact that he did not actually receive any land, not even a footstep, but was always a stranger and a pilgrim therein."[30]

After the lesson, Irenaeus's hearers unpacked themselves from the Sheepfold and went on their way. I took time to summarize what I had learned in my journal before returning to the Crux. Justin Martyr had taught that by listening to the call of Christ and leaving the world behind, we show ourselves to be God's chosen people. As an apologist, he found common ground for dialogue with the Jewish man and could be persuasive.

Next, Ambrose had highlighted the customs of Abraham's ancestors, especially astrology. This was surprising to me, since I had assumed that only modern biblical scholars interpreted Scripture in the light of its historical context. Ambrose, however, was primarily a preacher, relating the details of Abraham's story to the

---

29 Based on Irenaeus, *Against Heresies*, V.XXXII (ANF 1, 561).

30 See previous note.

Christian life and pointing to faith and obedience as the primary means of knowing God.

Finally, Irenaeus's teaching had helped me to see the big picture of the Story of God, filling me with hope for the future. He had begun with *the creature waiteth for the manifestation of the sons of God* passage from Romans, using it as a kind of lens to explain Abraham's experience of God's promises. In other words, he connected the promise of God described in the Old Testament to the theme of hope mentioned in the New, thereby making the link between the two testaments very clear.[31]

The Exodus and the Covenant at Sinai

By the time I had returned to the Crux my friends had already arrived but Mentor was not there. I shared the books I had discovered with them and asked Father Greg what he thought about Irenaeus' teaching.

"Irenaeus is—or, rather, was—a great systematic theologian," he explained.

---

31 That is, in Rom. 8:19, and this was an important connection to make since many people in Irenaeus's day denied the essential unity of the Bible. The heretic Marcion, for example, rejected the Old Testament, teaching that the creator god was an inferior being to the god whom Jesus called his Father. Irenaeus insisted on the unity of the Godhead and, therefore, of the two testaments. Specifically, ever present with the Father were His "Word and Wisdom," that is "the Son and the Spirit, by whom...He made all things, to whom also He speaks, saying, "Let Us make man after Our image and likeness" (*Against Heresies* IV, XX.1). Moreover, the Church Father asked, "How could the (Old Testament) Scriptures testify of Him (Jesus Christ), unless they were from one and the same Father? (V.X.1).

Even clearer, perhaps, is this statement in his *Demonstration of the Apostolic Preaching*: "This is our rule of faith, the foundation of the building, and what gives support to our behavior.

God the Father uncreated, who is uncontained, invisible, one God, creator of the universe; this is the first article of our faith. And the second is:

"What makes a theologian a *systematic* theologian?" I asked.

"They discover patterns within and connections between biblical passages," he explained.

"Can you give me an example?" I asked.

"Have you noticed," said Father Greg, "that events in the lives of the patriarchs often foreshadow later events in the life of Israel as a nation?"

"I'm not sure," I admitted.

"Do you remember where Abraham traveled after following God's call to Canaan?" he asked. I could not remember, so we opened Joseph's Bible to Genesis 12, and he asked me to read verses 10-20.

"I remember this story now," I said. "Abraham hides Sarah's true identity from Pharaoh to protect himself."

"True," he agreed, "but look at the plot: notice that Abraham goes to Egypt in the first place because of a famine. Then Abraham and Sarah are 'oppressed' by

---

The *Word of God*, the Son of God, our Lord Jesus Christ, who appeared to the prophets according to their way of prophesying, and according to the dispensation of the Father. Through him all things were created. Furthermore, in the fullness of time, in order to gather all things to himself, he became a human being amongst human beings, capable of being seen and touched, to destroy death, bring life, and restore fellowship between God and humanity. And the third article is:

The *Holy Spirit*, through whom the prophets prophesied, and our forebears learned of God and the righteous were led in the paths of justice, and who, in the fullness of time, was poured out in a new way on our human nature in order to renew humanity throughout the entire world in the sight of God." Quoted in Alister E. McGrath, *The Christian Theology Reader* (Oxford: Blackwell, 1995), 93.

Irenaeus, therefore, was Trinitarian in his theology and thereby recognized the unity of the Old and New Testaments.

Pharaoh in that she is taken into Pharaoh's house to be his concubine. Then God judges Pharaoh's house, striking it with plagues. After that, Abraham and Sarah go free from Egypt, but wealthier than when they arrived, because of all the livestock Pharaoh gives to them for Sarah's sake.[32] Isn't that the story of the Exodus itself?" asked Father Greg.

"I see!" I said. "It's a famine that brings the children of Israel to Egypt; then, the Egyptians oppress them; then come the plagues, and finally redemption from Egypt along with taking their silver and gold utensils."

"Precisely," said Father Greg, "so Abraham's experience in Egypt anticipated what would happen in the lives of his offspring. The fathers noticed these patterns and believed they were prophetic for the new people of God—the Church."

By now the others were listening, and Mentor had returned to discuss what we had seen and heard.

"Mentor, can you help me understand the plagues?" asked Joseph.

"They were signs and wonders from God," said Mentor.

"I know," said Joseph, "but my uncle, who is a college professor, says the children of Israel were able to cross the red sea only because the wind dried it up, making it shallow."

"That's modern thinking," said Father Greg, "the people of our time interpret Exodus through their scientific world view."

---

32 Compare the following passages: Gen. 12:10 & 41:56-42:2; Gen. 12:14-15 & Exod. 1:9-16; Gen. 12:17 & Exod. 7-11; Gen. 12:16, 20 & Exod. 12:35-36.

The fact that Father Greg referred to "the people of our time" made me wonder if he had finally accepted the miracle of our passage back in time.

"My uncle also believes that the Nile River turning into blood was probably an algae infestation that only looked like blood," said Joseph.

"Thank God, the Church Fathers didn't have to worry about science!" said Preacher.

"They had their own sciences," Father Greg corrected, "not as advanced as ours, but the ancient Greeks had medical sciences, biology, physics, and others."

"Truly," agreed Mentor, "our preeminent philosophers are also scientists.[33] Yet, as you have heard for yourselves, the witnesses always interpret Scripture in the light of Scripture."

Mentor excused himself from the Crux for a few moments, returning in the company of two witnesses he said would help us understand their beliefs.

"The elemental principles of creation," explained Mentor, "are themselves creatures of God, compelled to obey their Master."

He introduced the two witnesses as Bishop Cyril of Alexandria, whom we had not yet heard, and Bishop Augustine of Hippo whom we had.

"Listen carefully," said Mentor, "as they testify to the Exodus,"

Cyril was the first to speak. He read from the lectern Bible in a thick accent I could hardly understand. Toward the end of a long passage I realized he was reading from

33 Plato and Aristotle, for two examples.

the book of Isaiah, the prophecy of God's judgment on Babylon.[34] After reading the chapter, he repeated this verse,

> *Therefore, I will make the heavens tremble and the earth will be shaken out of its place, at the wrath of the* Lord *of hosts in the day of his fierce anger.*

"The Holy Prophets speak in parables," Cyril explained, "and in interpreting God's ineffable power and glory they raise their voices aloft and ponder remarkable things in their description."[35]

I understood why Cyril described Isaiah's poetic language as being "in parables," but why was he reading from Isaiah if our subject was the Exodus?

"Created nature are his servants," continued Cyril, "and wrath is stirred in them when the wrath of God arouses them. He was wrathful toward the Egyptians, for example, and creation could not fail to respond; the water was changed into blood, the land gave birth to frogs, as Scripture tells, heaven sent down hail, and total darkness spread over the whole land for three days. So, he says, *heaven will be moved and the earth shaken, from its depths*, as it were, *on account of the anger of the wrath of the Lord;* creation joined in combating the foolish people, and since its Master was offended, it too was aroused. In fact, everything conspires with the supreme design, and there is nothing that exists that does not move in accordance with the divine decisions and design."[36]

---

34 Isa. 13. Isa. 13:13 is the "repeated verse."

35 Robert Hill, *Cyril of Alexandria: Commentary on Isaiah*, vol.1, 288.

36 "So he says…" could refer to God or the Prophet Isaiah (who speaks for God). Robert Hill, *Cyril of Alexandria: Commentary on Isaiah*, vol.1 288.

Cyril excused himself and left the Crux, so there was no chance to ask him a question. I understood now why he had applied Isaiah to the Exodus, but I wondered if this was a case of proof-texting, so I asked Father Greg. [37]

"The Church Fathers often dialogue one passage of Scripture with another," he explained. "Scholars call this *intertextuality*.[38]

"Is that sort of interpretation legit?" asked Cesar.

"I admit the historical contexts differ in the two passages," said Father Greg. "One is the Exodus, of course, and Isaiah prophesied to the nation of Israel near the time of the exile. The theme of judgment runs through both passages, however, and in this case the later passage sheds light on the earlier one."

"The Prophet Isaiah knows the Story of God from beginning to end," added Mentor.

"But what exactly was Cyril teaching?" asked Joseph.

"I got this," said Preacher before Mentor could reply, "the water, the frogs, even the hail—they got God's back! If the Almighty's angry with you, they'll be on you too, cause they all do His will!"

Preacher had nailed it, we all agreed. In my journal I wrote that Cyril applied Isaiah's oracle to the Exodus to show how the pride and arrogance of the wicked bring on God's judgment as expressed through nature.

---

37 Proof-texting is quoting a Scripture out of context (i.e. without explanation of its historical context) in order to prove a point that is not supported by the passage.

38 Intertextuality is the use of one passage to explain another. For a concise survey of various forms of intertextuality see Dr. Steve Moyise, "Intertextuality and Biblical Studies: A Review" in *Verbum et Ecclesia JRG* 23 (2), 2002 (418-431). Posted online at the following link: http://www.ve.org.za/index.php/VE/article/viewFile/1211/1653

Augustine spoke next.

"I agree" he began, "that things which appear to happen by chance in nature really declare the praises of their Creator and point to divine providence. But what do you make of this: the Egyptians were struck with ten plagues and the people of God were given Ten Commandments"?[39]

Having piqued our curiosity, Augustine began comparing the plagues with the commandments.

"The first commandment was to worship God alone, as it says, "For you, there shall be no other gods than me" (Ex.20:3). The first Egyptian plague was water changed to blood (Ex. 7:20). If you compare the first commandment with the first plague you will see that the water is like God, from whom all things derive,[40] and that the blood represents humanity. Now, water turned to blood is corrupted water, that is, water emptied of its divine nature. And isn't this what the Egyptians had done? As Paul explained to the Romans, they "changed the glory of the incorruptible God into the likeness of corruptible man and birds and beasts and serpents."[41] They did this only in their minds, of course, for God himself is unchangeable."[42]

---

39 Augustine, Sermon 8, chapter 2 (not in NPNF) but see Edmund Hill and John Rotelle, *The Works of Saint Augustine A Translation for the Twentieth First Century* (Brooklyn: New City Press), 240ff. My translation is based on the text in *Patrologia Latina*, volume 38, column 67.

40 God made the water before vegetation, beasts, and man; in that sense they are all derived from water. See Gen. 1:9-26.

41 Rom. 1:23.

42 Paraphrase based on Augustine, *Sermon 8*, chapter 2, *Patrologia Latina*, 38, columns 67-74.

"But sir," asked Cesar, "isn't blood symbolic of life in many places throughout Scripture?"

"An excellent observation," said Augustine. "But what does the water represent here in this passage?"

"Before the Nile was turned to blood the Egyptians drank it and bathed in it," said Joseph, studying the passage, "but the blood made it undrinkable and even killed the fish."

"In truth," said Augustine, "and water-changed-into-blood mirrors what the Egyptians did to God: they made him into a creature of blood, and so *their minds were darkened.*"

"But where does it say all that?" asked Cesar.

"In the Apostle's letter to the Romans," replied Augustine, "or have you forgotten that the New in the Old is concealed, and the Old in the New is revealed?"[43]

It took me a moment to realize that Augustine was referring to the New and Old Testaments.

"Another commandment forbids taking the Lord's name in vain, correct?" asked Augustine, without waiting for our response. "This I match up with the plague of frogs, whose croaking is a symbol of vain babbling!"

Preacher was delighted with Augustine's parallels but Cesar seemed skeptical. The great Bishop began speaking more quickly and we had little time to think about his interpretation.

---

43 In other words, the message of the New Testament is concealed or hidden in the Old Testament, and obscure events of the Old Testament are revealed or explained in the New Testament. From Augustine, *Questions from the Heptateuch*, Question 73, *Patrologia Latina* 34, 623. The original Latin reads: *in Vetere Novum lateat, et in Novo Vetus pateat*, literally "in the old the new is concealed, and in the new the old is revealed."

"The Sabbath rest commandment can be matched to the plague of gnats," said Augustine, "since they swarm restlessly and without ceasing;

"The command against adultery I pair with the death of cattle, since they reproduce by instinct alone, and mate whenever, and with as many mates as they like;

"The command not to murder seems to me related to the plague of boils on the flesh, as an outward symptom of the soul inflamed with hatred;

"The command not to steal matches the plague of crops;

"The command against false witness is like the plague of locusts, whose biting teeth devour;

"Coveting the wife of one's neighbor is like the plague of darkness, since seducing another man's wife is thick darkness;

"And the commandment to honor father and mother is like the plague of dog flies since dogs reproduce without concern about their pedigree and since puppies are born blind and thereby fail to recognize their mother and father!

"That leaves only the command not to covet anything else belonging to one's neighbor, and the plague of the death of the first born. We have already mentioned stealing, but what is more valuable that one's first born? So, as the Egyptians coveted, they lost their most valued possession—their own first born."

"All this is speculative," Augustine concluded, "but I have compared the commandments to the plagues to encourage you to guard your own treasures in God's commandment. Do this, and you will be like God's chosen people among the wicked Egyptians, continually led out of Egypt by means of your own exodus! For, while the original exodus happened only once, the exodus of faithful believers never stops happening."

I'm pretty sure none of us had ever heard a sermon like Augustine's, whose comparisons were creative but fanciful.

"Thank you," said Mentor to Augustine.

"Never forget," said Augustine as he excused himself from the Crux, "the new in the old is concealed, and the old in the new is revealed!"

Preacher's stomach was making noises, probably because we had not eaten anything since entering the Athenaeum. At the lectern, Mentor was studying his Bible in preparation for the next episode. The lesson, he announced, would be on the Passover, which he called the *Pascha*. He directed us to follow along in Joseph's Bible.

"At the time of the final plague," said Mentor, "the children of Israel were commanded to guard their households from the death angel and to prepare for a journey. How did they make their preparations?"

"They slaughtered a lamb and put its blood on their door posts," said Joseph.

"And they roasted the lamb," added Preacher, "it was a Passover barbeque!"

"What else, asked Mentor.

"I know something," I said, "but may I read it from your Bible?"

Mentor nodded, and I went to the three-sided lectern to read aloud:

> *The blood shall be a sign for you, on the houses where you are. And when I see the blood, I will pass over you,*

and no plague will befall you to destroy you, when I strike the land of Egypt. This day shall be for you a memorial day, and you shall keep it as a feast to the Lord; throughout your generations, as a statute forever, you shall keep it as a feast. Seven days you shall eat unleavened bread. On the first day you shall remove leaven out of your houses, for if anyone eats what is leavened, from the first day until the seventh day, that person shall be cut off from Israel. Exodus 12:13–15

"Mentor," asked Cesar after I return to our bench, "why couldn't they eat the leaven?"

"It is the mystery of *Pascha*," replied Mentor.

"You mean no one knows, not even you?" asked Cesar.

Mentor did not reply.

"Leaven is mentioned in the New Testament too," said Joseph, "but I guess we have to find our answers in the Old Testament for now."

"But the Old in the New is revealed!" I said, recalling the principle Augustine had taught us. Mentor gave permission to read from the New Testament. After skimming his Bible, Joseph read from 1 Corinthians.

Cleanse out the old leaven that you may be a new lump, as you really are unleavened. For Christ, our Passover lamb, has been sacrificed (1 Corinthians 5:7).

"Correct me if I'm wrong," he said, "but this leaven had to do with the Corinthian's sinful past."

"What does that have to do with the Hebrews?" asked Cesar.

"Maybe the leaven symbolized their life of servitude in Egypt," said Joseph.

"What's the big deal about yeast anyway?" said Preacher.

"That's what *I* want to know!" said Cesar.

"It's the mystery of *Pascha*," I repeated, "just like Mentor says."

"Why guess?" said Father Greg. "The witnesses are here to help."

"Is there a witness that can help us with this question, Mentor?" I asked.

"There is a book in the reading room that will help," he replied.

We followed Mentor back to the reading room where he pulled a book entitled *On Pascha* from the shelf.

"You will be joining the Passover celebration led by Bishop Melito of Sardis," he said. [44]

"That's fantastic!" said Father Greg, who told us a little about ancient Passover meals. We arranged ourselves around the table and put our heads down again. In a few moments I found myself in a darkened basilica or church, lit only by candle light. Small groups of ancient worshipers were seated around low tables set with flat bread and various small vessels. I was hungry and wanted to break off a piece of flat bread and eat it, but I waited. Near the altar, someone was reading aloud the story of Exodus in Hebrew, which began, "*Hachodesh hazeh lachem rosh*: This month shall be for you the

44 The churches led by Bishop Melito celebrated Easter on the Jewish feast day of the Passover (the fourteenth of the Jewish month Nisan), rather than on the traditional Sunday following Passover used by most Gentile Christians in Rome at that time. They were called "quartodecimans" after the Latin term for fourteen.

beginning of months." Another reader followed him, reading the passage in Greek.[45]

Then Melito stood up to preach. His voice was pleasing and his words were measured, like the ticking of a clock.

He began,[46]

> *Now that the Scripture of the Hebrews concerning the Exodus has been read, and the very words of the Mystery openly declared—concerning the sacrifice of the sheep, the salvation of the people, and the disciplining of Pharaoh by means of the mystery—take note, beloved: that you may grasp how this is new and old, eternal and temporary, perishable and imperishable, mortal and immortal, this mystery of the Pascha.*

In his opening words, the preacher had declared he would explain the Paschal mystery.

---

45 The ancient Sardis dream sequence is based in part on Alistair Steward-Sykes, *Melito of Sardis On Pascha* (Crestwood, NY: St. Vladimir's Seminary Press, 2001), 20-21. Those who have participated in Christian Passover celebrations will find elements of the traditional Seder in this liturgy. For example, Christ's coming is described using the word *aphikomenos*, which, as Steward-Sykes notes, is reminiscent of the word *aphikoman*, a portion of bread broken off from the main loaf at the Passover Seder of Judaism, and hidden as a symbol of the coming Messiah. The value of the liturgy is apparent in its content and form, the rich, biblical imagery by which it conveys the story of Passover.

46 All the following quotations are my translation of the Greek text found in Melito of Sardis, *On Pascha and Fragments*, Stuart G. Hall (translator), Oxford Press, 1979. Compare his English translation in the same volume, and Alistair Stewart-Sikes, *Melito of Sardis On Pascha* (Crestwood, NY: St. Vladimir's Seminary Press, 2001. Melito is not in NPNF.

It is old in that it is the law,
new in that it is the word;
temporary in that it is a type,
eternal in that it is grace;
perishable through the slaughter of the sheep,
imperishable through the life of the Lord;
mortal by means of the burial of the sheep in earth,
immortal by means of the rising of Christ from the dead.

His poetic stanzas were filled with pictures, especially of sheep and their sacrifice.

The law is old, but the word is new;
the type is temporary, but the grace is eternal;
the sheep is perishable, but the Lord is imperishable—
not as a lamb, broken, but as God resurrected!
For though he was led off to the slaughter as a sheep,
yet he was not a sheep;
although he remained speechless, as a lamb,
he was not really a lamb.
For the type indeed existed, but then the reality appeared.

His recitation was dramatic: the pace of his words and the tone of his voice rose and fell as he narrated the Exodus.

As a son he was born, as a lamb he was led,
as a sheep he was slain, and as a man he was buried,
he rose from the dead as God, being in very nature
God and Man.

With a crescendo in his voice, Melito announced the thesis of his sermon:

He is Jesus, the Christ, to Him be glory for all ages. Amen.

"Amen, amen!" resounded from the gathered worshippers. Several children at my table asked questions of their parents or elders, and recited scriptures they had memorized. Then came a blessing and the serving of a first course, unlike anything I had ever been served at a Jewish Seder. After a while, the assembly grew quiet and Melito continued:

This is the mystery of the Pascha, as it is written in the
law, and just read.
But I shall narrate the story from scripture,
how God commanded Moses in Egypt,
when he decided to subject Pharaoh to discipline
and to free Israel from servitude by Moses' hand.

By *narrate the story*, Melito obviously meant more than just reading the Bible passage, which the first two readers had done. *Narrate* seemed to be Melito's word for telling the story as it unfolds. His dramatic retelling of the Exodus emphasized the judgment that came upon the Egyptians.

The strangest and most fearful matter you have yet to hear:
In groping darkness, death lurked untouchable,
as the miserable Egyptians stumbled in darkness,
death, commanded by the angel, took hold of the
Egyptians' first born.

Grasping darkness they were taken by death.
A first-born Egyptian reaching for darkness
screamed aloud,
"Who is holding my hand?
Who terrifies my soul?
Who covers my life in darkness?
Is it a father, then help me!
Is it a mother, then comfort me!
Is it a brother, then speak to me!
Is it a friend, then encourage me!
Is it an enemy, then leave me alone for I am a first-born."

The firstborn son, I knew, was specially privileged in ancient societies, "their most valued possession" as Bishop Augustine had described in his sermon. But Melito's sermon raised haunting questions: What was it like to experience the plagues? What had Pharaoh's people suffered on account of his hard heart? I pictured the death angel coming alongside, taking hold of my hand and whispering in my ear,

Firstborn, you are mine!
I, the silence of death, am your fate.

Near the conclusion of his sermon the preacher finally mentioned the leaven.

The feast of unleavened bread has become bitter to you
just as it was written:
You will eat unleavened bread with bitter herbs.

With a historical fast-forward, Melito turned the Egyptian judgment full-force on the Jews.[47]

Bitter to you are the nails which you made pointed.
Bitter to you is the tongue which you sharpened.
Bitter to you are the false witnesses whom you brought forward.
Bitter to you are the fetters which you prepared.
Bitter to you are the scourges which you wove.
Bitter to you is Judas whom you furnished with pay.
Bitter to you is Herod whom you followed.
Bitter to you is Caiaphas whom you obeyed.
Bitter to you is the gall which you made ready.
Bitter to you is the vinegar which you produced.
Bitter to you are the thorns which you plucked.

47 Specifically, those responsible for the persecution of Jesus, as described in John's Gospel. See John 5:16,18, and many other verses.

Bitter to you are your hands which you bloodied,
when you killed your Lord in the midst of Jerusalem.

Just as quickly, Melito concluded by returning the scene to Egypt.

Egypt was left childless in a moment of time,
But Israel was kept by the sacrifice of sheep,
and together they were illuminated through the spilling of blood,
for the death of the sheep was found to be a hedge for the people.

At the mention of the word *illuminated*, two ministers of the assembly quietly began resetting the altar furnishings. A young man and two women were recognized as having been baptized into the community earlier that day. They had already been immersed in "living water"—a nearby river. Now they repeated their vows with the assembled worshipers crowded around them. This included a simplified version of the creed, *"I believe in God, the Father Almighty,"* which we all recited together. They were asked to renounce the devil and his works. They were anointed with oil on the ear, the hand, and the foot, and with the sign of the cross made on their foreheads. Much was said by various ministers about the meaning of baptism in light of the Exodus—both in relation to the blood of the lambs on the doorposts, and Israel's passing through the waters of the Red Sea. At some point the baptized were directed to face toward the East, "the direction from which the Lord will come again" one of the ministers explained. He then pressed a pinch of salt into the palm of their right hands.

"Our Lord has commanded you to be salt!" declared the minister.

Lengthy prayers were offered on behalf of the baptized. Eventually we returned to our places reclining at the table, where more food and wine dilute with water were served.

At last Melito concluded his message:

O, mystery—strange and indescribable!
Yet the sacrifice of sheep was found to be Israel's salvation,
since the death of the sheep became life for the people,
and the blood persuaded the death angel.

But the service was not over. More lamps were lit until the sanctuary glowed brightly. The music of stringed instruments and drums rang out. I looked for the others but was caught up in the celebration, replying *He is risen indeed*, to everyone who greeted me with *The Lord is risen!*

Chapter 5: The Unfolding of Time, Part 2

When we returned to the Crux, Mentor asked us to share what we had learned about the mystery of the Pascha, but none of us had an answer.

"I'm still wondering why they couldn't eat leaven," said Cesar.

"There was no time for bread to rise," said Preacher, "they had to get out of town fast."

"That was *literally* true," said Joseph, "but leaven is a metaphor for something else—that's the mystery."

"Leaven is not the mystery," I said, "the Passover is the mystery."

"Of course," said Joseph, "but it involves leaven; Mentor only mentioned the mystery of the Passover after Cesar asked about leaven."

"I suggest you begin with *mystery*," said Father Greg, "what is your understanding of the term?"

"Something that's unknown," said Cesar.

"There's more to the Bible's use of *mystery* than that," advised Father Greg.

"Like what?" asked Joseph.

"Biblically speaking," replied Father Greg, "a mystery is something hidden which is now being revealed."

"I get that," said Joseph, "leaven is hidden when it's mixed into the dough; only when it begins to rise do you know it's there."

"But they couldn't eat leaven," said Preacher.

"Maybe the Israelites were like leaven among the Egyptians," I said.

"*There's* your metaphor, Joseph!" said Cesar.

"That's a good insight, Ari" agreed Father Greg, "but what was it that was hidden and yet came to light through the exodus?"

"God's mighty arm and His outstretched hand!" declared Preacher.

"That's right," agreed Joseph, "the salvation of God's people became visible through the exodus."

"And the Egyptians were judged," added Cesar.

"Melito said the feast of unleavened bread was bitter," I replied, "like the judgment on Egypt."

"Or on Israel at the exile," added Joseph.

"And especially on Jesus at the cross," said Preacher.

"Mentor, what do other witnesses beside Melito say about leaven?" asked Cesar.

"The witnesses testify to the leaven of their own day," explained Mentor, "the heresy of Marcion."

"What heresy is that?" asked Joseph.

"May I answer this one, Mentor?" asked Father Greg. Mentor nodded.

"Marcion taught that the Old Testament is corrupt, revealing a god who is inferior to Jesus," explained Father Greg. "His theology was based only on Luke's Gospel and Paul's letters."

"What kind of theology ignores the Old Testament?" asked Joseph.

"Not the theology of the Apostles," replied Father Greg.

Mentor excused himself from the Crux. He returned in a few moments with Irenaeus.

"The Greek and Hebrew Scriptures testify of One God," explained Mentor, "so I have asked brother Irenaeus to share his insight on the genuine teaching of the Apostles."

From the lectern, Irenaeus read aloud from a small book.[1]

> *In the desert Moses received the law from God, and the commandments and statutes which He commanded the sons of Israel to keep. The Ten Commandments were written upon tablets of stone with the finger of God, and the finger of God is the Holy Spirit who is issued from the Father.*[2]

"*The Unfolding of Time*," explained Irenaeus, "tells of the sweep of salvation's history from Adam to Christ, demonstrating that our *two* testaments make *one* great

---

1 The book was Irenaeus's own *Demonstration of the Apostolic Preaching*."

2 Paraphrase of John Behr, *St. Irenaeus of Lyons: On the apostolic preaching* (Crestwood, N.Y.: St. Vladimir's Seminary Press, 1997), 57. The work's traditional title is *Demonstration of the Apostolic Preaching* (it is not in ANF).

picture.[3] Now, if you have studied the covenants, you know that creation and redemption are part of one great story."

I saluted, and Mentor called on me.

"I've always found the covenants confusing," I admitted, "there are so many of them in the Old Testament; how do they all connect with the New?"

"I'll tell you," replied Irenaeus, "they are lessons in the training of God's people, first Israel and later the Church. This all began, as you have seen, with the call of Abraham, Isaac, and Jacob, and continued with the Exodus, as Melito shows. Then came the wilderness wanderings, the conquest, and so on, when God was preparing His people for the way of salvation. He educates humanity, if you will, gradually guiding them by means of covenants made with Adam, Noah, Moses, and, in time, the covenant of the Gospel itself."

"Israel was in school," said Preacher.

"They graduated to the next grade with each covenant," added Cesar.

"I think they flunked out," said Joseph, "anyway, I don't remember reading about a school in Exodus."

"It *does* say God wrote the commandments on tablets of stone," said Father Greg. [4]

"Does that mean he literally wrote with his finger?" said Joseph.

"How do *you* write?" asked Irenaeus.

---

3 The statement is based on Joseph Lienhard, *Ancient Christian Commentary on Scripture, Vol. 3 Exodus—Deuteronomy* (Downers Grove: InterVarsity Press), xviii.

4 Exod. 31:18.

Joseph did not reply but looked at his hand.

"You use your finger, do you not?" asked Irenaeus.

"I use my fingers to hold a pencil," said Joseph, confused.

"Do you find it strange that our God, like a wise teacher, would write something for our instruction?" asked Irenaeus.

"Not at all," replied Joseph, "it's just that I was trying to picture God writing with his finger."

"You pictured God's finger like a drill or jack hammer, didn't you?" said Preacher, "I know cause that's what I was thinking!"

"God's ways are always suited to the time and place," explained Irenaeus, "Moses was in the wilderness, so the Almighty's lessons were on tablets of stone."

"I see now," said Joseph.

"God is our wise teacher," Irenaeus continued, "he trains humanity so they will grow from infancy to maturity.[5] Sadly, Israel failed to keep the commandments and statutes."

Irenaeus began listing examples of disobedience from Adam until the coming of Christ, the *Second Adam.* He then described a pattern of obedience and blessing in relation to Adam, Noah and Noah's sons, as well as Abraham, Moses, David, and Christ.[6] Those who obeyed, such as Noah and his sons Shem and Japheth, were

---

5 Based on Rowan A. Greer, *Broken Lights and Mended Lives: Theology and Common Life in the Early Church* (Pennsylvania State University Press, 1986), 39.

6 This pattern in Irenaeus' writings was first identified by Susan L. Graham, in "Zealous for the Covenant: Irenaeus and the Covenants of Israel" (PhD dissertation, University of Notre Dame, 2001), 98-106.

blessed, while those who disobeyed such as Noah's son Ham were cursed.[7]

"The significance of the blessing is this," explained Irenaeus, "that the Lord and God of all became for Shem a peculiar possession of worship. For, the blessing bore fruit in the tenth generation of the seed of Shem—namely, in Abraham. Thus, the Father and God of all was pleased to be called the God of Abraham, the God of Isaac and the God of Jacob, for the blessing of Shem extended to them."[8]

Irenaeus reminded us that Abraham's ancestors had been idol worshippers.

"But Shem was absolutely faithful to God," he explained, "so God became for Shem not an idol, but a unique possession of worship. Thus, He is the God *of Abraham*, because Abraham's call began with his ancestor Shem's obedience, and the blessing of that obedience was passed from generation to generation, from Abraham to Isaac to Jacob."

"In the same way," Irenaeus continued, "Japheth was blessed when his father Noah declared, *May God enlarge Japheth, and let him dwell in the tents of Shem, and let Canaan (Ham) be his servant.*[9] This blessing of Japheth was seen in the incarnation of our Lord Jesus. And the blessing bore fruit when God enlarged the Gentiles by calling them and their descendants into the Church."[10]

---

7 See the account in Gen. 9:20-27.

8 Behr, *St. Irenaeus of Lyons*, 52.

9 Gen. 9:27.

10 John Behr, *St. Irenaeus of Lyons, On the apostolic preaching* (Crestwood, N.Y.: St. Vladimir's Seminary Press, 1997) 52-53.

"This is what the Scripture means when it says *the blessing was enlarged to Japheth*," he concluded, "because through the Gentiles, the future Church, receives its fruit."

The Promise Land

Having outlined lessons learned by the Patriarchs and Moses, Irenaeus went on to Joshua and the Conquest of the Promised Land. The topic of fruit came up again—this time the gigantic grapes that the spies discovered and brought back, further supporting the pattern of obedience and blessing.[11]

"The grapes are blessings God had prepared for Israel in the Conquest," Irenaeus explained, "to motivate them to take the land."

"I remember that story from Sunday school," said Preacher, "but why couldn't Moses go into the promised land?"

Irenaeus's lengthy explanation left Preacher scratching his head.

"Mentor," he asked, "can you please get Turtle to answer my question?"

"He means Tertullian," said Father Greg.

Mentor left the Crux, returning in a few moments with Tertullian, who offered this answer,

"Moses could not go in, not because he sinned,
He's the discipline, so he could not go in;
He's the law, not the grace,
That's a whole different case;
Joshua used a flint knife,

11 See Num. 13:23.

Jesus offered his life;
There's a Promised Land lock,
Jesus Christ is the Rock,
Moses down on one knee,
Joshua-Jesus the key."[12]

"I love that guy!" said Preacher.

"What'd he say?" asked Joseph.

"Joshua was the Old Testament *type* of Jesus," explained Father Greg, "he led Israel into the Promised Land, while Jesus leads the New Testament people of God into eternal life and adds them to the Church.[13]

Mentor thanked Tertullian and Father Greg, and Irenaeus continued his teaching.

"Moses died according to the word of the Lord, and Joshua succeeded him. Joshua parted the waters of the Jordan and made the people pass over into the Promised Land. Now, when he had overthrown and destroyed the seven nations that dwelt therein, he assigned the people to *temporal Jerusalem*, where David was king, and Solomon his son built the temple to the name of God, according to the likeness of the tabernacle which had been made by Moses after the pattern of the heavenly and spiritual things."[14]

---

12 Based on Tertullian, *An Answer to the Jews*, 9 (ANF 3, 163).

13 Moses failure—the basis on which he was excluded from entering the Promised Land—is explained in Num. 20:1-13. The "rock knife" refers to the flint knives Joshua used to circumcise Israel as second time in accordance with God's command (Josh. 5:2). Joshua's activities thereby prefigure Jesus and the inclusion of the "new people" of God into the Church.

14 John Behr, *St. Irenaeus of Lyons, On the apostolic preaching* (Crestwood, N.Y.: St. Vladimir's Seminary Press, 1997), 59.

Irenaeus continued his summary of Old Testament history, following the pattern of command-obedience, and blessing-fruit.

"Moses, who received the blessing of a vision of the heavenly tabernacle and the command to build according to that vision, obeyed by constructing the earthly tabernacle, which in turn bore fruit in the lives of David, Solomon who built the Temple, and ultimately the Church."[15]

City, Temple, and Throne

Mentor thanked Irenaeus as he left the Crux.

"Let us now consider the roles of prophet, priest, and king in Israel as the basis for our Lord's ministry in the *Fullness of Time*," said Mentor.

"Wait," said Preacher, "what did Irenaeus mean by *Temporal Jerusalem*?"

"Do you recall the *heavenly Jerusalem* mentioned in Revelation?"[16] replied Mentor.

"Sure," said Preacher.

"*Temporal Jerusalem* is the earthly city the Lord chose to represent His name," explained Mentor, "as we read in the books of the Kings, *that David my servant may always have a lamp before me.*[17] This is the place from which David ruled as king, and where Solomon built the Temple of the Lord. If the Promised Land is a *type* of the

---

15 In an earlier citation, Irenaeus noted that "at the command of God he (Moses) constructed the tabernacle of testimony, a visible structure on earth of things which are spiritual and invisible in the heavens—and the figure of the form of the Church."

16 In Rev. 3:12 and also in Heb. 12:22.

17 1 Kings 11:36.

Kingdom of God that will be established in the future, then the throne of David and the Temple of Jerusalem are signs of His rule in the midst of his people."[18]

Preacher nodded.

"The books of the Kings..." continued Mentor until Cesar interrupted,

"Do you mean First and Second Kings from the Old Testament?"

"We have *Four* Books of the Kings," replied Mentor.

"Don't forget," said Father Greg, "in the Septuagint—the Greek translation of the Old Testament used by many of the Fathers—*First and Second Samuel* was called *First and Second Kings*, and our 1 and 2 Kings became *Third and Fourth Kings*.

"The books of the Kings," Mentor continued, "make clear that the Lord reigned in the midst of a faithless people. Yet, in his faithfulness he promised an ultimate King in the line of David, and he continually sent his servants the prophets to warn the people. As our brother Irenaeus has written, *Here in Jerusalem, the prophets were sent from God by the Holy Spirit, teaching the people and turning them to the Almighty, the God of their fathers...*".[19]

Joseph saluted and Mentor called on him.

"The role of the prophets seems pretty straightforward," said Joseph, but what about the priests and kings?"

---

18 Based on Suzanne de Dietrich, *God's unfolding purpose; a guide to the study of the Bible* (Philadelphia: Westminster Press, 1960), 85.

19 Irenaeus, *The Demonstration of Apostolic Preaching* (30). Translation by Armitage Robinson, (ed), *St. Irenaeus, The Demonstration of the Apostolic Preaching, translated from the Armenian with an Introduction and Notes* (London: Society for the Promotion of Christian Knowledge, and New York: MacMillan Co), 1920.

"The priests ministered on behalf of God," Mentor explained, "directing worship—offerings and sacrifices—first in the Tabernacle and later in the Temple and maintaining the guidelines for holiness among God's people."

"And the kings?" asked Joseph.

"As I have explained," Mentor emphasized, "the throne was a *type* of God's sovereign rule. However, the kings of Israel and Judah were anointed by God to shepherd the people, as we read in the Gospels, our Lord had compassion on the people because they were like sheep without a shepherd."

"The Old Testament kings were bad shepherds!" said Cesar.

"In truth," agreed Mentor, "yet the Prophet tells of One who is to come who will *tend his flock like a shepherd.*[20]

Our brief study of the roles of prophet, priest, and king in Israel brought up many negative examples. There were conflicts between the Temple and the throne, and between prophets, priests, and kings. Joseph recalled that Samuel anointed Saul as king, but later clashed with him over the matter of his presumptive offering.[21] Preacher reminded us that as long as King Saul lived, he hated and opposed David, his successor.[22] Mentor himself had already pointed out that God had dispatched the prophets to admonish the kings of Israel and Judah.

---

20 See Isa. 40:11.

21 See 1 Sam. 10:1; 13:11-14.

22 See 1 Sam. 18—29.

"But there are also hopeful signs," Mentor reminded us, "like King David—a man after God's own heart—to whom God promised a descendant on his throne forever."

"That also points to Jesus in the New Testament," Cesar reminded us, "since he will be called the son of David."

"Before we go further in the *Fullness of Time*," said Mentor, "what examples can you offer of Jesus himself fulfilling the roles of prophet, priest, and king?"

"In Matthew's Gospel" I said, "you can see Jesus' prophetic ministry in his preaching against the unbelieving cities, against the Temple, and against Jerusalem itself."[23]

Joseph added that Hebrews 4 describes Jesus as a great high priest, and other New Testament passages identify him as king.[24]

The Exile

Our lesson on the roles of prophet, priest, and king in Israel as the basis for our Lord's ministry in the *Fullness of Time* had been a success. Mentor excused himself from the crux, but soon returned with two witnesses, Origen and Cyril, who carried a large folio volume.

"When are we finished with the *Unfolding of Time*, Mentor?" asked Preacher.

"Two episodes remain," said Mentor.

"Are these long lectures?" I asked.

---

23 See, respectively, Matt. 11:20-23; 12:6; 13:2; and 23:37.

24 John 19:19 and Rev. 1:5.

"There are no more lectures," said Mentor, "you must engage the witnesses in dialogue if you wish to hear their testimonies."

The two witnesses stood silently by.

"What can you tell us about the Exile?" I asked them.

"What can you tell us?" asked the elderly Origen, smiling.

"God judged his people for their idolatry and kicked them out of the Promised Land," replied Joseph.

"God stirred up foreign armies to conquer Israel, taking the people captive into Assyria and later into Babylon," added Cesar.

"God indeed sentenced Jerusalem for her sins," agreed Origen, "and the condemned were given over to their captors.[25]

"They had it comin' to 'em," said Preacher.

"But God was ready to show mercy," replied Origen, "even to those who deserve punishment. For though he could punish anyone without warning, yet he always warns first, in order to turn the disobedient from their sin.[26]

"There's always an opportunity for repentance with God," agreed Joseph.

"Right," said Cesar, "he sent Jeremiah to warn Judah long before the fall of Jerusalem."

---

25 Paraphrase of John Clark Smith (translator), *Origen, Homilies on Jeremiah, Homily on 1 Kings 28*, in The Fathers of the Church, A New Translation (Catholic University of America Press, 1998), 4.

26 John Clark Smith (translator), *Origen, Homilies on Jeremiah, Homily on 1 Kings 28*, in The Fathers of the Church, A New Translation (Catholic University of America Press, 1998), Homily, 3.

"The patient God was offering them mercy," agreed Origen, "and this is true for us also, because if we sin, we become captives. And handing the captives of Jerusalem over to Nebuchadnezzar was no different than delivering someone to Satan—our Nebuchadnezzar.[27]

"Delivering *who* to Satan?" asked Preacher.

Origen did not reply, nor did Cyril. Now Father Greg joined the dialogue.

"Do you remember that passage in 1 Corinthians where Paul talks about handing a disobedient member of the congregation over to Satan?" he asked.[28]

"I remember," said Preacher, "but what does it mean?"

"It was the final step in church discipline," explained Father Greg. "So, when a disobedient Christian refused to repent and be restored to the congregation, Paul taught that the Church has authority to hand over the willfully disobedient member to Satan for the sake, ultimately, of his or her salvation.[29]

"The Old *is* revealed in the New!" declared Preacher.

"Precisely," agreed Father Greg, "God delivered Israel into the hand of Nebuchadnezzar to teach them to hate the servitude that resulted from their idolatry."

"God's patient love manifests itself through all these means," added Origen. "The Law, the Prophets, and the Apostles, and finally through his own Son—all speak to us about repentance and encourage us toward

---

27 John Clark Smith, 4-5.

28 See 1 Cor. 5:4-5.

29 1 Tim. 1:18-20.

conversion. If we hear, let us believe in Him who said, *I will repent of all the evil which I planned to do to them.*"[30]

The Remnant

"This is going more quickly than I expected," I said, "can we dialogue about the Remnant now?"

Neither Mentor nor the witnesses replied.

"We have to work for our answers," Joseph reminded me.

"Right," I agreed, "so where is Remnant mentioned in Scripture?"

Joseph checked the concordance at the back of his Bible and read aloud,

> *Grace has been shown from the Lord our God, to leave us a remnant.*

"It's Ezra 9:8," he said.

"What's the context?" I asked.

"I think it's Ezra's prayer of repentance," he said, turning to the passage and reading aloud,

> *From the days of our fathers to this day we have been in great guilt. And for our iniquities we, our kings, and our priests have been given into the hand of the kings of the lands, to the sword, to captivity, to plundering, and to utter shame, as it is today.*[31]

"He's talking about the Exile" explained Joseph, "but here's where he mentions the Remnant..."

---

30 Here, Origen quotes Jer. 18:8, in John Clark Smith, 5-6.

31 Ezra 9:7.

> *Now for a brief moment favor has been shown by the Lord our God, to leave us a remnant and to give us a secure hold within his holy place, that our God may brighten our eyes and grant us a little reviving in our slavery. For, we are slaves. Yet our God has not forsaken us in our slavery but has extended to us his steadfast love before the kings of Persia, to grant us some reviving to set up the house of our God, to repair its ruins, and to give us protection in Judea and Jerusalem.*[32]

"The Remnant helps to rebuild Jerusalem after the Exile," explained Father Greg.

"The Prophet also speaks of the Remnant," said Cyril. Stepping up to the lectern, he read from Isaiah,

> *On that day the remnant of Israel will no longer be associated with those who wronged them and the survivors of Jacob will no longer trust in them. Instead, they will trust in God, the Holy One of Israel, in truth. The remnant of Jacob will remain with the mighty God.*[33]

"Israel was keepin' bad company!" Preacher commented.

"In truth," agreed Cyril, "God was provoked by Israel when they sent ambassadors to the Egyptians at one time and to the Assyrians at another, begging help from them.[34]

---

32 Ezra 9:8–9.

33 Isa. 10:20-21, quoted from the Septuagint version in the commentary of Cyril of Alexandria. Robert Charles Hill, *Cyril of Alexandria, Commentary on Isaiah*, vol.1 (Brookline, M A.: Holy Cross Orthodox Press), 237. The Hebrew text says "the House of Jacob will no longer lean on him who struck them, but will lean on the Lord" (ESV).

34 Robert Charles Hill, *Cyril of Alexandria, Commentary on Isaiah*, volume 1 (Brookline, M A.: Holy Cross Orthodox Press), 238-239

"How does all this relate to the Remnant?" I asked.

"Not all Israel offended God," said Cyril, "some refused to compromise, and only the sinners were called to account."[35]

"Are we finish with this session now?" I asked, eager to move on to the New Testament.

"Do you understand the Remnant?" asked Mentor.

"They were the Israelites who refused to compromise," I said, repeating what Cyril had said.

"And they helped rebuild Jerusalem," added Joseph, recalling Father Greg's words.

"What does this teach you about *The Unfolding of Time*?" added Mentor.

None of us could answer, and I had to admit I didn't really understand this final theme very well.

"Bishop Cyril," I asked, "what else does the Prophet say that could help us understand the Remnant?"

"God has broken the rod of the oppressor as on the day of Midian," said Cyril, quoting Isaiah.[36] "He rescued the Israelites by driving off Midian, just as He saved the Exiles from the nations by breaking the rod of their oppressors."[37]

Cyril could see by my expression I did not understand.

"What do you know about winnowing and threshing?" he asked.

---

35 Paraphrase of Robert Charles Hill, 239.

36 Isa. 9:4.

37 See Isa. 9:4 and Hill, vol. 1, pages 205-206.

"They separated the grain from the chaff by rolling a heavy stone over it," I answered.

"Correct," replied Cyril, "Isaiah's day illustrates the threshing—the purifying of believers."

"They are the remnant?" I asked.

"Among the Exiles," Cyril agreed, "but what winnowing took place in the day of Midian?"

"I'm not sure about winnowing *or* the day of Midian," I admitted.

"Before you can thresh grain," explained Father Greg, "you must separate it from the straw like this," he said, pretending to toss hay into the air with a pitch fork.

"I know about winnowing in the day of Midian," said Preacher, "God told Gideon he had too many soldiers, so he handpicked three hundred of them and they whipped the whole Midian army!"[38]

"How did you remember that?" I asked.

"Gideon & Midian?" rhymed Preacher, "everybody knows that!"

Bishop Cyril thanked Father Greg and Preacher.

"God works through a select and purified few," I said to Mentor, refining my definition of the remnant.

"But what have we learned about *The Unfolding of Time*?" asked Joseph.

"Mentor told us to watch for Good News about the seed of the woman," said Preacher.

"Do the Old Testament prophets announce any good news?" asked Cesar.

---

38 See Josh. 7.

"O my threshed and winnowed one," quoted Cyril from Isaiah, "what I have heard from the LORD of hosts, the God of Israel, I announce to you.[39] With these words," explained Cyril, "the Prophet announces the destruction of Israel's enemies."

39 Isa. 21:10.

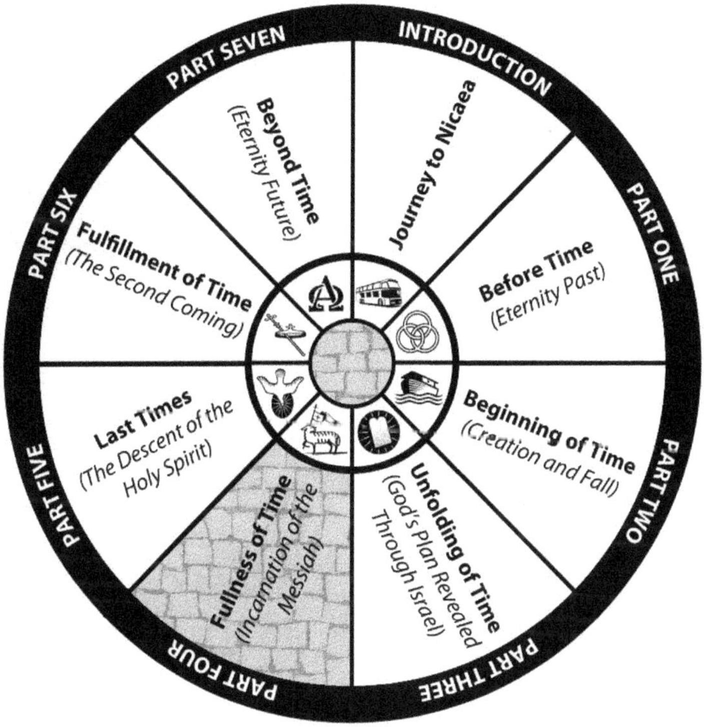
INTRODUCTION
Journey to Nicaea
PART ONE
Before Time
(Eternity Past)
PART TWO
Beginning of Time
(Creation and Fall)
PART THREE
Unfolding of Time
(God's Plan Revealed Through Israel)
PART FOUR
Fullness of Time
(Incarnation of the Messiah)
PART FIVE
Last Times
(The Descent of the Holy Spirit)
PART SIX
Fulfillment of Time
(The Second Coming)
PART SEVEN
Beyond Time
(Eternity Future)

Chapter 6: The Fullness of Time

In our survey of the Story of God we had at last arrived at the four Gospels. *The Incarnation*—Christ Jesus, the Word of God, come in the flesh—was our subject. As the Apostle Paul explains,

> *But when the fullness of time had come, God sent forth his Son, born of woman, born under the law, to redeem those who were under the law, so that we might receive adoption as sons. Galatians 4:4-5*

Mentor was talking with some witnesses, so Cesar and I went to look at the books he had checked out for the upcoming session. On the table next to the lectern were commentaries on the gospels of Matthew and Luke, a book entitled *Agreement among the Evangelists*, and another entitled *Proof of the Gospel*. Two other volumes had strange titles—one was *Diatessaron* and the other *Opus Imperfectum*. We waited for the authors to claim their works, hoping to make conversation with them.

Four Gospels Versus One

Augustine came up to claim his *Agreement among the Evangelists.*

"So many interesting books," I said, hoping he would tell me about his.

"The Gospel outshines them all, even the other sacred authorities," he said, "for what the law and the prophets foretold comes to light in the Gospel."

Sacred authorities was how Augustine described the books of the Bible. To him, all books were authorities which he ranked according to value.

"What about this book?" I asked, handing him the volume entitled *Diatessaron.*

"That's the four-in-one," he said, "which, in the Syrian churches, has replaced the four gospels."

"How could any book replace the Gospels?" I asked.

"It is a *harmony of the gospels,*" he explained.

"How do you harmonize gospels?" asked Cesar.

"You combine them," explained Augustine. "Father Tatian took the overlapping passages found in all four gospels—including the ministry of Jesus, his crucifixion and resurrection—and then added other passages unique to each Gospel, in their order.

"What was the point of that?" asked Cesar.

"To remove the differences between the four," explained Augustine, "because some believe the four gospels cannot all be accurate if they differ from one another."

"I know people who say that," said Cesar.

"They must understand there are four Gospels for a reason," replied Augustine.

"What reason?" I asked.

"The four authorities correspond with the four corners of the world," replied Augustine, "or perhaps the number is a sign that Christ's Church is everywhere throughout the world. In either case, the four Gospels do not disagree with one another, as I have shown in my work, *Agreement Among the Evangelists*."

"But they do disagree at points, don't they?" asked Cesar.

"No," said Augustine, "that claim is only made by those who say they honor Christ but who do not believe the Gospels."[1]

"Could you give us an example?" I asked.

The Bishop directed me to the opening words of Matthew's Gospel…

The book of the genealogy of Jesus Christ, the son of David, the son of Abraham. Abraham begot Isaac, Isaac begot Jacob, and Jacob begot Judah and his brothers. Judah begot Perez and Zerah by Tamar, Perez begot Hezron, and Hezron begot Ram. Ram begot Amminadab, Amminadab begot Nahshon, and Nahshon begot Salmon. Salmon begot Boaz by Rahab, Boaz begot Obed by Ruth, Obed begot Jesse, and Jesse begot David the king.[2]

---

1 Augustine's words on this page are paraphrased from his *Agreement Among the Evangelists* 1.1-1.2, and his Revisions II, 16 (43). For both of these see John Rotelle, The Works of Saint Augustine, New Testament 1 & 2 (I/15, I/16), 133-139.

2 Matt. 1:1-6 NKJV.

He asked me to compare this with the genealogy of Jesus in Luke's Gospel, which begins

Now Jesus Himself began His ministry at about thirty years of age, being (as was supposed) the son of Joseph, the son of Heli, the son of Matthat, the son of Levi...[3]

"The two genealogies follow a different order," I said.

"Truly," said the Bishop, "Luke begins with Joseph and traces his line all the way back to Adam, but Matthew begins with Abraham and goes forward in time down to Joseph."

"Some of the names are different too," I added.

"Agreed," said Augustine, "Luke mentions Levi and many other priests, but not King Solomon. And you will find David's name mentioned only once in Luke."

"Here in Matthew, David is mentioned three times, at least once as David the king" I said.

"Therefore you can see," said Augustine, "that Matthew traces Jesus' genealogy through Solomon the king, following the order of the kings. But Luke is more concerned with the priestly line and character of the Lord. Both Gospels are needed, for the Lord Jesus Christ is the one true king and the one true priest—as king he rules us, as priest he atones for us."

"That's interesting!" I said.

"There's more," said Augustine, "for, in following the order of the kings, Matthew has preserved their mystical number."

"What number?" asked Cesar.

"Notice," explained Augustine, "that Matthew lists *forty* names, excluding Christ himself, spanning *forty*

---

3 Luke 3:23-24.

generations, and that identifies our Lord with Israel and speaks of His rule as king."

"Why do you say that?" asked Cesar.

"*Forty* signifies both discipline and rule," explained the Bishop, "for both the Law and the Prophets mention forty-day fasts—the humbling of the soul—in the persons of Moses and Elijah.[4] Moreover, both good and evil men are disciplined: the good are ruled by discipline—for "God punishes every son he receives"[5]—while the evil are crushed by it.[6] Our Lord, too, was tested by the devil for *forty days* since he humbly took our mortality upon himself.[7] And after his resurrection he remained with his disciples for *forty days*.[8] *Forty days*, then, is a sign of that laborious period during which, under the discipline of Christ the King, we have to fight against the devil.[9] And Matthew's Gospel alone presents the record of Christ the King who endured this sweaty, earth-bound existence in order to reign over us sin-oppressed creatures."[10]

---

4 See Exod. 34:28 and 1 Kings 19:8.

5 Heb. 12:6.

6 Ps. 2:9.

7 Matt. 4:1-2.

8 Acts 1:3.

9 Paraphrase based on Augustine, *Harmony* 2.4.9 (*Patrologia Latina* 34, 1075; NPNF I, 6:105).

10 A paraphrase of *Ad huncigitur mundum, et ad istam terrenam mortalemque vitam hominum, ad nos regendos in tentatione laborantes…* Augustine, *Harmony* 2.4.10 (*Patrologia Latina* 34, 1075; NPNF I, 6:106).

I had, of course, noticed that the number forty is often mentioned in Scripture, though I could not say why. In Augustine's view the "mystical number," like God's promises to Abraham, predicted the emergence of a people—Israel—specially set apart to God, and this in turn predicted the emergence of a champion—the Messiah, Jesus.

"Notice," continued Augustine, "that Matthew marked out three sets of fourteen generations each, stating that from Abraham until David there were fourteen generations, and from David until the carrying away into Babylon another fourteen generations, and another fourteen from that period on to the nativity of Christ.[11]

"But that totals *forty-two* generations," I said, "not *forty*."

"Ah," the Bishop countered, "but Matthew did not add them up, saying they make forty-two all together, for one of the ancestors—Jechonias—is counted twice to compensate for the extra nations at the time of the Babylonian exile."[12]

Cesar and I were confused by this, as Augustine probably noticed from our expression.

"Be that as it may," he continued, "both Matthew's and Luke's Gospels mainly set forth the humanity of Christ: for it was according to His humanity that Christ was made both King and Priest. To Him, too, God gave the throne of His father David, in order that of His kingdom there should be no end. And this was done with the purpose

11 Same as previous note.

12 Same as previous note.

that there might be a mediator between God and men, the man Christ Jesus, to make intercession for us."[13]

This last point I understood clearly: Christ's humanity displayed both his royal lineage as well as his priestly role as mediator between God and man.

The Incarnation

Ephrem of Syria came to the table to claim his *Commentary on the Diatessaron*. He was the Eastern Church father who had conducted the choir during the *Beginning of Time*. When I told him we had just been discussing the humanity of Christ, he broke out in song:

> *Why did the Lord clothe himself with humanity?*
> *Why did he dress himself in our flesh?*
> *How else could he conquer the passions Adam had put on?*
> *And how else could he overcome the oppression Adam now wore?*
> *Samson killed many with the jawbone of an ass,*
> *But the serpent killed the entire human race through Eve;*
> *So, with the flesh the Lord received from Eve—the same equipment used by the enemy to attack us—the Lord joined the battle, and conquered the world!*
>
> *Why did the Lord clothe himself with humanity?*
> *Why did he dress himself in our flesh?*
> *If God had been victorious without the flesh,*
> *Then what praise could this flesh offer Him?*

13 Augustine, *Harmony*, I.3.6 (*Patrologia Latina* 34, 1044-1045; NPNF I, 6: 79). It was the Gospel of John and its emphasis on Christ's divinity that alerted Augustine to the theme of humanity in Matthew and Luke. Just prior to the statement quoted above, he says, "John…had in view that true divinity of the Lord…in which he is the Father's equal" (NPNF I.4.7).

He did it so that this flesh might experience victory,
And that we humans might know and understand the gifts of God.[14]

Drawn by Ephrem's hymn, the others gathered round the table. I shared with them what Augustine had taught us about the genealogies of Matthew and Luke, that they portrayed Jesus as king and priest. Ephrem's hymn, we agreed, portrayed Christ as a warrior and champion.

"No one has claimed this book yet," I said, holding up the *Opus Imperfectum*.

"That is *not* a catholic commentary," said Augustine.[15]

"What kind of commentary is it?" I asked, but he turned away from the table.

"*Opus Imperfectum*—the *Incomplete Commentary*—is an ancient commentary on eighteen of the twenty-eight chapters of Matthew's Gospel," said Father Greg.

"What happened to the other ten chapters?" I asked.

"No one knows for sure," he said, "but probably they were destroyed."

Father Greg explained that some passages in the commentary taught heretical ideas.

"Is that why no one has claimed the book?" I asked.

"No one knows the author's identity," said Mentor.

"Why did you checked it out?" I asked.

14 Paraphrase based on Carmel McCarthy, *Saint Ephrem's Commentary on Tatian's Diatessaron* (Oxford University Press, 1993), 39-40.

15 By catholic, Augustine meant universal or true Church.

"The Gospel contains mysteries which this commentary reveals," said Mentor, "and the Apostle teaches us to test everything and hold fast to the good."[16]

"Does the *Incomplete Commentary* say anything about the genealogy of Jesus," I asked, "or is that chapter missing?"

Mentor opened the *Incomplete Commentary* for us to examine. There were in fact many pages explaining Matthew's genealogy of Jesus. He read a passage aloud for us.

"*The book of the genealogy of Jesus Christ, the son of David, the son of Abraham.* Why does he say *the son of David, the son of Abraham*, and not the son of Abraham alone, or the son of David alone? It is because a promise had been made to both of them that Christ would be born as one of their descendants. To Abraham it was said, 'And by your descendants shall all the nations of the earth bless themselves.'[17] To David the promise was spoken, 'One of the sons of your body I will set on your throne.[18] Therefore he calls him the son of both Abraham and David in order to show that the promises to both were fulfilled in Christ."[19]

"Interesting!" said Joseph.

---

16 1 Thess. 5:21.

17 Gen. 22:18.

18 Ps. 132:11.

19 James Kellerman and Thomas Oden, *Incomplete Commentary on Matthew* (*Opus Imperfectum*), Ancient Christian Texts (Downers Grove: IVP Academic, 2010), volume 1, page 2.

"Does the *Commentary* say anything about how the roles of prophet, priest, and king relate to Jesus?" asked Cesar.

Mentor replied by reading from the *Commentary*,

"Matthew also calls him the son of both Abraham and David because Christ would have three titles: king, prophet, and priest. Abraham had two sons and two titles: he was a prophet and a priest. He is a priest, as is clear when God says to him in Genesis, 'Bring me a heifer three years old.[20] And he was a prophet, as the Lord testified to Abimelech about him: 'He is a prophet, and he will pray for you, and you shall live…you and all that are yours.'[21] Therefore he was called the son of Abraham and David, so that he might be understood to be a prophet and priest because he is of Abraham; and a king because he is of David. Thus, he was called the son of both, that the threefold office from each ancestor might be recognized in Christ by right of his lineage."

Signs Accompanying Christ's Birth

"What else does the *Commentary* say?" asked Cesar.

"The signs surrounding the birth of Christ are also revealed," said Mentor.

"What about the wise men," asked Joseph, "I've always been curious about them." [22]

Mentor turned in the *Commentary* until he found this passage:

---

20 Gen. 15:9.

21 Gen. 20:7.

22 Matt. 2:1-12.

"With their words, their motives, and their worship, the wise men revealed the greatness of God in the tiny infant."[23]

The five of us huddled around Mentor to listen to more of the *Commentary*.

"Their words revealed his greatness because they asked 'Where is he who is born king of the Jews? We have seen his star in the east and have come to worship him.' Their motives revealed it because when they saw him they adored him. What faith they had, able to perceive greatness in the lowliest of things! Their array of gold, frankincense and myrrh displayed his greatness... their gold reserves, I say, in recognition of his royalty, himself a precious offering beloved by the saints; their frankincense, like prayer offered in the fragrance of the Holy Spirit, in recognition of his divine, celestial rank; and their myrrh, in recognition of his human death and burial."[24]

"This commentary does reveal mysteries!" said Cesar.

"Truly," commented Mentor, "because with their attention and their gifts, the wise men pointed to Christ's royal standing."

---

23 The ancient commentary is known as the *Opus Imperfectum* or *Incomplete Commentary on Matthew*, as it will be referred to in the following passages. The Commentary is divided into "homilies" or sermons. The original Greek text is in *Patrologia Graeca*, volume 56. The best available English translation is that of James Kellerman, in James Kellerman and Thomas Oden, *Incomplete Commentary on Matthew* (*Opus Imperfectum*), in two volumes, Ancient Christian Texts (Downers Grove: IVP Academic, 2010).

24 *Opus Imperfectum*, Second Homily (PG 56, 636-638) my translation. The ellipsis joins two distinct passages in the second Homily. For the complete English translation, see Kellerman and Oden, *Incomplete Commentary on Matthew*, vol.1, pages 31, 38.

"But the prophets had already said that, right?" asked Joseph.

"The wise men sought out and confessed the king though they had not yet seen him," explained Mentor, "and this was a sign of the coming faith of the Gentiles."

"How so?" asked Joseph.

"The wise men were blessed to become the first fruits of the faithful from all the Gentiles," read Mentor, "and they bore the image of the Church that was coming to be."[25]

Joseph still seemed puzzled.

"The wise men weren't Jews," explained Cesar, "but they were a sign to the Jews."

"What does the commentary say about King Herod?" asked Preacher.

Mentor turned to another passage in the *Incomplete Commentary* and invited Preacher to read.

"Taking Christ for a mortal king," read Preacher with expression, "Herod was disturbed at the prospect of a successor. Great power always succumbs to greater fear. Indeed, as a high branch sways at the slightest breeze, so men at the top are shaken by the messenger's word; yet, the lowly dwell peacefully in the valley. For this reason, then, Herod was disturbed, having learned of the birth of a king among the Jews in Judaea. And being himself of Idumean descent, he did not want to see a return to Jewish rule or, for that matter, himself banished from Judaea and his descendants thereafter expelled from ruling."[26]

---

25 *Opus Imperfectum*, Second Homily (PL 56, 639) my translation. For comparison see Kellerman and Oden, 31.

26 Herod was of mixed (Idumean) and not purely Jewish descent; he feared the possibility of his family's loss of rule in Judea. Quotation, same as previous note.

"So, Herod was shaking at the good news," said Cesar.

"Like a twig blowing in the breeze!" agreed Preacher.

Something in the *Commentary* caught my eye, and I read aloud over Preacher's shoulder.

"Greater than Herod's fear was the fear inspiring the devil: Herod was fearful of what he thought might be true, but the devil's fear was based on what he knew to be true. The one whom Herod believed to be a man, the devil knew to be God, for he had heard the angels cry, "Glory to God in the highest and on earth peace to men of good will."[27]

"So the devil was afraid too," said Joseph, "I never thought about that!"

"Listen to this," I read further, "while Herod's fears were earth-bound, the devil's were heavenly. For if Herod had believed a heavenly king was to be born, he would not have greatly feared. Nor would the devil have feared an earthly king."[28]

"I don't get that," said Preacher.

"It makes sense," said Cesar, "because the devil would only be afraid of God, not a human. And Herod didn't believe Jesus was God, but he hated the idea of a human successor to his throne."

"Herod's fear was inspired by the devil who knew Christ's true identify," explained Father Greg.

"But Herod must have believed the wisemen," said Cesar, reading Joseph's Bible—*Then Herod, when he had secretly called the wise men, determined from them what*

27 *Opus Imperfectum*, Second Homily (PG 56, 639) my translation.

28 Same as previous note.

time the star appeared.[29]—so why didn't he believe the prophecies about the king of the Jews?"

"According to the *Commentary*," said Mentor, "Herod was blinded by the devil who knows the Scriptures are true but who deceives others into thinking the Scriptures lie." Mentor read,

"Men cannot change what God has ordained, can they? Yet Herod relied on the Scriptures for evil and not for good. He accepted what they said about the place of the king's birth but he did not recognize his own powerlessness to oppose the one God sent. Herod was bound by the devil's chains, not guided by his own reason."[30]

Signs at the Beginning of Christ's Ministry

"The *Incomplete Commentary* also describes mysterious signs of the beginning of Christ's ministry," explained Mentor, reading about John the Baptist.

"Even before it rises, the sun brightens the eastern sky and makes brilliant the morning star which announces the coming of day. Now, before the Lord was born into this world—and before he appeared in glory—his Spirit bestowed a glorious light on John who announced the coming of the Savior. Thus, the advent of God's Son did not dawn unexpectedly, catching men off guard, nor did the Son have to announce his own arrival."[31]

---

29 Matt. 2:7 NKJV.

30 *Opus Imperfectum*, Second Homily (PG 56, 639) my translation.

31 Same as previous note.

"John's witness was very credible too," agreed Father Greg, "because his birth was miraculous[32] and he was well respected in his generation as the son of Zacharias the priest."

"The *Commentary* says that?" I asked. Father Greg replied by reading,

"John was like the king in the circumstances of his birth: like Christ, he was born out of grace, not nature; his conception was announced by an angel and his name was heard before his birth; his virtue was evident before his birth, as was Christ's power."[33]

"Is the *Commentary* saying there was no difference between John and Jesus?" I asked.

"Not at all" said Father Greg, reading further,

"When Christ was conceived, his faithful mother gave thanks to God, saying 'Behold, the handmaid of the Lord; be it unto me according to your word,' but when John was conceived, his unbelieving father was struck dumb. Furthermore, when John was born the law was silent in other respects, but when Christ was born a little later, grace was about to speak."[34]

"I love that!" said Joseph, "John's heritage was the law, but Christ was born of a grace-filled confession, and with his birth *grace was about to speak!*"

---

32 See Luke 1:57-80.

33 These assertions are supported by Luke's Gospel, including John's miraculous conception (Luke 1:7), the announcement of his name by an angel (Luke 1:13), and his unusual virtue (Luke 1:44).

34 My translation here follows James Kellerman and Thomas Oden, *Incomplete Commentary on Matthew* (*Opus Imperfectum*) in Ancient Christian Texts (Downers Grove: IVP Academic, 2010), volume 1, page 43).

"John was no ordinary prophet," added Mentor, "he is the messenger who prepares the way for the coming of the king.[35] In other words, he lives on the threshold of the coming reign, yet his greatness consists in the fact that he wishes to be nothing more than the precursor of the one greater than he. Do you recall what John said when Christ presented Himself for baptism?"

"I need to be baptized by you, and do you come to me?"[36] quoted Joseph.

"Truly," agreed Mentor, and the *Commentary* suggests what John's objections might have been. Mentor read,

"The place I desire to arise to—you've already come down from! It is more reasonable that I should be baptized by you, so I might be made righteous and, therefore, worthy of heaven. And what would my baptism do for you, who are the very root of righteousness? Would it secure heaven for you? You, by your very nature, are heavenly!"[37]

"Did John the Baptist really say that?" asked Preacher.

"That's how the *Commentary* interprets John's words," said Mentor.

"Later on," added Mentor, "as John was awaiting execution in prison, he sent his disciples to Jesus to ask, *Are you the one who is to come, or shall we look for another?*[38] This was not idle curiosity on John's part; he

---

35 Susanne de Detrich,161.

36 Matt. 3:14.

37 *Opus Imperfectum*, Fourth Homily (PG 56, 657), my translation. Compare Kellerman and Oden, vol.1, 56.

38 Matt. 11:3.

knew very well who Jesus was, but he had the welfare of his disciples in mind. As the *Commentary* says,

"John, now in prison and knowing his own departure was imminent, wanted his disciples to follow Christ. So, like a wise father anticipating his death he entrusts his children to a trustworthy guardian, desiring to see them no longer doubting but fully trusting Christ. A more pleasant end he could not hope for than to know his disciples were now complete in Christ. So he asked his question—"are you the one?"—through the disciples, not for his own benefit but so that they might see with their own eyes and believe."[39]

"If John was in prison," said Father Greg, "how could he know it was Jesus?"

"Listen to Jesus's response," said Joseph, reading from his Bible,

> *And Jesus answered them, "Go and tell John what you hear and see: the blind receive their sight and the lame walk, lepers are cleansed and the deaf hear, and the dead are raised up, and the poor have good news preached to them. And blessed is the one who is not offended by me" (Matthew 11:4–6).*

"Jesus was saying to John's disciples, 'look for yourselves and learn that the blind see, the deaf hear, and blessed are you if you take no offense in me,'" said Joseph.

"After his baptism," Mentor continued, "Jesus was immediately led by the Holy Spirit into the wilderness

---

39 *Opus Imperfectum*, Homily 26 on Matt. 11 (PG 13, 772), my translation; compare Kellerman & Oden vol.1,196

to be tempted by the devil.[40] According to the *Incomplete Commentary*, this leading should not be understood as the command of a superior authority, as if the Holy Spirit ruled over Jesus. Rather," Mentor read,

"When a military advisor informs a king that an enemy has entered his realm, and advises him to draw him out for battle lest the kingdom perish, such a king will be guided by the advisor though he is in no way inferior to him.

"Moreover," Mentor continued, "the devil lures people in order to tempt them, but people do not pursue the devil in order to be tempted. Yet, the devil could not lure Jesus, so Jesus came out against him."[41]

"You know what's comin' next don't you?" asked Preacher, "the temptations of Jesus!"

We had been reading alongside Mentor for a long time. Now he called on Origen, and as the elder witness made his way to the lectern, Mentor invited us to be seated as he read from the Bible. After reading the account of the temptations of Jesus, first in Matthew's Gospel and then in Luke's,[42] Origen recited in his distinctive voice the verse that describes the first temptation of Jesus.

"*If you are the Son of God, say to this stone that it should become bread.*' What sort of temptation is that?" asked Origen, who spoke as if addressing the entire Athenaeum and not just those of us seated in the Crux.

---

40 Matt. 4:1; Luke 4:1.

41 *Opus Imperfectum*, Fifth Homily (PG 56, 661); Kellerman and Oden, *Incomplete Commentary on Matthew*, vol. 1, 61.

42 Matt. 4:1-11, Luke 4:1-13.

"Say to this stone?" he pointed to an imaginary stone on the floor. "Or say to *that* stone?" he pointed to another spot. "Say to *which* stone?" he paused.

"Of course our Lord was tempted so that once he conquers we too might conquer," Origen continued. "Yet, if we are to learn from Christ's testing, we need to understand the nature of his temptation. When a son asks a father for bread, he does not give him a stone does he?"

"That's from Matthew 7," whispered Joseph, "Which one of you, if his son asks him for bread, will give him a stone?"

"But the Adversary," said Origen, "fickle and deceptive as he is, offers stone in place of bread. What a cruel temptation! Our heavenly Father supplies all our needs, but the Adversary offers stone in place of bread!

If you are the Son of God, say to this stone that it should become bread. Is this all that the devil wanted, that a stone might become bread? No, but that men should eat the stone pointed out by the devil instead of bread."[43]

"And what about you?" asked Origen, looking directly at us, "for I think that even to the present day the devil points out a stone and urges each of us, just tell this stone to become bread! Marcion spoke and the devil's stone became his bread, Valentinius spoke, and another stone was turned into bread for him. Basilides also had bread of this sort, and so did the rest of the heretics. We

43 Quotation adapted from Joseph T. Lienhard, *Origen Homilies on Luke*, Homily 29:3 in The Fathers of the Church, vol. 94, 120; and *Patrologia Graeca* 13, 1875).

must take care lest we eat the devil's stone and believe we are eating God's bread!"[44]

Origen paused to wipe his brow.

"He just named the most infamous heretics of the Second Century," whispered Father Greg.

"What did they teach?" I asked.

"Marcion taught that the Creator god was evil," he replied, "and that he was an entirely different god than the Father of Jesus Christ. Valentinius and Basilides taught various forms of Gnosticism in place of the Gospel, meaning they denied that God's Son could have come in the flesh."

"But what is Origen saying about their bread?" I asked.

"They compromised God's word," explained Father Greg, "Jesus refused to accept the devil's suggestion to turn stones into bread, but the heretics followed the evil suggestion, rejecting God's bread, God's word."

Origen went on to the second temptation, calling on Preacher to read the next verse in Luke's account of the temptations. Joseph handed his Bible to Preacher who stood and read,

> *The devil took him up and showed him all the kingdoms of the world in a moment of time, and said to him, "To you I will give all this authority and their glory, for it has been delivered to me, and I give it to whom I will. If you, then, will worship me, it will all be yours." And*

---

44 Adapted from Joseph T. Lienhard, *Origen Homilies on Luke*, Homily 29:3 in The Fathers of the Church, vol. 94, 120; and *Patrologia Graeca* 13, 1875).

> *Jesus answered him, "It is written, 'You shall worship the Lord your God, and him only shall you serve.'"*[45]

"He showed Christ the kingdoms of the world in a moment of time," explained Origen, "because compared with eternity, the present age lasts only a moment. Moreover, Christ would permit only a brief glance of what the devil was offering: what our Savior saw was sin reigning, all the people ruled by sin, and the ruler of this world reveling in their destruction!"[46]

"This temptation, "Origen continued, "shows us two rival kings striving to reign—the devil is king of sin over sinners; Christ is King of Justice over the just! [47]

"Amen!" said Joseph, and Origen prompted Preacher to read the next passage.

> *And he took him to Jerusalem and set him on the pinnacle of the temple and said to him, "If you are the Son of God, throw yourself down from here, for it is written, 'He will command his angels concerning you, to guard you,' and "'On their hands they will bear you up, lest you strike your foot against a stone.' And Jesus answered him, "It is said, 'You shall not put the Lord your God to the test.'"*[48]

The elder witness launched into his next point with greater passion than before.

---

45 Luke 4:5-8. (NKJV)

46 Adapted from Joseph T. Lienhard, *Origen Homilies on Luke*, Homily 29:3 in The Fathers of the Church, vol. 94, 123-124; and *Patrologia Graeca* 13, 1878).

47 Same as previous note.

48 Luke 4:9-12. (NKJV)

"Listen, my children to this blasphemous corruption of Holy Scripture! Does the devil really want our Lord to display the Father's glory by throwing himself from the Temple? —No, I tell you, he wishes to diminish his glory—as if the Son of God needed any help from the angels!" he added, with disgust in his voice.

"This is like the heretics who ensnare those who grasp only a simplistic, literal reading of Holy Scripture," added Origen. "Marcion, Basilides and Valentinius—all these insist on the simple, literal sense in order to destroy those who are friends of the letter."[49]

Puzzled by this saying, we all looked to Father Greg.

"The friends of the letter were those who took a literal approach to interpretation," he said, "but Master Origen prefers allegorical readings."

"*Spiritual* interpretation is what we practice," said Origen, correcting Father Greg.[50]

"What does he mean by that?" I whispered to our professor.

Father Greg shook his head and said nothing for a moment, then quietly added,

"He means discovering deeper meaning in the passage, but I can't explain how."

---

49 Adapted from Joseph T. Lienhard, *Origen Homilies on Luke*, Homily 31 in The Fathers of the Church, vol. 94, 126; and *Patrologia Graeca* 13, 1880).

50 Origen represents Alexandrian exegesis which employed allegory in the interpretation of Scripture. Antiochene interpretation ("friends of the letter"), on the other hand, emphasized historical, contextual interpretation. Both schools practiced "spiritual interpretation," searching for deeper meaning beyond the basic narrative.

As if to demonstrate his spiritual interpretation, Origen imitated Satan taunting Christ:

"Have you come out to fight against my authority, to take my subjects for your own? Don't trouble yourself. Why risk the battle? Go ahead and take the entire kingdom for yourself, only first bow down and worship me, then it will all be yours!"

"And yet," Origen continued, "our Lord and Savior wants to reign in truth, with all people serving him out of righteousness. He will reign righteously and rule blamelessly, but he will *not* rule if he himself is subject to the devil."[51]

Signs of the Coming Kingdom of God

Origen, exhausted from preaching, excused himself from the Crux as Mentor returned to the lectern.

"The incarnation revealed Christ as the legitimate heir who has come to take possession of what belongs to him,[52] said Mentor, summarizing Origen's teaching. "Christ is victorious in his initial battle against the devil. The *Incomplete Commentary* describes Christ's further preparations for battle." Mentor again read from the *Commentary*,

"Every king preparing to fight an adversary assembles his troops before engaging the battle. So also the Lord,

51 Adapted from Joseph T. Lienhard, *Origen Homilies on Luke*, Homily 30 in The Fathers of the Church, vol. 94, 124; and *Patrologia Graeca* 13, 1878).

52 Susanne de Dietrich, 154.

preparing to combat the devil, assembled his Apostles before declaring the gospel throughout all Galilee."[53]

"Christ attacked his enemy," Mentor continued, "as the *Commentary* says, by declaring truth, for the preaching of righteousness shoots a deadly arrow into Satan's heart, miraculous signs undo him, and the salvation of the faithful destroys his very power!" [54]

"*Christos Victor!* shouted the witnesses gathered in the Crux.[55]

"Christ came preaching the kingdom of God," added Mentor, "but what are the *signs of God's kingdom revealed in the Gospels?*"

Ephrem of Syria returned to the lectern.

"Even our Lord," he began, "when questioned by the Pharisees, said simply, 'The kingdom of God is not coming in ways that can be observed, nor will they say, 'Look, here it is!' or 'There!' for behold, the kingdom of God is among you.'"[56]

"I've always wondered what Jesus meant by *the kingdom of God is among you*," said Joseph.

"He meant that the kingdom of God is *in your heart,*" answered Ephrem.

---

53 Paraphrase based on Kellerman and Oden, *Incomplete Commentary on Matthew*, vol. 1, 80 and *Patrologia Graeca* 56: 676-677.

54 Same as previous note.

55 The ancient Church rallying cry means "Christ the Victor."

56 Luke 17:20-21. Quotation in C. McCarthy, *Saint Ephrem's Commentary on Tatian's Diatessaron, an English Translation of Chester Beatty Syriac MS 709 with Introduction and Notes* (Oxford University Press, 1993), 272.

"Why do you say that?" asked Joseph.

"Did you know the Pharisees kept account of the times to discern when the Messiah would appear?" asked Ephrem.

"Not really," admitted Joseph, "but that makes sense."

"Rumors were spreading concerning Christ's birth as much as thirty years before his coming, explained Ephrem, "and that's when Theudas and his companions were at large. They had come before the Lord in order to rob and usurp the name of the Messiah for themselves. This is why our Lord said the Pharisees sought him through observations, not in a hidden way.

"A hidden way?" said Joseph.

"Inwardly," replied Ephrem, "for they had not accepted Christ with an inward acceptance."

"They didn't have Jesus in their hearts," said Preacher.

"Indeed, they did not," agreed Ephrem.

"But who is Theudas?" I asked.

"Theudas, is mentioned in the book of Acts," said Father Greg. Reaching for Joseph's Bible, the priest turned to chapter 5 and read,

> *But a Pharisee in the council named Gamaliel, a teacher of the law held in honor by all the people, stood up and gave orders to put the men outside for a little while. And he said to them, "Men of Israel, take care what you are about to do with these men. For before these days Theudas rose up, claiming to be somebody, and a number of men, about four hundred, joined him. He was killed, and all who followed him were dispersed and came to nothing."*[57]

57 Acts 5:34-36.

Father Greg explained that the passage was Gamaliel's advice to the Jewish Ruling Council that they should take no action against the preachers but make careful observations to see whether the preaching of Peter and the Apostles would come to anything.

"Is that what you meant by *observations*, Father Ephrem?" asked the priest.

"Yes," Ephrem agreed, "the Pharisees believed they could discern all truth through their subtle observations. Theudas had shown himself to be no messiah since he sought to rob people in secret. Yet the Pharisees were no better than thieves and robbers who never show themselves in daylight. The true Lord of the flock had come to them, entering his sheepfold by the gate. That is, He was coming into his inheritance with confidence and strength, by reason of his miracles. Still, the Pharisees could not identify him by their astute observations."

"I see what you mean," said Father Greg, "the Pharisees' corrupt hearts were shown by their inability to recognize their own Messiah: Jesus said *the kingdom of God is in your hearts*, because one perceives God's kingdom from one's heart."

"But the disciple's hearts weren't right, were they?" asked Cesar.

"That's true," agreed Joseph, "besides, Jesus said they were given the knowledge."

"Where does it say that?" I asked.

"Right here in Matthew," said Joseph. Turning the pages of his Bible he read,

> *To you it has been given to know the secrets of the kingdom of heaven, but to them it has not been given.*

For to the one who has, more will be given, and he will have an abundance, but from the one who has not, even what he has will be taken away. This is why I speak to them in parables, because seeing they do not see, and hearing they do not hear, nor do they understand.[58]

"Isn't that unfair?" asked Cesar.

"He is speaking about their hearts," replied Ephrem.

"With all due respect to Father Ephrem," said Cesar, "I'd like to know what the *Incomplete Commentary* say about that."

Mentor looked for the passage and read,

"The fault is not Christ's for not wanting to speak openly, but theirs for not wanting to hear what they were hearing. For it was not because Christ spoke in parables that they did not see, but because they chose not to see that Christ spoke to them in parables."[59]

"In other words," said Father Greg, "Christ spoke in a fitting way to those who did not want to hear what they were hearing, like Isaiah said—'Hear and hear, but do not understand.'"[60]

"What about the other part," asked Preacher, "he who has will be given more?"[61]

Mentor continued the reading:

---

58 Matt. 13:11-13.

59 My translation of *Opus Imperfectum*, Homily 32 in *Patrologia Graeca* 56, 798. See Kellerman, 2, 249.

60 Isa. 6:9.

61 Matt. 13:12.

"Whenever you see a person who delights in hearing about the good, even if he does not do good works, God does not take away what he has, but waits for him to repent and do good. But when you see a person who not only does not do good but does not even delight in hearing about the good, understand that God has already removed from him his ability to understand the good; and he is dead as far as God is concerned.[62]

"So then, concluded Mentor, "the one who does not rightly exercise his God-given knowledge of good and evil receives what he deserves: what he has is according to nature, and what he loses is according to his will.[63]

"In other words, *it is* a matter of the heart," said Cesar, echoing Ephrem's words.

One of the three Church historians saluted Mentor. He was a distinguished-looking man in stylish vestments, whom Mentor introduced as Eusebius of Caesarea.

"You are speaking of the hearts of the disciples," said Eusebius, "but what about the heart of our Savior?"

"Illuminate us, please" said Mentor. Eusebius came the lectern and read from Matthew's Gospel:

> *The Pharisees went out and conspired against him, how to destroy him. Jesus, aware of this, withdrew from there. And many followed him, and he healed them all and ordered them not to make him known. This was to fulfill what was spoken by the prophet Isaiah: "Behold, my servant whom I have chosen, my beloved with whom my soul is well pleased. I will put my Spirit upon him,*

---

62 *Opus Imperfectum*, Homily 32 in *Patrologia Graeca* 56, column 797.

63 Same as previous note.

> *and he will proclaim justice to the Gentiles. He will not quarrel or cry aloud, nor will anyone hear his voice in the streets; a bruised reed he will not break, and a smoldering wick he will not quench, until he brings justice to victory.*[64]

"Everything in the passage fulfills the prophecy of Isaiah," explained Eusebius, "including Jesus' yielding to those who plotted against him, and also His command to those that were healed not to make Him known."

"What did the Prophet mean by saying 'he did not break the bruised reed?" I asked.

"Not only did Jesus *not* break the bruised reed," replied Eusebius, "but, in a manner of speaking, he repaired it—strengthening the weak and the bruised in heart. He did not neglect the sick and sinful, who needed his medicine, nor did he bruise the repentant with hard judgment. He did not quench those whose evil smoked with the fire of passion by preventing them from following their sinful ways, nor did he punish them before the time, but left that for the general Judgment. This is why the Scripture says, *and the smoking flax he shall not quench*."[65]

"This is the heart of our Savior," concluded Eusebius, returning to his place.

"Another sign of the kingdom was seen when our Lord commanded his disciples not to make him known," said Mentor. He read another passage from Matthew's Gospel.

---

64 Matt. 12:14–20, quoting from Isa. 42:1-3.

65 Eusebius, *Demonstration IX*, 15. Eusebius of Caesarea and W.J. Ferrar (ed), *The Proof of the Gospel, vol.1* (Grand Rapids: Baker, 1981), 182-183.

> *He said to them, "But who do you say that I am?" Simon Peter replied, "You are the Christ, the Son of the living God." And Jesus answered him, "Blessed are you, Simon Bar-Jonah! For flesh and blood has not revealed this to you, but my Father who is in heaven. And I tell you, you are Peter, and on this rock I will build my church, and the gates of hell shall not prevail against it. I will give you the keys of the kingdom of heaven, and whatever you bind on earth shall be bound in heaven, and whatever you loose on earth shall be loosed in heaven." Then he strictly charged the disciples to tell no one that he was the Christ.*[66]

Mentor invited Cyril of Alexandria to the lectern to explain why Jesus charged his disciples not to make him known.

"I believe that the disciples were not sufficiently prepared or experienced to testify," said Cyril. "There were things yet unfulfilled which must also be included in their preaching about him."

"His miracles?" asked Father Greg.

"The cross, the passion, and the death in the flesh," replied Cyril, "all these they must proclaim. They must also preach the resurrection of the dead, that great and glorious sign that testifies he is Emmanuel, truly God and by nature the Son of God. Our Lord utterly abolished death and wiped out destruction itself. He robbed hell and overthrew the tyranny of the enemy. He took away the sin of the world, opened the gates above to the dwellers upon the earth, and united earth to heaven. These things proved him, in truth, to be God. Yet, he commanded them to keep the mystery by a seasonable

66 Matt. 16:15–20.

silence until the whole plan of the dispensation should arrive at a suitable conclusion."[67]

"Since their knowledge was lacking," I asked, "why did Jesus bother to ask them 'Who do you say I am?'"

"What did the Savior ask before he asked them 'Who do *you* say I am?'

None of us knew, and Cyril invited me to the lectern where he pointed out a verse before the passage read by Mentor.

"He asked, 'Who do *the people* say that the Son of Man is?'" I answered.[68]

"Indeed," said Cyril, "he asked this question in order to deliver them from the wrong thinking that was typical of their day, and to implant in them a correct faith. Just imagine the disciples' confusion when they see our Lord Jesus Christ working miracles like God but praying like a human. 'What strange behavior! Should we consider him to be God or man? We could say that he is a man like ourselves or like one of the prophets, yet we see from his inexpressible miracles that he far transcends the limits of human nature, and in many ways he performs wonders as God. If we say he is God, then surely to pray is unnecessary for one who is, by very nature God.'"[69]

Cyril was reserved in his manner, but he became animated as he explained the Scriptures. We listened closely as he continued his teaching.

---

67 Cyril of Alexandria and R. Payne Smith, A *Commentary Upon the Gospel According to St. Luke, by St. Cyril, translated into English from an ancient Syriac version*, (Oxford: Univ. Press 1859), 219. Available online at Google books. The translation is modernized.

68 Matt. 16:13, parallel with Luke 9:18b.

69 Cyril of Alexandria and R. Payne Smith, Sermon 49, 214, modernized.

"To dispel such confusing thoughts," he explained, "and to calm their storm-tossed faith—this is why Jesus asked his question, and not because he was unaware of what the crowds were saying about him. Consider the skillfulness of his question. He did not first say 'Who do *you* say that I am?' but asks what the people were saying about him. Once that was shown to be false, he could bring them back to the truth. For once the disciples had said, *some say you are John the Baptist, others Elijah, and others a prophet.* Then he said to them, *But you, who do you say that I am?* How full of meaning is that 'you'! In this way he separated the disciples from all others, so they could avoid their errors and, in effect, he says to them, 'You who have been chosen, who by my decree have been called to the apostleship, and who are the witnesses of my miracles, who do you say that I am?'"[70]

I returned to our bench and wrote in my journal that Jesus' two-fold question pushed the disciples to think for themselves and not just accept what the crowds were saying. Cyril continued his explanation:

"Notice that it was Simon Peter who correctly answered Jesus' question by saying, *You are the Christ, the Son of the living God.* This was a remarkable answer, for Jesus never would have said *Blessed are thou, Simon* if Messiah's true identity was known by the crowds. And we must study Peter's answer closely, for he does not simply say that He is 'a' Christ of God; but rather 'the Christ.' For, there are many who have been called 'Christ,' from

---

70 Cyril of Alexandria and R. Payne Smith 1859. *Commentary upon the Gospel according to St. Luke* (Oxford: Univ. Press), 215, modernized.

having in various ways been anointed of God.[71] For some have been anointed as kings and some as prophets, but He who is God the Father's Christ is unique, because He alone has as His Father Him that is in heaven."[72]

Cyril paused to make sure we had understood.

"Peter's definite answer," he continued, "identified Jesus as *the Messiah* among many who previously were described as anointed ones— *messiahs*—of God. But how did Peter receive this wisdom? Jesus himself identifies the source of Peter's knowledge as the revelation of God: *Blessed are you, Simon Bar-Jonah! For flesh and blood has not revealed this to you, but my Father who is in heaven.*[73] So, the disciple was taught by God, for he did not make this profession of faith according to his own thoughts, but because divine light shown on his understanding, and the Father led him to a correct knowledge of Christ.[74]

"Now then," Cyril concluded, "Peter believed that He who was in the likeness of mankind as part of creation was God, Who transcends all created things. He who dwells in the high and lofty place was abased from His glory to be in poverty like us. And He who, as God, is Lord of all and King of all, was in the likeness of a slave!

---

71 Messiah means "anointed of God," *Christos* (Christ) being the Greek translation of the Hebrew *meshiach* (messiah). Cyril's point is that while many were anointed by God (e.g. Saul and David), only Jesus earned the title *'O Christos* (the Christ) of God.

72 Cyril of Alexandria and R. Payne Smith 1859. *Commentary upon the Gospel according to St. Luke* (Oxford: Univ. Press), 216

73 Matt. 16:17.

74 Cyril of Alexandria and R. Payne Smith 1859. *Commentary upon the Gospel according to St. Luke* (Oxford: Univ. Press), 216

This is the faith that our Savior praises—*Blessed are you, Simon Bar-Jonah.*"[75]

"When *do* the disciples get to tell what they know about Jesus?" asked Preacher.

"When he rose from the dead," replied Cyril, "he commanded that the mystery should be revealed to all the inhabitants of the earth, setting before every man justification by faith, and the cleansing efficacy of holy baptism. For he said, *All power is given unto me in heaven and in earth. Go ye, therefore, make disciples of all nations, baptizing them in the name of the Father, and of the Son, and of the Holy Spirit, teaching them to obey all those things which I have commanded you. And Lo! I am with you always, even unto the end of the world.*"[76]

The Transfiguration

"Peter's confession of Christ as Lord is followed by Jesus' glorious appearance with Moses and Elijah on the mountain, while Peter, John and James look on," said Mentor.[77] He then read the account from Matthew's Gospel and invited Cyril to continue his teaching.

> *If anyone would come after me, let him deny himself and take up his cross and follow me. For whoever would save his life will lose it, but whoever loses his life for my sake will find it. For what will it profit a man if he gains the whole world and forfeits his soul? Or what shall a man give in return for his soul? For the Son of Man is going to come with his angels in the glory of his Father, and*

---

75 Cyril of Alexandria and R. Payne Smith, 218

76 Cyril of Alexandria and R. Payne Smith, 220.

77 See Matt. 17:1-8; Mark 9:2-8; Luke 9:28-36.

> *then he will repay each person according to what he has done. Truly, I say to you, there are some standing here who will not taste death until they see the Son of Man coming in his kingdom.*[78]

"The command to follow Christ," Cyril began, "is for both the salvation and honor of the saints, and the cause of the highest glory, and the means of perfect joy. Choosing to suffer for the sake of Christ is not a thankless duty but makes us sharers in everlasting life and the glory that is prepared.[79]

"Even so," continued Cyril, "the disciples had not yet been empowered by the Holy Spirit, and had no doubt fallen into various human weaknesses. They were probably asking themselves 'How does a man deny himself? Or 'how having lost himself does he find himself again? And what reward will compensate those who thus suffer?' To rescue them from such timid thoughts and to mold them into manliness and birth in them a desire for the glory about to be given them, our Lord says, *there are some standing here, who shall not taste death until they have seen the kingdom of God.*[80]

"In saying this," explained Cyril, "the Lord does not mean that he is prolonging their lives until the kingdom comes in its fullness. Rather, by *the kingdom of God* he means the sight of the glory in which he will appear at his manifestation to the inhabitants of the earth. For he

---

78 Matt. 16:24–28.

79 Cyril of Alexandria and R. Payne Smith 1859. *Commentary upon the Gospel according to St. Luke* (Oxford: Univ. Press), Sermon 51, 227.

80 Same as previous note.

will come in the glory of God the Father, and not in low estate as he previously came to us.[81]

"How did Christ help them glimpse this future glory?" continued Cyril, "He goes up into the mountain taking with him three chosen disciples and is transformed to so surpassing and godlike a brightness, that his garments even glittered with rays of fire, and seemed to flash like lightening. And Moses and Elijah stood at Jesus' side, and spoke of his departure, which he was about to accomplish at Jerusalem—by which is meant the mystery of the dispensation in the flesh, and of his precious suffering upon the cross.[82]

"And this," said Cyril, "was the method which our Lord Jesus Christ used for the benefit and edification of the holy Apostles. Allowing them to become spectators of splendid and glorious changes—Peter appears to have believed that the kingdom had come already in fullness—"Lord, it is good that we are here"[83]—Christ thereby equipped his followers to be made partakers of the hope prepared for the saints, to joyfully undergo combat for piety's sake toward Christ, and to lead elect lives, not complaisant or shy but manfully resisting every temptation, and nullifying violent persecutions, while they count it gain to suffer on his behalf.

"Such disciples," Cyril concluded, "are skillful in battle and roused to a glorious height of courage"![84]

---

81 Same as previous note.

82 Same as previous note, 227-228.

83 Matt. 17:4.

84 Cyril of Alexandria and R. Payne Smith 1859. *Commentary upon the Gospel according to St. Luke* (Oxford: Univ. Press), Sermon 51, 226.

"The vision of the transfiguration," added Mentor, "is given to the disciples as a foreshadowing of the resurrection. For a moment the veil is pulled aside, yet almost immediately it closes again. Once more, God affirms his good will toward the One who comes to take up his cross, by enfolding him in his glory."[85]

"And our Lord Jesus showed his disciples his transfigured face before his death, so that when he would rise from the dead and be changed, they would not be in doubt," explained Ephrem.[86]

"What about the two men who appeared with Jesus on the mountain?" asked Cesar.

"The Law was represented by Moses and the word of the holy prophets was represented by Elijah," explained Cyril. "Both foreshadowed the mystery of Christ—Moses by types and shadows, painting it, so to speak, as in a picture. The prophets, with diverse expressions, declared beforehand that in time he would appear in our likeness, and for the salvation and life of us all, would consent to suffer death upon the tree."[87]

"That reminds me of the first verse of Hebrews," said Joseph, "*Long ago, at many times and in many ways, God spoke to our fathers by the prophets*. You're saying that the Law pictures the mystery of salvation while the prophets prophesy the coming death and resurrection of the Messiah?" he asked Cyril, who agreed.

---

85 See Mark 9:2-13 and Susanne de Deitrich, 185.

86 Paraphrase based on Carmel McCarthy, *Saint Ephrem's Commentary on Tatian's Diatessaron* (Oxford University Press, 1993), 39-40 (XIX, 8).

87 Cyril of Alexandria and R. Payne Smith 1859. *Commentary upon the Gospel according to St. Luke* (Oxford: Univ. Press), Sermon 51, 228.

"If you picture Moses and Elijah as bodyguards for the Lord Jesus," concluded Cyril, "Moses representing the Law and Elijah the Prophets, then you have the right idea."[88]

The Garden of Gethsemane

At Mentor's invitation, Ephrem returned to the lectern, standing next to Cyril.

"The scene at the Garden of Gethsemane is quite different from the glory of the transfiguration," said Mentor. "Just before His arrest, we again find the three chosen disciples accompanying the Savior, and we hear him say to them, *Sit here, while I go over there and pray*. Mentor read,

> *And taking with him Peter and the two sons of Zebedee, he began to be sorrowful and troubled. Then he said to them, "My soul is very sorrowful, even to death; remain here, and watch with me." And going a little farther he fell on his face and prayed, saying, "My Father, if it be possible, let this cup pass from me; nevertheless, not as I will, but as you will" (Matt.26:36–39).*

"Think of our Savior's grief!" said Ephrem, "and notice that He was not ashamed to confess his grief, hiding nothing beneath a deceptive appearance. This, in part, was to show that he had clothed himself with weak flesh, and was united to a soul capable of suffering."[89]

---

88 Same as previous note.

89 McCarthy, *St. Ephrem's Commentary*, 292. (XX)

"Amen," added Cyril, "and of the profoundness of the dispensation in the flesh and the height of its wisdom, no words can tell."[90]

"Dispensation in the flesh?" asked Joseph.

"His incarnation," explained Cyril, "God's plan or arrangements for the *Fullness of Time*.

"Father Cyril," asked Cesar, "did Jesus understand everything his death would accomplish?"

"Certainly," replied Cyril, "our Lord understood that by agreeing to suffer the passion of the cross he would deliver everyone from every evil and be the cause of unending blessings to the inhabitants of the whole earth!"

"But the passage says he was troubled and very sorrowful," said Cesar.

"It is true," said Cyril, "and why were you troubled, O Lord? Were you terrified at death? Did you being seized with fear draw back from suffering? And yet you taught the holy apostles not to worry about the terrors of death, saying "Do not fear those who can kill the body but cannot kill the soul."[91]

"What's the answer?" asked Cesar.

"Only what the prophets teach," Cyril replied, "for I hear our Lord saying 'It grieves me that Israel the firstborn, henceforth, is not among the servants, and that the portion of the Lord will be the portion of foxes; that the beloved, who had the promises, is utterly stripped of

90 Cyril of Alexandria and R. Payne Smith 1859. *Commentary upon the Gospel according to St. Luke* (Oxford: Univ. Press), Sermon 146, 684.

91 Matt. 10:28, and Cyril, 684, translation modernized.

my gifts, and the pleasant vineyard with its rich grapes henceforth will be a desert land."[92]

"I don't understand," said Cesar.

"Christ grieved for Israel, his chosen people," replied Cyril, "and he pitied Jerusalem. He wept over the city because he knew that it would endure much misery because of its crimes against him."

"I see," said Cesar.

"This is the passion of grief!" said Ephrem.

"Yes," agreed Cyril, "but this grief does not flow from the divine and impassive nature of the Word, because the Word transcends all passion. Yet, the Incarnate Word willed also to submit himself to the measure of human nature, by suffering what belongs to it. For it would not have been fitting for him who emptied himself to be unwilling to endure human suffering. So, while God the Father is altogether free from passion, the Son wisely and for the dispensation's sake submitted himself to the infirmities of mankind."[93]

The Betrayal and Arrest of Jesus

Mentor thanked Cyril and Ephrem and walked them back to their section in the Athenaeum. He returned with two witnesses we had not met before, both of them tall and aristocratic in appearance.

"John's Gospel does not include the account of Jesus' sorrow and prayer in the Garden of Gethsemane," said

---

92 Cyril of Alexandria and R. Payne Smith 1859. *Commentary upon the Gospel according to St. Luke* (Oxford: Univ. Press), Sermon 51, 685, translation modernized.

93 Same as previous note, 686, translation modernized.

Mentor, "but it does describe Jesus's betrayal and arrest. Judas leads a cohort of soldiers and temple guards to the place he expects to find Jesus and the disciples. In John we read,

> *Then Jesus, knowing all that would happen to him, came forward and said to them, "Whom do you seek?" They answered him, "Jesus of Nazareth." Jesus said to them, "I am he." Judas, who betrayed him, was standing with them. When Jesus said to them, "I am he," they drew back and fell to the ground. So he asked them again, "Whom do you seek?" And they said, "Jesus of Nazareth." Jesus answered, "I told you that I am he. So, if you seek me, let these men go." This was to fulfill the word that he had spoken: "Of those whom you gave me I have lost not one." Then Simon Peter, having a sword, drew it and struck the high priest's servant and cut off his right ear. (The servant's name was Malchus.) So Jesus said to Peter, "Put your sword into its sheath; shall I not drink the cup that the Father has given me?"*[94]

"The other Gospels," added Mentor, "have a description of the sign of Judas' betrayal, for example as we read in Matthew,

> *Now the betrayer had given them a sign, saying, "The one I will kiss is the man; seize him." And he came up to Jesus at once and said, "Greetings, Rabbi!" And he kissed him.*[95]

"This passage," explained Mentor, "shows the false disciple's use of the traditional greeting—the kiss of peace—to identify Jesus to the soldiers."

---

94 John 18:4–11.

95 Matt. 26:48-49.

"It's pure irony," said Father Greg.

"What do you mean?" I asked.

"Irony means things are different than they appear to be," explained Cesar.

"Precisely," agreed Father Greg.

At this point, one of the unfamiliar witnesses spoke up.

"Wicked Judas," he said with a voice deep and dramatic, "that raving wolf no longer concealed by sheep skin but exposed, unleashes his treachery with a kiss of peace—a betrayal more deadly than any weapon!"[96]

Mentor introduced the witness as Leo, Bishop of Rome.

"We know him as Leo the Great," replied Father Greg, "and remember him for his *Tome*."

"What's a tome?" asked Preacher.

"A large book," said Cesar, "may I have a look at it?"

"In this case the *Tome* is a letter," explained Father Greg.

"Too bad," said Preacher, teasing Cesar.

"Do we know what the letter was about?" I asked.

Mentor stepped back and offered the lectern to Bishop Leo.

---

96 From a sermon preached on Easter, AD 441. My paraphrase of Leo the Great, Sermon 52.3 in *Corpus Christianorum Series Latina* 138a, 309. Compare the English translation of Freeland and Conway, *St. Leo The Great, Sermons*, in The Fathers of the Church (FOTC), vol. 93, 228. The latter phrase, "more deadly than any weapon," follows FOTC. Note also that Leo's description of Judas as "a wolf in sheep's clothing" follows Jesus' description of false prophets in Matthew 7:15.

"I believe we were speaking of the traitor, Judas" said Leo, "my letter—my Tome, as you call it—concerns another traitor, who has departed from the catholic tradition by teaching what he does not understand—the incarnation of the Word of God."

"What do you mean, he departed from the catholic tradition?" I asked.

"He should have studied the Holy Scriptures and listened to the confession," replied Leo, "*We believe in God, the Father Almighty, and in Jesus Christ, His only Son, our Lord, who was born of the Holy Spirit and the Virgin Mary*."

"The Apostle's Creed," said Father Greg.

"By which the heretics are over thrown," added Bishop Leo.

"Which heretics?" I asked Father Greg.

"Eutyches for one," he replied, "who taught that Jesus' humanity was swallowed up by his divine nature so that he did not really suffer what we humans suffer."[97]

"Shall we return to the topic at hand?" suggested Mentor.

"Judas' kiss identified Jesus," said Cesar, recapping.

"Yet that sign was missed by the mob that came to capture the Lord," said Leo, "because they could not tell true light from torches and shadows.[98] Therefore our Lord identified himself by declaring, 'I am he.'"[99]

---

97 His name is pronounced ***you***-tick-ees.

98 Leo the Great, Sermon 52.3 in *Corpus Christianorum Series Latina* 138a, 309.

99 John 18:5.

"That's right," said Joseph, who was following along in his Bible.

"At the hands of this confession," Bishop Leo continued, "the mob was thrown back and retreated.[100] What happened to their conspiracy? Where was their violent rage and their drawn weapons? More than this, what will happen to those who were unable to endure his incarnate humility, when His Majesty returns in judgment?"[101]

"Amen!" said Preacher, "if the power of the God came through 'I am he,' then just wait 'til he returns in glory!"

"The Lord, knowing the mystery he had chosen to endure, and not relying on his own power, allowed his persecutors to carry out their evil plan," Bishop Leo continued. "Indeed, he would not have been taken if he had not permitted it, but what man could be saved if that man had not been arrested?"[102]

"Amen!" said Joseph.

Leo's preaching portrayed the drama of the gospel, even the drama of the two natures of Christ—he was *fully God* and *fully man*—in the one person of Jesus Christ. "Which human being," Leo had asked, "could have been saved if *that* human being (Jesus, who was *fully man*) had not been arrested?"

"We need to understand that two natures coalesced in our Redeemer," Leo explained, "each retaining its own character, so that a truly remarkable unity of these two natures emerged when, as human nature required, the

100 John 18:6.

101 *Corpus Christianorum Series Latina*, vol. 138a, 309.

102 *Corpus Christianorum Series Latina*, vol. 138a, 310.

Word became flesh in the blessed virgin's womb. Indeed, scarcely can we think of him as God apart from his humanity, nor his humanity apart from his divinity."[103]

"The *two natures*," Mentor reminded us, "are Christ's divine and human natures, which, as the Bishop explains, became unified in our Redeemer when the Word was made flesh. Those who rightly understand the words of our Lord in the garden and at his betrayal and arrest will find it impossible to think about Jesus *as human*, without also thinking of him *as God*.

"Each of Christ's two natures," added Leo, "kept its own characteristics: each nature expresses its own truth in its own distinct actions, but neither separates itself from its connection with the other. Neither nature lacks anything: his lowliness was apparent in his majesty, and his majesty in his lowliness. Unity brings no confusion, nor does the distinctiveness ruin the unity. One is subject to suffering, the other is unmoved."[104]

"Will this be on the test?" whispered Preacher.

"We are nearing the end of what our brother Cyril calls the *dispensation in the flesh*," explained Leo. "So, when everything God allowed to be done in the limiting veil of flesh had been carried out, Jesus the Son of God was nailed to a cross which he himself had carried—along with two thieves, one on his right, the other on his left, crucified in the same way.[105]

---

103 Same as previous note, vol.138a, 317.

104 Freeland and Conway, *St. Leo the Great, Sermons*, in The Fathers of the Church, vol. 93, 233.

105 Leo the Great, Sermon 55, Fathers of the Church vol.93, 237. Latin original in *Corpus Christianorum Series Latina*, vol. 138a, 310.

"Christ's crucifixion was the culmination of his Incarnation and earthly ministry," added Mentor.

"Yes," Bishop Leo agreed, "and his passion contains the very mystery of our salvation. Notice that the cross itself, though designed for torture, became for us a step up to glory. For this is what the Lord Jesus undertook for the salvation of all when, as he was being held to the wood by the nails, he implored his Father's mercy for his murderers, saying, *Father, forgive them, for they know not what they do.*[106]

"Notice also," he continued, "that the very arrangement of the gallows—one on his right hand and one on his left—shows the criterion that will be applied when he comes again to judge all humans. On the one side, the faith of the believing thief prefigured those who were to be saved, while wickedness on the part of the blasphemer foreshadowed those who were to be condemned."

"Thank you, Bishop," said Mentor, who summarized, "Surveying the crucifixion scene, we behold God's forgiveness extended by his Son from the cross. Here, too, is the destiny of believers, in the person of the believing thief, and unbelievers—the blaspheming thief.

Mentor now introduced the second witness, Bishop Peter Chrysologus, whose name he explained meant "golden-word."[107]

"The human mind can hardly grasp that God is born and dies!" began Chrysologus. "But why did the origin of the universe, the author of nature, will to be born,

106 Luke 23:34.

107 Chrysologus was a fifth century Bishop of Ravenna, Italy, known also as the *Doctor of Sermons*.

except that he willed to die? Why did God assume flesh with all its weakness, except that he chose to take on the indignities associated with the flesh? Why did the Lord of all creation enter the form of slavery except to endure all the indignities of slavery?"[108]

Christ had come in the flesh, Chrysologus had explained, in order to identify himself with human weakness. He had entered the form of slavery in order to suffer the same indignities of slavery that his children suffered.

"Why did God the Father send his own Son to death, and to this kind of death?" he continued. "And why did Christ submit to so shameful a passion? Consider: When is a king more glorious? When he is decked out in his purple, adorned with the crown, covered with gold, and high up on his throne? Or, is he more glorious dressed in armor, carrying his sword? When for his country, his citizens, and his children he destroys the enemy, despises danger, forget his own wounds, and endures death for the sake of his people, so that he gains a greater victory?"[109]

Chrysologus was teaching us to see Christ's suffering on the cross as glorious warfare waged by the King on behalf of his subjects. His questions and creative scenarios held our attention. His sermons also made use of strongly contrasting themes.[110] When he came to the

---

108 Peter Chrysologus, Sermon 72b, Fathers of the Church, vol. 110, pages 6-7. *Corpus Christianorum Series Latina vol. 24a.*

109 Same as previous note, page 8.

110 Known as antithesis. Patristics scholar B. Düler, in Siegmar Döpp and Wilhelm Geerlings, *Dictionary of Early Christian Literature* (page 481), describes Chrysologus's sermons as emphasizing antithesis (contrasting themes) throughout, "to the point that whole sermons have an antithetical structure" in "what amounts to a dialogue."

subject of Christ's resurrection, for example, he began by emphasizing "our Christian Passover in contrast to the Jewish customs" because "in contrast to the Jewish commemoration of Passover, God was doing a new thing as a sign pointing to Christ's return." Likewise, about the Passover he explained that,

"Today's feast, brothers, does not connect the old with the new, nor does it keep the flesh of the lamb for tomorrow, but while it makes the past a partner with the present in solemn devotion, and joins our Passover with the Jewish Passover, it weans the infants newly regenerated, because as the Apostle says, "The old has passed away, and see all things have been made new."[111]

Chrysologus strongly emphasized the radical new thing God was doing. He spoke of the Christian commemoration of Easter as "today's feast," and he referred to newly baptized believers as the "newly regenerated."

"Today's feast," he added, "does not connect the old with the new, nor does it keep the flesh of the lamb for tomorrow." [112] In this way the Bishop interpreted the warning in Exodus not to allow any of the Passover lamb to remain until the next day.

The Resurrection

In the place of the annual Jewish festivals, Chrysologus emphasized the Church year calendar.

111 2 Cor.5:17. Peter Chrysologus, Sermon 73 in the Fathers of the Church vol. 110, 12.

112 See Exodus 12:10.

"The year of the Lord progresses through seasons," he explained, "it does not grow old, since it repeats its cycle for as long as it takes to lead us to the day of recompense." [113]

Chrysologus was not rejecting Old Testament practice but emphasizing its future fulfillment. Speaking of Abraham's celebration of the weaning of Isaac, and of Hannah's return of Samuel to the temple following his weaning, he explained that

"Today's celebration of Easter leaves off the milk of those who gave it birth, so that it might be strengthened by eating solid food and be made into the perfect man of Christ."[114]

Chrysologus now read the biblical account of the resurrection, beginning in Matthew 28:1-3,

> *Now after the Sabbath, toward the dawn of the first day of the week, Mary Magdalene and the other Mary went to see the tomb. And behold, there was a great earthquake, for an angel of the Lord descended from heaven and came and rolled back the stone and sat on it. His appearance was like lightning, and his clothing white as snow.*

"When Christ rises, day begins to dawn for believers," declared Chrysologus, "and for disciples, night is changed into day."[115] But for unbelievers, spiritual

---

113 Day of recompense refers to the Lord's return. Peter Chrysologus, Sermon 73, *Corpus Christianorum Series Latina vol. 24a*, 447.

114 Gen. 21:8, 1 Sam. 1:23-28, and Eph. 4:13 respectively. To wean a child is to feed it solid food instead of its mother's milk—a biblical metaphor seen, for example, in 1 Cor.3:2 and 1 Pet. 2:2.

115 Peter Chrysologus, Sermon 73, Fathers of the Church vol. 110, page 15.

darkness descended even as literal darkness fell for the space of three hours during the crucifixion."[116]

In Chrysologus's teaching, every word of the Scriptures held a deeper meaning.

"In coming to the tomb," he continued, "Mary came to the womb. She came to the womb of the resurrection and to the birthing of life, in order that Christ who came from a womb of flesh, would now come forth from the tomb of faith; and that the sealed-up tomb would give back, for all eternity, him whom the sealed-up womb of the virgin had brought forth.[117]

"Tomb-womb," said Preacher, "I like that!"

I wrote down many of Chrysologus's amazing insights in my journal. Christ's tomb had become a "womb" by bringing forth the giver of eternal life. And He who was born of a virgin's (sealed-off) womb, had now been born a second time from a tomb of faith!

"Two Marys came to the tomb," Chrysologus continued.

"Two Marys?" asked Cesar.

"*Mary Magdalene and the other Mary*," said Mentor, quoting Matthew 28.[118]

"The women beat the men!" declared Preacher.

---

116 Matt. 27:45.

117 Peter Chrysologus, Sermon 73, Fathers of the Church 110, 16-17. *Corpus Christianorum Series Latina vol. 24a*, 460.

118 Matt. 28:1.

"They came not as women," said Chrysologus, "but as a type of the Church to the Lord's tomb.[119]

"Is he dismissing the role of women in the gospel?" asked Cesar.

"No," said Father Greg, "he's following the biblical pattern of identifying types with their antitypes."[120]

"But isn't an Old Testament type usually matched to a New Testament fulfillment?" asked Joseph.

"That's true," agreed Father Greg, "but here Chrysologus is describing the Marys as a kind of double-anticipation of the birth of the Church at Pentecost."

"Mary, the Mother of Christ, is doubled in two women," explain Chrysologus, "because here the Church, coming from two peoples, is prefigured as from the gentiles and the Jews, since *the first shall be last and the last first*." [121]

"What's he talking about?" asked Preacher.

"Listen to the angel's charge to the women," said Chrysologus, *Go tell his disciples that he has risen and goes before you into Galilee, where he will appear to you.*'[122] The angel is not just sending women, but sending the one Church in the two women, sending her—the Church—to

---

119 Peter Chrysologus, Sermon 73, Fathers of the Church vol. 110, (75.3). In that socially, very conservative Middle Eastern setting, attention was not focused on a woman apart from her role as a virgin, a mother, or a widow.

120 Greek: *tupos*, matched with antitypes, *antitupos*.

121 Matt. 19:30. Paraphrase of Peter Chrysologus, Sermon 73, Fathers of the Church vol. 110, 16. *Corpus Christianorum Series Latina vol. 24a*, 459-460.

122 Matt. 28:7.

spread her fame far and wide, and sending the bride to the Bridegroom!"[123]

"Do you understand?" asked Father Greg. "The angel sends the bride, which is the Church, to the Bridegroom, who is Christ."

Chrysologus now read and commented on Matthew 28:8-9,

> *So they departed quickly from the tomb with fear and great joy, and ran to tell his disciples. And behold, Jesus met them and said, "Greetings!" And they came up and took hold of his feet and worshiped him.*

"While on their way," the Bishop explained, "the Lord met them—Greetings!—and in greeting them, he did not overawe them with his power, but lovingly presented himself. In confronting them, he did not confuse them but honored them as the beloved, not domineeringly, but as a loving bridegroom with his bride."[124]

The angel, Chrysologus explained, rolled back the stone from the tomb in order to build the faith of the women, the faith of the disciples to whom they will be sent, and the faith of all Christ's future witnesses. Here, as elsewhere in his sermon, Chrysologus used repetition to drive home his point.

"An angel rolled away the stone, not to help the Lord out of the tomb, but to show the world that the Lord had already risen. He rolled away the stone, not to help the Lord resurrect, but to give his servants the faith to

---

123 Same as previous note, 76.2, page 465.

124 Same as previous note. In his resurrection appearance to the women, Christ acted gently and in accordance with "the law of betrothal." See Deut. 22:23-28; and compare 1 Cor.7:25-38.

believe. He rolled away the stone for faith's sake, since on account of faithlessness it had been rolled there. He rolled away the stone to give notice of his life, since it had guarded over his death."[125]

"Pray brothers," Chrysologus concluded his message, "that the angel may descend now and roll away all hardness from our heart and remove the barriers to our understanding. For our heart is a heaven in which Christ lives and reigns, unless our breast remains a tomb in which Christ is dead and buried!"

Mentor thanked the two Bishops, Leo and Chrysologus, as they returned to their places. Meanwhile, I wrote down as many of their comments as I could recall with the help of my friends' recollections.

---

125 Peter Chrysologus, Sermon 73, Fathers of the Church vol. 110, 17. *Corpus Christianorum Series Latina vol. 24a*, 460-461. (75.4).

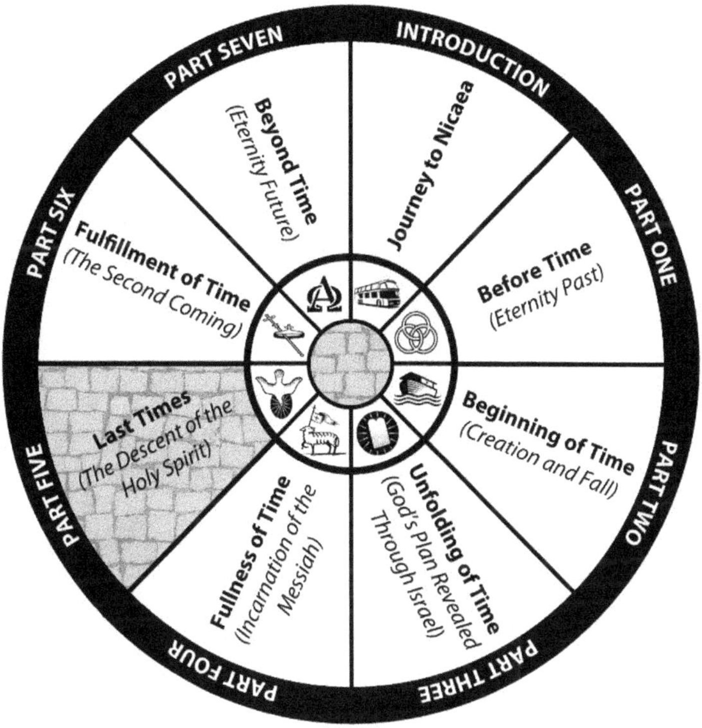

INTRODUCTION
Journey to Nicaea
PART ONE
Before Time
(Eternity Past)
PART TWO
Beginning of Time
(Creation and Fall)
PART THREE
Unfolding of Time
(God's Plan Revealed Through Israel)
PART FOUR
Fullness of Time
(Incarnation of the Messiah)
PART FIVE
Last Times
(The Descent of the Holy Spirit)
PART SIX
Fulfillment of Time
(The Second Coming)
PART SEVEN
Beyond Time
(Eternity Future)

Chapter 7: The Last Times

"Shouldn't we be getting back to the hotel?" asked Joseph, after we discussed what we had learned during the *Fullness of Time*.

"But there are so many witnesses we've not heard from yet," said Father Greg.

"Besides, time begins as soon as we leave," Cesar reminded us.

"What's left in the Story of God?" asked Preacher.

"The *Last Times*," announced Mentor,

"Yes, the rapture!" replied Preacher.

"No," Mentor corrected, "that falls during the following episode—the *End Times*.

"What's the *Last Times* about?" asked Preacher.

"The Holy Spirit is poured out," called Irenaeus, from his place in the pre-Nicene choir.

"The birth of the Church," added Justin Martyr.

"This is our own age," explained Father Greg, "and it's what we have in common with the ancient witnesses because we all live in the Last Times."

As before, Mentor began by reading aloud from the Scriptures,

> *And it shall come to pass afterward, that I will pour out my Spirit on all flesh; your sons and your daughters shall prophesy, your old men shall dream dreams, and your young men shall see visions. Even on the male and female servants in those days I will pour out my Spirit.*[1]

"Luke the evangelist records the fulfillment of this prophecy," Mentor continued,

> *When the day of Pentecost arrived, they were all together in one place. And suddenly there came from heaven a sound like a mighty rushing wind, and it filled the entire house where they were sitting. And divided tongues as of fire appeared to them and rested on each one of them. And they were all filled with the Holy Spirit and began to speak in other tongues as the Spirit gave them utterance.*[2]

The Pre-Nicene witnesses commented again,

"Now it is possible to see women and men among us who possess gifts of the Spirit of God!"[3] said Justin Martyr.

"Truly," agreed Irenaeus, "the God who promised by the prophet that he would send His Spirit upon the whole human race has fulfilled His own promise."[4]

---

1 Joel 2:28-29.

2 Acts 2:1-4.

3 Justin Martyr, *Dialogue with Trypho, a Jew* 88 (ANF 1, 243).

4 Irenaeus, *Against Heresies*, 3.12 (ANF 1, 430).

Mentor acknowledged them and introduced a third witness, "Chrysostom," whose name he explained means "Golden Mouth."

"He must have a lot of gold fillings!" teased Preacher.

"The esteemed Chrysostom has preached fifty-five memorable sermons from the book of Acts," said Mentor, ignoring Preacher's joke.

Unlike the Roman witnesses, who were clean-shaven, Chrysostom had a long white beard. His robe was embroidered with large crosses on each shoulder, and his bronze skin and narrow nose made him the very picture of eastern Church father. Speaking on the passages Mentor had just read, Chrysostom began,

"What is this Pentecost? It is the time when the sickle was put to the harvest, and the ingathering was made. Now, let us consider what has been said from the beginning."[5]

Chrysostom began explaining Pentecost in light of the Joel 2 prophecy, emphasizing the pouring out of the Spirit. The pitch of his voice rose as his sermon took shape.

"When the day of Pentecost had come in fullness," he said, looking up at heaven, "the Spirit filled the house and that Spirit was a very pool of water. For, the pouring out of water signifies for us the abundance of the Spirit, just as fire signifies intensity. Such a forceful, overflowing Spirit was not seen among the prophets, for to unsatisfied souls the abundance had not yet been poured out."

---

5 This and following words of Chrysostom are paraphrased from *The Acts of the Apostles*, Homily IV (NPNF 1.11.25-31), and *Patrologia Graeca* vol.60.

"Is he saying the Old Testament saints didn't have the Holy Spirit?" asked Joseph.

"Not in abundance like the New Testament saints," replied Father Greg.

"Elijah received the grace through a mantle," explained Chrysostom, "David by anointing oil, and Moses by fire, as we read about him at the bush. But in Acts the tongues of fire sat on every one of them, and this fire was able to kindle an infinite amount of fuel!"

"Dang," said Preacher, "he makes the Holy Spirit sound like a blowtorch!"

"Moses was the greatest of the Prophets," added Chrysostom, "yet when he shared the Spirit with elders of Israel, there was less for himself.[6] But at Pentecost it was not so. For as a flame lights many fires, at Pentecost the abundance of the Spirit was shown—each disciple receiving a fountain of the Spirit, as the Lord himself foretold, that those who believe in Him should have *a well of water springing up into everlasting life*.[7] And for good reason, since the disciples did not go out to argue with Pharaoh, but to wrestle with the devil."[8]

"Amen!" agreed the gathered witnesses.

---

6 See Num. 11:16-17. Paraphrase of Chrysostom with highlight added, *The Acts of the Apostles*, Homily IV (NPNF 1.11.26), which reads as follows: "Thus Moses was the greatest of the Prophets, yet he, when others were to receive the Spirit, himself suffered diminution."

7 John 4:14.

8 See previous note.

The Birth of the Church

As the sermon concluded, another witness came forward and stood next to Chrysostom. He was a clean-shaven Roman with a proud expression and a heavy, prominent brow. He wore a plain brown robe and carried a leather journal, such that he looked like a scribe. Mentor introduced him as Arator, an author whose epic commentary on the book of Acts had been read before the bishop of Rome.

"I was hoping we would hear more from Chrysostom," I whispered to Father Greg.

"I believe we will," he replied, "but Arator brings a western perspective to balance out Chrysostom's eastern Church view."

"Long ago," Arator began his testimony,

Malicious men wished to raise their tower of Babel up to the heavens,
But their wicked hearts confused the language and thwarted their building.
Until the coming of the Church reversed the trend,
And one language again prevailed.[9]

"Is he talking about Pentecost?" asked Cesar.

"Yes, he's illustrating it from the story of the Tower of Babel," explained Father Greg.

The Holy Spirit, descending from the ethereal hall, illumined with splendor the place where the blessed pedigree of the nascent church was; with fire as their teacher, a glow suffused their mouths, and from their flowing words came forth an abundant harvest of

9 Paraphrase of Schrader, *Arator's On the Acts of the Apostles*, page 29.

> *languages; no letter did its duty but faith alone was the teaching and the rich theme of the words given from heaven, a new source of speaking which comes in many forms and alone is sufficient for the speech of eloquent persons from the whole world.*[10]

"What's an ethereal hall?" asked Cesar.

"It's a classical name for heaven," said Father Greg, "and blessed pedigree refers to the disciples in the upper room."

"Their teacher was fire!" said Joseph, "I like that!"

"Their mouths were glowing," added Preacher.

The poem reminded me of Ephrem's hymns, and since he was at his place in the Post-Nicene choir stalls, I asked Mentor if he would share a verse from a Pentecost hymn for comparison.

"The upper room shook as the blessed Apostles came together," sang Ephrem, "and Paradise recognized its home, pouring forth its perfume, delighting the heralds as they invited guests to come to His banquet; eagerly He awaits their arrival for He is the Lover of mankind."[11]
"There was a banquet at Pentecost?" asked Cesar.

"The hymn is eschatological," said Father Greg.

"That means it's about the future," said Preacher.

"Precisely," said Father Greg, "Pentecost anticipates the wedding feast of the Lamb described in the book of Revelation."[12]

---

10 Schrader, *Arator's On the acts of the Apostles*, 28, lines 119-129.

11 Ephrem of Syria, *Hymns on Paradise*, 11.14 in Brock and Kiraz.(St. Vladimir's Seminary Press, 1990), page 159.

12 See Rev. 19:9.

"The eastern and western views are not so different," I suggested to Father Greg, "both Chrysostom and Arator interpreted Pentecost in light of the past—the anointing of the Old Testament figures, and the building of the tower of Babel."

"Agreed," said Father Greg, "but Ephrem's interpretation points to the future."

The Church Militant

"Speaking of the future, the disciples will be arrested in Acts 4," said Joseph, reading from his Bible,

> *The priests and the captain of the temple and the Sadducees came upon them, greatly annoyed because the Apostles were teaching the people and proclaiming in Jesus the resurrection from the dead. And they arrested them and put them in custody…*
> *Acts 4:1–3*

"As glorious as Pentecost was," he added, "the apostles had lots of enemies."

"That's why they're called the Church Militant,"[13] added Cesar, "and the next passage names their enemies..." he read,

> *Sovereign Lord, who made the heaven and the earth and the sea and everything in them, who through the mouth of our father David, your servant, said by the Holy Spirit, "Why did the Gentiles rage, and the peoples*

---

13 *The Church Militant* comes from the Latin *Ecclesia Militans*, and is the body of Christ comprised of members currently alive (and therefore who struggle against sin and the devil), in contrast to the *Church Triumphant* (*Ecclesia Triumpans*) comprised of those who have died in the Lord and are now with Christ in heaven. See also Susanne de Dietrich, *God's Unfolding Purpose*, 222.

> *plot in vain? The kings of the earth set themselves, and the rulers were gathered together, against the Lord and against his Anointed" for truly in this city there were gathered together against your holy servant Jesus, whom you anointed, both Herod and Pontius Pilate, along with the Gentiles and the peoples of Israel, to do whatever your hand and your plan had predestined to take place.* Acts 4:24–28

"The prayer quotes Psalm 2," explained Father Greg, "the Anointed—the Messiah—was the royal descendant of David, whom the rulers opposed."

"They are taking God at his word," said Chrysostom, "to comfort themselves and to ensure that their opponents' threats come to nothing.[14] They flee, in prayer, to the true Help, lifting up their voices to God with one accord, addressing Him as Sovereign."

"We could learn a lot from the prayers of early Christians," said Preacher.

"Consider this," added Chrysostom, "when they prayed for the wisdom to choose a replacement for Judas they said, 'You, Lord, who knows the heart of all men, show us…' for that was a subject for foreknowledge. But here, the thing needed was that the mouths of their adversaries should be closed, and so they speak of lordship—Lord, the God who made heaven and earth, and the sea, and all that in them."[15]

---

14 The phrase: *Ac si pacta a Deo exigerent, prophetiam in medium afferent, seipsos simul consolantes, quod omnia frustra meditentur inimici* answers the question, "Why this prophesy?" Answer: This prophecy they point to in order to take God at his word, both to comfort themselves and to ensure that opponents threats come to nothing.

15 Acts 1:24; Chrysostom, *Acts of the Apostles*, Homily 11, *Patrologia Graeca* 60, 93. (NPNF 1.11.70).

Summarizing the event, Arator added:

> *The glorious army of the Church now five thousand strong and growing, Judea tried to withstand, as wrath moved the Jews to complete their wickedness against saints deserving reverence. O ever rebellious ones! They saw the gifts, yet set violence in motion. Why do you so often fall, Judea?*[16]

"Why are the witnesses so hateful toward the Jews?" whispered Cesar.

"It is the Enemy whose hatred is focused on them," replied Arator. He then recited,

> *By Pilate's judgment Christ was willing to substitute his limbs for the trials of the world, that his flesh might get rid of fleshly evil, and that the fierce Enemy, by whose contrivance the poisonous weapons streamed forth, might fail to obtain the lamentable expiation of the ancient war, now that a matching substance had overcome, lest the burden of Adam's crime go forward longer through his offspring. The condemnation of the righteous One has become the setting free of the guilty.* [17]

"Did anybody get that?" asked Preacher.

---

16 Arator, *Acts of the Apostles*, lines 33-34, in *Corpus Scriptorum Ecclesiaticorum Latinorum* (CSEL) vol. 72, page 29: *Agmine iam viveo per milia quinque virorum /Ecclesiae crescebat apex; Arecere laborat/ Hunc Iudaea coli cuius de muneri fluxit/.* See Schrader, Arator's *Acts of the Apostles*, 33-34.

17 Arator, lines 348-349 CSEL vol. 72, page 33: *Quis dolus Herodis cum tristia bella moveret/Infantum mandata neci! Quos ubere raptos/Vulnera suscipiunt parvis errentia membris.* See also, Schrader, *Arator's On the acts of the Apostles*, page 35.

"The righteous one, Jesus, was willing to substitute his life for ours," replied Father Greg.

"I got that," said Preacher, "but what was he saying about crime going forward?"

"His point was that it did *not* go forward," said Cesar.

"That's right," agreed Father Greg, "you recall the *proto-evangelium* of Genesis 3:15, Edward?"

"The first announcement of the Good News?" asked Preacher.

"Precisely," replied the priest, "and according to Arator's poem, the good news is that the burden—the guilt—for Adam's rebellion won't be passed on to his offspring."

"I like the part about enemy's poison weapons meeting their match," I said.

"We were speaking about what may be learned from their prayers," said Chrysostom.

Overhearing this, Arator continued his recitation.

Wherever the beautiful feet shone the earth shook,
Shimmering from the life-giving Spirit;
Fluency fired their faltering tongues,
So that powerful prayers sounded,
And able supplications took.

Human stock is from the soil,
"Born of clay" means Adam's name,
Sermons set the earth in motion,
With Apostolic faith as their aim.

Why this place more than all others? Scripture tells,
"How beautiful are the feet that bring a pardon,"

How joyful the earth beneath their tread,
Till the Master's words through them to all lands spread.[18]

The "beautiful feet" passage sparked much discussion and many questions. In my journal I summarized that Arator had described the proclamation of the gospel by recalling Isaiah 52:7—*how beautiful upon the mountains are the feet of him who brings good news*—as well as Psalm 114, where the mountains *skipped like rams and the hills like lambs*. He tied the passage together, however, with the theme of *soil* and *earth*.

The Gospel Treasure

As Arator and Ephrem sat down, Chrysostom was joined by two new Roman witnesses, Marius Victorinus and Ambrosiaster.[19] The dark-skinned Romans stood on either side of Chrysostom, creating an image like a Russian icon.

Having examined Pentecost—the out-pouring of the Holy Spirit and the birth of the Church—Mentor now turned our attention to the message of the Gospel itself, which he described as the treasure of the ancient Church.

---

18 My paraphrase of lines 370-382 in Arator, *Acts of the Apostles*, in CSEL vol. 72, pages 33-35: *Qua sancti fulsere pedes, concurrere visa est/Pondere terra gravi, moxque almus Spiritus illis/Splenduit, et linguis facundia crevit abortis./Auditae valuere preces. Humana propago/Materies terrena sumus, limumque patrentem/Nomine proidit homo. Vis flexit et impulit arva/Vocis apostolicae quae de tellure creatos/Fecit habere fidem; sed quod magis exsilit unus/Concutitureque locus, cecinit Scriptura decoros/Pacem ferre pedes; horum sub gressibus ergo/Laeta movetur humus, quibus est sermone Magistri/Pax commissa pii, quae deportata per illos/Exiit in Cunctas veloci munere terras*. Compare Schrader, *Arator's On the acts of the Apostles*, page 36.

19 This father's identity was unknown by the ancient Church. The writings he left were attributed to "Ambrosiaster" beginning in the sixteenth century.

He opened the topic by putting the following question to us pastors:

"If you could choose one passage to represent the message of the gospel, which would you choose?"

"That's easy," said Preacher, "John 3:16, *For God so loved the world, that he gave his only Son, that whoever believes in him should not perish but have eternal life.*"

"Preacher's got it," said Joseph, "but I vote for the heart of the Gospel."

"What's that?" asked Cesar.

"Romans 3:19-26," replied Joseph, "which says something like, 'apart from the law the righteousness of God has now appeared.'"

"What about Romans 1:16?" I asked, *for I am not ashamed of the gospel, for it is the power of God for salvation to everyone who believes...*"

"That's good too," agreed Joseph, "but what about you Father Greg, what's your choice?"

Father Greg pondered the question for a moment, and then replied,

"*For by grace you have been saved through faith, and this is not from you; it is the gift of God.*"[20]

We all agreed that Father Greg's choice was best, especially when Mentor announced that Ephesians would be our focus for the gospel message. Mentor now read from Ephesians 2 phrase by phrase, inviting comments from the three Fathers.

Mentor: ***And you were dead in the trespasses and sins in which you once walked, following the course of this world...***

20 Eph. 2:8.

Chrysostom: This reminds us of the difference between physical death and spiritual death: it is no sin to die physically, and there is no blame in it since physical death is a matter of nature and not of deliberate choice.[21]

Marius Victorinus: Yet as the passage shows, death can be taken in a second way when the soul, established in this very body, acts out of the desires of the flesh and lives in its sins.[22]

Ambrosiaster: Paul is saying that those who follow the errors of this age are dead. Whoever turns away from confessing the one God is considered to be dead because he does not remain in the root from which he derived his origin.[23]

Chrysostom: Paul indeed shows us what a terrible thing is spiritual death: to heal a dead soul is a far greater thing than to raise the dead![24]

Each witness offered his commentary in turn, though the Roman witnesses deferred to Chrysostom and he set the agenda for the commentary.

---

21 Paraphrase of Chrysostom, *Homilies on Ephesians*, Homily IV (NPNF I.13, 65).

22 Marius Victorinus, *Commentary on the Letter to the Ephesians*, Book 1, 2:1-2. Published in Stephen Andrew Cooper, *Metaphysics and Morals in Marius Victorinus' Commentary on the Letter to the Ephesians* (New York: Peter Lang, 1995), 63.

23 Ambrosiaster, *Commentaries on Galatians-Philemon*, in Gerald Bray, Ambrosiaster, Ancient Christian Texts, page 38.

24 Paraphrase of Chrysostom, *Homilies on Ephesians*, Homily IV (NPNF I.13, 65).

Mentor: ***Among whom we all once lived in the passions of our flesh…***

Chrysostom: Observe the gentleness of Paul, how on all occasions he encouraged the hearer, not bearing too hard upon him, since men are put to shame when their former misdeeds are brought forward, though they are now cancelled.[25]

Marius Victorinus: By saying we all once lived that way, the apostle included himself in this, so as not to hurt the Ephesians' feelings, since he had told them "you were dead in trespasses…"[26]

Ambrosiaster: But the Apostle lived a clean life because he acted according to the righteousness of the law without any problem. It is because he persecuted the faith of Christ that he says "we all lived in the passions of our flesh." Good works and purity are of no use to anyone who is an unbeliever, because his unbelief taints everything else.[27]

25 Paraphrase of Chrysostom, *Homilies on Ephesians*, Homily IV (NPNF I.13, 65).

26 Marius Victorinus, *Commentary on the Letter to the Ephesians*, Book 1, 2:3. Published in Stephen Andrew Cooper, *Metaphysics and Morals in Marius Victorinus' Commentary on the Letter to the Ephesians* (New York: Peter Lang, 1995), 64.

27 Paraphrase of Gerald Bray, Ambrosiaster, Ancient Christian Texts, page 39.

Mentor: ***But God, being rich in mercy, because of the great love with which he loved us...***

Chrysostom: What we have done is not deserving of love but of wrath and punishment! Why did He love us?[28]

Ambrosiaster: The true riches of mercy are that it was freely preached to those who were not looking for it, as Isaiah says: *I have made myself known to those who were not looking for me*. To abound in mercy is to grant it to those who have not asked for it. The love of God for us is such that because he made us he does not want us to perish, since he loves what he made. Nobody hates his own work.[29]

Marius Victorinus: But we made ourselves alien to God by our sins, thus God redeemed us for Himself, dealing leniently with our trespasses, through His Son whom he did not spare, that He might liberate us. Great without doubt are God's riches! Great also is His love! So much love that He emptied out His Son for our sake that He might redeem us by His passion! So, this is love.[30]

---

28 Paraphrase of Chrysostom, *Homilies on Ephesians*, Homily IV (NPNF I.13, 66).

29 Isa. 65:1 and paraphrase of Gerald Bray, Ambrosiaster, Ancient Christian Texts, page 39.

30 Marius Victorinus, *Commentary on the Letter to the Ephesians*, Book 1, 2:4. Published in Stephen Andrew Cooper, *Metaphysics and Morals in Marius Victorinus' Commentary on the Letter to the Ephesians* (New York: Peter Lang, 1995), 66.

Mentor: ***For it is by grace you have been saved, through faith—and this is not from yourselves, it is the gift of God—not by works, so that no one can boast.***

Ambrosiaster: So we must give thanks to God who has given us his grace to recall sinners to life even when they were not looking for the true way.[31]

Marius Victorinus: The Apostle explains plainly that there ought to be faith on our part, but that we ought to believe only in Christ. For if this salvation is ours in this way alone, we have not been saved by our merit but by the grace of God.[32]

Chrysostom: On the other hand, so that our free will is not impaired, he mentions our part in the work: faith. Yet, he cancels the work again by adding "this is not from yourselves." For faith is not of ourselves: If he had not come, if he had not called us, how would we have believed? As he says elsewhere, "how can they believe in the one of whom they have not heard? So even the work of faith is not our own.[33]

---

31 Ambrosiaster, *Commentaries on Galatians-Philemon*, in Gerald Bray, Ambrosiaster, Ancient Christian Texts, page 40.

32 Marius Victorinus, *Commentary on the Letter to the Ephesians*, Book 1, 2:8. Published in Stephen Andrew Cooper, *Metaphysics and Morals in Marius Victorinus' Commentary on the Letter to the Ephesians* (New York: Peter Lang, 1995), 67.

33 Rom. 10:14. Paraphrase of Chrysostom, *Homilies on Ephesians*, Homily IV (NPNF I.13, 67).

Will All Israel Be Saved?

Aside from an occasional "amen" from one of the witnesses, the preceding comments on salvation by faith through grace were made without interruption. But the calm was disturbed when Cesar asked a question.

"What about the Jews who don't confess Christ, what will happen to them?" he asked.

"Faith in Christ is the only basis of salvation, as the witnesses have described," replied Mentor.

"And without faith it is impossible to please God!" called another witness, out of turn.

Several "amens" rang out in agreement.

"God hasn't rejected his own people—the Jews—has he?" objected Cesar, "Doesn't the Apostle say that all Israel will be saved?"[34]

Before Mentor could reply, the witnesses were up on their feet, clamoring to be recognized. Other witnesses then entered the Crux uninvited, arguing with one another in the passageways as the commotion grew louder and as Mentor tried in vain to restore order.

"What's this all about?" Joseph called to Cesar.

"Replacement theology," he replied.

"What's that?" asked Joseph

"Ask Ari," said Cesar, "he should know."

It was difficult to hear in the midst of the uproar, let alone think clearly. But arguments like these were common place in the neighborhood I grew up in. The claim that the Church had replaced Israel was, as my father would have said, just one more way the Christians have of disrespecting the Chosen. Listening to the

---

34 Rom. 11:26.

witnesses' many negative judgments on the Jews, Cesar had become offended on my behalf. Being ethnically Jewish, I was embarrassed at not having raised the issue myself, but as a Christian believer I was not sure what to say.

Suddenly, a loud imprecation was screamed from a distant corner of the Athenaeum—someone pronounced a curse on the Jews! I felt myself flush with emotion. Preacher looked as if he was ready to find the man and fight him. We heard the noise of a scuffle as other witnesses subdued the man who had shouted the curse, and calm was restored. Mentor, collecting himself, reminded the gathered witnesses that they must be called upon to speak. Any recognized witness, he explained, would be welcome to state his view regarding the Jews. A line quickly formed at the front.

Mentor, however, went to the pre-Nicene choir and led an elderly witness to the lectern. The man's voice, in contrast to the ancient lines of his face, was youthful.

"As one who loves you as my own soul, brothers," the ancient witness began, "I beg of you to take care not to be like those who claim that their covenant with God remains valid, when in fact they forfeited it through disobedience. For when Moses was fasting on the mountain top for forty days and nights and receiving the covenant from the Lord—the tablets of stone written with the finger of God—they turned away to idols and lost it. For the Lord said to Moses, go down quickly, for the people you led out of the land of Egypt have sinned. And Moses cast the two tablets from his hands and their covenant was broken. But this was in order that the covenant of the beloved Jesus might be sealed upon our heart, in the hope which flows from believing in Him."[35]

The elderly witness believed that the Jews had forfeited their covenant with God on account of the sin with the golden calf at Mount Sinai.

"What about the renewed covenant?" asked Cesar, "didn't God continue to deal with his people throughout their wilderness wanderings and even long after that?"

The ancient witness offered no reply, and Mentor helped him back to his seat, as Justin Martyr returned to the lectern. After saying many positive things about the Hebrew Scriptures, he concluded that,

"There shall be a final law and preeminent covenant, which everyone seeking the inheritance of God must obey. For, as the prophets foretold, the Law given on Mt. Sinai is now obsolete and pertains to the Jews alone, but the new covenant is universal. This latter covenant cancels the first, putting an end to it. In its place an eternal and final law, namely Christ, has been given to us, and this covenant is trustworthy, after which shall be added no further laws, commandments, or ordinances."[36]

Justin Martyr, it seemed, also believed that God's covenant with the Jews was cancelled, but that this had happened when the new covenant—presumably the one prophesied by Jeremiah[37]—was given. While these two witnesses were testifying, I read through Romans chapter 11 in Joseph's Bible. When they were finished, I saluted

---

35 Epistle of Barnabas 4:6-9 (ANF 1, 138).

36 Justin Martyr, *Dialogue with Trypho*, 11 (ANF1, 199-200).

37 See Jer. 31:31-34.

Mentor and he graciously invited me into the speaker's line-up. I began by reading these two verses,

> *So I ask, did they (i.e. the Jews) stumble in order that they might fall? By no means! Rather through their trespass salvation has come to the Gentiles, so as to make Israel jealous. Now if their trespass means riches for the world, and if their failure means riches for the Gentiles, how much more will their full inclusion mean!*[38]

"These verses," I explained, "say that the Jewish rejection of Jesus has led to salvation for the Gentiles, but that this in turn will make the Jews jealous and, presumably, they will later seek to be saved. So it seems to me that Paul was *not* describing the Jews as permanently rejected."

Chrysostom saluted and was called on by Mentor.

"It is no surprise that Paul speaks this way," he said, "he wants to comfort the fallen souls of these Jews, for even if they had fallen a thousand times, the Gentiles would not have been saved unless they had shown faith. And the Jews likewise would not have perished unless they had been unbelieving and disputatious.[39]

"In other words," Chrysostom continued, "Paul is comforting them so they can be confident in their salvation *if* they change."

"May I comment on the Romans passage?" asked Origen. Chrysostom stepped aside as Origen limped to the lectern and opened a volume which, we soon learned,

---

38 Rom. 11:11-12.

39 Chrysostom, *Commentary on Romans*, Homily XIX (NPNF 1. 11, 488-489).

was his commentary on Romans. I braced myself for what I assumed would be more negative comments about the Jews, but he took a different course.

"In the verses just read," Origen began, "Paul asks *did they (i.e. the Jews) stumble in order that they might fall?* But note well his answer: *By no means!*"

Origen paused to let the answer to sink in.

"Let us suppose," he continued, "that a righteous man is overcome by some weakness of the flesh. If he continues seeking God, can we really say that he has fallen with no chance for repentance? *By no means!* And Israel, though it persecuted those sent by God to preach salvation, still have something that remains."[40]

"This is why the Apostle Paul says they have not stumbled so as to fall," concluded Origen, "that is to say, they have not turned completely away. Besides this, if their offense toward Christ means riches for the world, and if their forfeit means riches for the Gentiles, how much more will their fullness mean!"

Origen closed his commentary and returned slowly to his choir stall.

"Ari," said Joseph, encouraging me, "I think he's saying that God's not done with the Jews, that He still has something for them."

"Okay," I agreed, "but what is that something?"

Chrysostom, who had not left the lectern, spoke up.

40 Origen, *Commentary on the Epistle to the Romans*, Book 8, chapter 9, in Thomas Scheck, Fathers of The Church 104, pages 168-169.

"Paul has already shown the Jews to be guilty of more evils that can be counted! He simply says what he says[41] to make his condemnation less harsh, but I agree with the esteemed Master," he indicated Origen, "that their fall is not incurable."

If their forfeit means riches for the Gentiles, how much more will their fullness mean?" recited Origen, once more from his place.

"But Paul does not say *when* they return or *how much more their* return will mean," countered Chrysostom, "or even *their changing*, but simply, *how much more their fullness*."

The debate continued without consensus for some time. Aside from Origen, the Pre-Nicene witnesses were uniformly harsh in their view of Israel, while the later fathers—especially Augustine and Ambrosiaster—refused to dismiss Israel as having no place in God's future salvation. There were witnesses still waiting to testify when Mentor announced a break.

One Holy, Catholic, and Apostolic Church

After this, Mentor called for us to recite the Nicene Creed, toward the end of which comes the line, *We believe in one holy, catholic, and apostolic Church.* As we were seated he invited the witnesses to testify to the four marks of the Church—*one, holy, catholic, and apostolic*. A fresh line formed, at the head of which was Irenaeus.[42]

41 i.e. *So I ask, did they (i.e. the Jews) stumble in order that they might fall? By no means!* In other words in verse 11 of Rom. 9.

42 The following selection of texts is indebted to Gregg R. Allison, *Historical Theology*, 566—572.

"The Church, though dispersed throughout the whole world," said Irenaeus, "has received from the apostles and their disciples this faith—occupying and preserving, as it were, one house. It also believes these points of doctrine just as if it had one soul, and one and the same heart. It proclaims them, teaches them, and hands them down, with perfect harmony, as if it possessed only one mouth."[43]

Irenaeus had portrayed the Church in its unity as one house, and as a body with *one soul, one and the same heart, and one mouth*. Clement of Alexandria, who spoke next, emphasized unity itself.

"The preeminence of the Church, as the principle of unity, is its oneness. In this, it surpasses all other things and has nothing like or equal to itself," said Clement.[44]

"What would he think of all our denominations and divisions?" Joseph whispered to me, shaking his head.

"*Holy*," said Mentor, calling on Theophilus who commented,

"God has given to the world, which is driven and tempest-tossed by sins, assemblies—we mean holy churches—in which survives the doctrines of the truth.[45]

Theophilus's mention of sin and holy churches got a reaction from two other witnesses.

"Let it be understood," said Justin Martyr, "that those who are not found living as Christ taught are not Christians, even though they profess with their lips the

43 Irenaeus, *Against Heresies*, 1.10.1-2, as quoted in Allison, *Historical Theology*, 567.

44 Clement of Alexandria, *Stromata (Miscellanies)*, 7.17.

45 Theophilus, To Autolycus, 2.14. (ANF 2.100).

teachings of Christ.[46] "After such audacious acts," agreed Hippolytus, "they lose all sense of shame, yet still attempt to call themselves a catholic Church![47]

Cyprian, next in line, advised patience with those who have fallen. Recalling Jesus' parable of the wheat and the weeds,[48] he said,

"Although there seem to be weeds in the Church, yet neither our faith nor our love ought to be hindered. Because we see that there are weeds in the Church, we ourselves should not withdraw from the Church. Rather, we only should labor that we may be wheat."[49]

"*Catholic*," said Mentor, "is the next mark we will consider."

"I knew they were Catholic!" said Preacher.

"He doesn't mean Roman Catholic," said Father Greg.

"What *does* he mean?" asked Cesar.

Father Greg saluted Mentor, asking for a demonstration of how the ancient witnesses used the term *catholic*. Mentor called on an elderly witness who read from his account of a famous Christian martyr.

"Now when at last Polycarp finished praying, remembering everyone who had ever come in contact with him, both small and great, known and unknown, and all the *universal* (*catholikos*) Church throughout the world, it was time to depart. Our Lord Jesus Christ is the Savior of our souls and Helmsman of our bodies and

---

46 Justin Martyr, *First Apology*, 16 (ANF 1.168).

47 Hippolytus, *The Refutation of all Heresies*, 9.7 (ANF 5, 131).

48 Matt. 13:24-30.

49 Cyprian, Letter, 50.3 (ANF 5, 327).

Shepherd of the *universal* (*catholikos*) Church throughout the world."[50]

These words, explained Mentor, contained the earliest use of the Greek term, *catholikos*, which referred to the Church throughout the world.

"*Apostolic* is the final mark," announced Mentor.

"This is our rule," said Tertullian, who had returned to the lectern, "the Lord Jesus Christ sent the apostles to preach and, therefore, none should be recognized as authoritative except those whom Christ appointed. As to what they preached, in other words what Christ revealed to them, this is known only by those churches which the apostles founded, declaring the gospel to them in person or, afterward, by their letters. If this rule is accurate, then it must also be the case that if any other church's doctrine matches the apostolic churches, it too must be considered true, holding to all that the apostolic churches received from the apostles, and the apostles from Christ, and Christ from God."[51]

Tertullian's rule of the apostolic Church, I summarized in my journal as follows: "An apostolic Church is an authoritative or true church, whose teaching come from or matches the twelve apostles, since their teaching in turn comes from Christ himself."

Tertullian reminded Mentor that, aside from the four marks of the Church mentioned in the Nicene Creed, the witnesses often spoke of the Church as their *mother*.

---

50 *The Martyrdom of Polycarp* (about AD 160). See Michael W. Holmes, *The Apostolic Fathers*, 3rd edition (Grand Rapids: Baker Academic, 2007), 315; 327.

51 Tertullian, *Prescription against Heretics*, 21 (ANF 3:252).

"Our one Father, God, lives; and so does our *mother*, the Church," said Tertullian, illustrating his point.[52]

"He can no longer have God for his Father, who has not the Church as his mother" agreed Cyprian.[53] Other witnesses mentioned biblical terms like *the temple of God*, a *house of living stones*, and *the body of Christ* to illustrate the Church. But when one of them spoke of *the people of God*, it seemed the debate about whether the Jews were still the people of God might erupt once more.

The Church and Society

So, Mentor invited Augustine to address the topic of the church and its relationship to society, and especially to worldly authorities, during the *Last Times*.

"Paul warns Christians who become puffed up with pride about the freedom they enjoy in Christ," began Augustine, "and who therefore think they no longer need to submit to governing authorities. Besides, I say, are we not made of soul and body?"[54]

"Are you saying our bodies are subject to earthly rulers?" asked Cesar.

"As long as we are in this life," replied Augustine, "we make use of temporal things as a means of living this life. So, it is fitting, as far as this life is concerned, that we be

---

52 Tertullian, *On Monogamy* 7 (ANF 4,64).

53 Cyprian, *Treatise 1.6* "On the Unity of the Church," quotation in Allison, 569, and ANF 5:423.

54 Augustine, *On Romans*. This and following passages are from Gerald Bray, *Romans*, in Thomas Oden (ed), Ancient Christian Commentary on Scripture, VI (Chicago: Institute of Classical Christian Studies, 1998), 325.

subject to the authorities, by which I mean those people who are recognized administrators of human affairs."

"Like when we pay taxes?" asked Cesar.

"If anyone thinks that because he is a Christian he does not have to pay taxes or tribute," replied Augustine, "nor show the proper respect to the authorities who take care of these things, he is in very great error. The balance which the Lord himself prescribed is to be maintained: render unto Caesar the things which are Caesar's but unto God the things which are God's."[55]

"But what if the authorities are corrupt?" asked Cesar.

"We are called into a kingdom where the present world has no authority, that's true enough," said Augustine. "Yet, while we are on the way there and until we have reached that state where every principality and power will be destroyed, we must put up with our condition for the sake of human affairs, doing nothing falsely and in this very thing obeying God, who commands us to do it, rather than men."[56]

"You're saying that when we obey corrupt authorities we're really obeying God," concluded Cesar, "but didn't Peter say *We must obey God rather than men*?"[57]

"Sorry to interrupt," said Joseph, "but you're taking that verse out of context—the Apostles were being commanded not to preach in the name of Jesus."

"Alright," said Cesar, "but aren't we Christians called to fight injustice?"

---

55 Matt. 22:21.

56 Same as previous note.

57 Acts 5:29.

"A wise man will wage just wars," replied Augustine, "but he will regret the war because of its evil cause."

"Of course," agreed Cesar, "but if we know a ruler is acting unjustly…"

"Ah, but those who pronounce judgment cannot see into the consciences of those on whom they pronounce it," replied Augustine "for darkness attends our life here in the city of man, ignorance is unavoidable, and the question remains as to whether the ruler is guilty or not."[58]

"Some of them are obviously guilty," said Cesar, "but what do you mean by the city of man?"

"I divide the human race into two parts," explained Augustine, "those who live according to man, and those who live according to God. These are two cities, figuratively speaking, one of which—the city of God—is predestined to reign eternally with God, and the other—the city of man—will suffer eternal punishment with the devil."[59]

"Is that biblical?" asked Cesar.

"Scripture tells us that Cain founded a city," affirmed Augustine, "whereas Abel, as a pilgrim, did not found one. For the city of the saints is above, although it produces citizens here below, and in them the city is on pilgrimage until the time of its kingdom comes."[60]

"The Bishop has written extensively about this subject," said Father Greg.

58 Adapted from Augustine, City of God, 19.6 (Knowles, 859-860).

59 Augustine, City of God, 15.1 (Knowles, 595).

60 For the city of Cain, see Genesis 4:17. Same as previous reference, 596.

"That's a book I'd like to read," said Cesar.

"It's *The City of God*," replied Father Greg.

"Precisely!" said Augustine, using Father Greg's expression and making us laugh.

The Bishop called two scribes who came forward carrying a huge book—too large, in fact, to set on the threefold lectern. One of the scribes got down on his hands and knees while his companion opened the enormous folio volume onto his back. Augustine turned the pages for a while and then read aloud,

> *Of the bliss of Paradise, of Paradise itself, and of the life of our first parents there, and of their sin and punishment, many have thought much, spoken much, written much. We ourselves, too, have spoken of these things in the foregoing books, and have written either what we read in the Holy Scriptures, or what we could reasonably deduce from them. The time remaining does not allow me to answer all the questions asked by curious men with too much time on their hands—those who are more ready to ask questions than they are able to understand the answers!*[61]

Joseph and I looked at each other, astonished that what Augustine had written hundreds of years so perfectly described people we knew today.

"Bishop," asked Cesar, "is justice possible in the city of man?"

"You remind me of Marcellus!" replied Augustine.

"Who?" asked Cesar.

"Long ago," explained Augustine, "I mentored a young man who rose to some prominence in the Roman

---

61 Same as previous reference, 596.

Church. Marcellus, for that was his name, had the gift of diplomacy, and Rome appointed him to come and make peace between the Donatists and the Church catholic in North Africa where I was the presiding bishop."[62]

"In the course of his negotiations," Augustine continued, "Marcellinus made friends with an important Roman official and shared the gospel with him. The official expressed genuine interest in Christ but resented Christianity because he believed it was responsible for all the empire's troubles. This was a common view among Romans, and Marcellinus turned to me for help in answering the official's doubts. I wrote him a long letter outlining my basic answer and promised him a more complete answer when I could devote time to writing. It only took me another fourteen years to finish it!" He pointed to the open book, *The City of God*, as his answer.[63]

---

62 In appealing to the authority of the entire Church against the Donatist schism, Augustine used the term *catholikos* (universal). Donatists refused to restore to full communion any who fled during the persecution, and rejected the authority of any church leaders willing to receive them back.

63 Augustine wrote *The City of God* to expose the inaccuracies of the provincial Roman view of Christianity, and offered in its place a detailed exposition of the grand biblical narrative as a blueprint of the relationship of the Church to Roman society. The heart of this blueprint was a "tale of two cities." One city—the "City of Man"—represented earthly cities like Babel in Genesis 11, set on exalting itself and its fortune, and having its origin in the rebellious will of Cain (Gen. 4). Rome, for Augustine, was synonymous with the City of Man. Another city—"the City of God"—had sprung from righteous Abel and represented redeemed humanity. Having their citizenship "above," they sought a city "whose designer and builder is God" (Heb. 11:10). Though strangers in the present world, Christians were exemplary citizens of the empire, praying for its rulers and seeking its best interests in accordance with the scriptural mandate (Jer. 29:7; 1 Tim. 2:1-3).

"So, justice *is* possible in the city of man?" asked Cesar.

"I believe that virtue—virtuously living—is possible."

"What is virtuous living?" asked Cesar.

"It is to enjoy such peace as we may have," explained Augustine, "and to find good even in the things we suffer."

"Then, are we not called to work for justice here?" asked Cesar.

"In this world," Augustine concluded, "not even the saints can escape the lies and temptations of demons. Yet, by God's grace, the anxiety we suffer sparks in us a fervent desire for that peace that passes all understanding—that ultimate bliss, in which the spirit is healed by wisdom and the body is renewed by resurrection. Here in this world we are called blessed if we have peace—even a little peace—but that's meager compared with the final bliss."

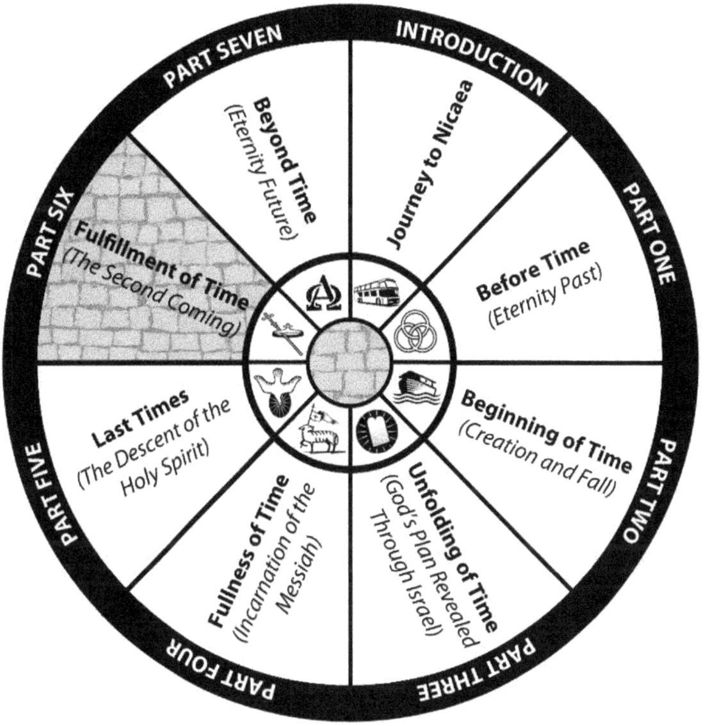
INTRODUCTION
Journey to Nicaea
PART ONE
Before Time
(Eternity Past)
PART TWO
Beginning of Time
(Creation and Fall)
PART THREE
Unfolding of Time
(God's Plan Revealed
Through Israel)
PART FOUR
Fullness of Time
(Incarnation of the
Messiah)
PART FIVE
Last Times
(The Descent of the
Holy Spirit)
PART SIX
Fulfillment of Time
(The Second Coming)
PART SEVEN
Beyond Time
(Eternity Future)

Chapter 8: The Fulfillment of Time

Mentor announced our final regular session, though he hinted at a "consummation" session to follow. I wondered what the witnesses could teach us about the Second Coming, since Jesus had warned his disciples that no one—not even he—knew the hour of his return. The *Fulfillment of Time*, Mentor explained, would give the witnesses time to explain their views on several passages related to the Second Coming of Christ. As a bonus, we students were invited to submit our own questions about the afterlife, with the understanding that not all them could be answered. Joseph suggested we write down our questions for clarity's sake and to avoid repetition. I offered sheets of blank paper from my journal and soon we were all scribbling furiously.

Deciding what to ask the witnesses turned out to be an interesting exercise. We tossed out many questions like, "Will I see my loved ones in heaven?" and "What will our resurrection bodies look like?" For who can answer such questions, even among the witnesses? Each of us finally decided on a single question to ask.

Joseph: *Where do we believers go, right after we die?*[1]

Preacher: *Will the Church be raptured before or after the tribulation?*[2]

Cesar: *Will there be a literal millennial kingdom here on earth?*[3]

Ari: *Is there a purgatory?*[4]

Several ancient witnesses were at the lectern as Mentor began reading aloud from the lectern Bible. After reading several verses in 1 Thessalonians 4, he came to the following verse, which he and the witnesses recited in unison from memory,

---

1 This question, discussed by Erickson, *Introducing Christian Doctrine*, 3rd edition (Hulstad, ed. 198-199), asks what happens to a believer after death but before the Lord's return and the resurrection of the dead. Some commentators point to Luke 23:43 and 16:19-31 to suggest an intermediate state between death and resurrection during which the believer is with the Lord but awaiting the resurrection of his body.

2 This question, also discussed by Erickson (444-445), assumes two "Second Comings" of the Lord separated by a seven-year period of tribulation on the earth. The first is a secret coming of the Lord to take his saints out of the world (known as the *rapture*), and the second is when the Lord comes with his saints to judge the world.

3 The belief in a literal millennial kingdom here on earth is the view of *premillennialism*, which teaches that Jesus Christ will be physically present to rule on earth for a period of a thousand years. This view is discussed by Erickson (see previous note) on pages 455-457.

4 Purgatory is a place of purification, according to Roman Catholic doctrine, for those who are going to heaven but not yet perfected. See Erickson, 435-436.

> *The Lord himself will descend from heaven with a cry of command, with the voice of an archangel, and with the sound of the trumpet of God....*[5]

A witness whom Mentor identified as Jerome came to the lectern.

"He's one of the four great doctors of the Western Church," whispered Father Greg, "he translated the entire Bible into Latin."

"At the sound of the trumpet the earth and its people shall tremble," declared Jerome, "but you shall rejoice! The world shall howl at the Lord who comes to judge it, and the tribes of the earth shall smite their breast. But you, though poor and country-bred, you shall rejoice and laugh, and say, behold my crucified Lord, behold my judge!"

I could feel a swell of emotion coming over me as I imagined the scene. Jerome stepped back from the lectern and Mentor introduced Prudentius, who led the assembly in a hymn he had composed on the theme, and which included this verse:

> *When at the awesome trumpet's sound*
> *The earth will be consumed by fire,*
> *And with a mighty rush the world*
> *Unhinged, will crash in dreadful ruin!* [6]

The witnesses sang with such gusto and conviction, it was as if the scene was unfolding before our eyes. We'd only begun the *Fulfillment of Time*, but already the drama of the Second Coming of Christ was overtaking us.

---

5 1 Thessalonians 4:16a.

6 Prudentius, *The Poems of Prudentius, A Hymn for Christmas Day* (FOTC 43, Hymn #11, 83; ACC IX, 89.

After the hymn, Ambrosiaster, whom we had met in the previous session, stepped up to the lectern and declared,

"Christ the Lord will himself come down by the will of the Father, like the chief angel of God with the heavenly host, as is written in the revelation of John, and will wage war in God's name against the antichrist."[7]

With these words I was reminded that the second coming of Christ is the beginning of the end for Satan.

"After the antichrist has been wiped out," continued Ambrosiaster, "the dead will rise again at Christ's command. God's trumpet will sound and war will be waged in the name of God. This is what Christ himself, the commander and chief of God's army, said to Joshua the son of Nun, for which reason he was called an archangel."[8]

Ambrosiaster was teaching that Christ himself had appeared to Joshua, and that the conquest of the Promised Land led by Joshua was a type of the Second Coming of Christ.[9]

Mentor continued his reading from 1 Thessalonians 4.

> *And the dead in Christ will rise first. Then we who are alive, who are left, will be caught up together with them in the clouds to meet the Lord in the air, and so we will always be with the Lord.*[10]

"The Lord, here, is Christ—the true Son of God," explained Ambrosiaster. "He is also the commander

---

7 Revelation 12:7. Gerald Bray, *Ambrosiaster, Galatians—Philemon*, Ancient Christian Texts (Downers Grove, IL:IVP Academic, 2009), page 108.

8 Same as previous note.

9 See Joshua 5:13-15.

10 1 Thessalonians 4:16b-17.

and chief, because he is the head of all things, since everything comes from him. Those who have died in Christ will rise first, and then we who are still alive will be caught up together with those processional clouds to meet Christ in the air. Thus, everyone will come with Christ to the battle: those who killed the saints will see them alive, because as the clouds accompany the Lord, so also will those whom he has been pleased to call his brethren. So, we shall always be with the Lord."[11]

The Rapture

For Ambrosiaster, the angelic shout and trumpet call will signal the final battle to be waged by Christ against Satan. Those who persecuted the saints will see them resurrected and, indeed, will find themselves conquered by Christ and those very saints!

"In this *rapture*," explained Ambrosiaster, "death will come as it were through sleep, and the soul which has departed will be given back in a moment. When they are taken away they die, and when they reach the Lord they receive their souls back again in his presence, because they cannot be dead if they are with Christ. Paul directs them to console one another with this hope, because they still thought they ought to mourn the passing of their loved ones as the Gentiles did."[12]

"But will they be raptured before or after the tribulation?" asked Preacher.[13]

---

11 Same as previous note, page 109 (paraphrasing Bray's translation).

12 Gerald Bray, *Ambrosiaster, Galatians—Philemon*, Ancient Christian Texts (Downers Grove, IL:IVP Academic, 2009), page 109.

13 See note 2.

Ambrosiaster did not reply but discussed the question with Mentor, who then spoke with Preacher.

"When the body dies, the soul leaves it—that's all the witness means by *rapture*," explained Mentor.

"But what about what the Bible says about the *rapture*?" asked Preacher.

"Are you thinking of the passage where two men are in the field, one is taken and the other is left?" asked Joseph.

"That's the one," agreed Preacher.[14]

"So, when you hear the word *rapture*, you think of the saints who have not yet died being snatched up into heaven, body and soul."

"What else?" asked Preacher.

"That's not what the witness means," explained Joseph, "besides, I think you're confusing Matthew 24 with 1 Thessalonians 4."

Joseph turned to Matthew 24 and read aloud.

> *They were unaware until the flood came and swept them all away, so will be the coming of the Son of Man. Then two men will be in the field; one will be taken and one left (Matthew 24:39-40).*

"That's is how it will be when Christ returns," said Preacher.

"Right," agreed Joseph, "but that passage is about the Second Coming and final judgment. Besides, it doesn't say where the man who disappears goes, or what happens to the man who is left behind."

"What do you mean?" he asked.

---

14 Matthew 24:40.

"Which one is saved, Preacher, the one who is taken or the one who is left behind?"

"Then two men will be in the field; one will be taken and one left," Preacher read again.

"The man who is left behind goes through the tribulation," he replied.

"It doesn't say that," objected Joseph.

"But I've always understood the verse that way," said Preacher.

"I know," said Joseph, "but that idea is not based on Scripture."

While Preacher continued studying the verse, Mentor offered to address my question next.

"Why do you want to know about purgatory?" asked Joseph.

"I caused an uproar when I asked about the Jews," I said, "so, I thought I'd ask about something less controversial."

"I like your question," said Joseph, "cause it's about what happens to believers between death and the resurrection."

Purgatory

Mentor invited Tertullian back to the lectern to represent the western Church view on purgatory, but as yet there was no witness for the eastern Church perspective.

"Mentor, may I represent the opposing view? asked Joseph.

"Do you understand what you are opposing?" asked Mentor.

"Not very well," admitted Joseph, "but I know someone who can help me, right prof?"

"This should be fun!" agreed Father Greg, and taking Joseph aside he began to rehearse him.

"Okay champ, what do Catholics believe about Purgatory?" asked Preacher when the two returned.

"All who die in God's grace but still imperfectly purified have salvation," said Joseph, quoting the catechism, "but after death they undergo purification, to attain the holiness needed to enter the joy of heaven."[15]

"And what do you Greeks believe?" I asked, but there was no more time to rehearse. As Joseph stood next to Tertullian at the threefold lectern, the contrast was striking. Both were dark skinned, but Joseph's street clothes and youthful swagger set the two men apart—the ancient Carthaginian professor and the Church history student.

Mentor prompted Tertullian to begin.[16]

"All believers will experience Hades for a season after they die," announced Tertullian.

"Wait," said Joseph, "I thought we were talking about purgatory."

"It's the same thing," said Father Greg, "the term purgatory wasn't coined until later."

Tertullian looked at Mentor, who requested the ancient witness to begin again.

---

15 Catechism of the Catholic Church, Section III, Article 12, 1030, and online at http://www.usccb.org/beliefs-and-teachings/what-we-believe/catechism/catechism-of-the-catholic-church/epub/index.cfm.

16 The dialogue is based on the concluding chapter (58) of Tertullian's *Treatise On the Soul.*

"All believers will experience Hades for a season after they die," repeated Tertullian.

"Everyone?" asked Joseph.

"Not the martyrs, of course," said Tertullian, "but everyone else."

"I don't buy that," said Joseph.

Tertullian, puzzled, looked at Joseph.

"Sorry," said Joseph, "I mean I don't accept that,"

"Whether you accept it or not," replied Tertullian, "after death and before the second coming, the soul experiences both punishment and comfort in Hades, awaiting gloom or glory—its final judgment."

"I like to say the soul is secure in God," replied Joseph, "but that it knows nothing of its final destination before the judgment."

"But what do you believe the soul *does* after the person dies and before Christ returns to judge?" asked Tertullian.

"The Bible says we are fallen asleep," explained Joseph.

"But souls do not sleep, bodies do," insisted Tertullian, "the soul is always awake."

"Okay," agreed Joseph, "the soul is awake, so what?"

"Then it recalls the rights and wrongs done in its past life and, as I have said, it gets an introduction—a foretaste—of its future in heaven or hell,"

"How can the soul know its destiny before it stands before Christ to be judged?" asked Joseph.

"Do you really believe that, in the interim, the soul is uncertain and without hope or any knowledge of its destiny? Does that uncertainty await us all when we die?" asked Tertullian.

"After death," said Joseph, "the soul waits to be reunited with the body, because judgment is judgment upon the whole man—body and soul."

"Please make your concluding statements," Mentor interrupted.

"In his teaching," concluded Tertullian, "our Lord described Hades as a prison and taught that one would not get out until he has paid the last penny—meaning the smallest offense we have committed against God.[17] In Hades, therefore, the soul endures discipline for its purification, while the resurrection works recompense in the body. This is my view."

"Maybe there is a Hades waiting for us," concluded Joseph, "but I thank God for grace and salvation through Christ!"

We cheered for Joseph, who thanked Tertullian and Mentor for allowing him to participate.

"I never dreamed of facing such an awesome opponent as Tertullian!" he said.

"You did well," said Father Greg.

"Is *Hades* just another word for Hell?" I asked Father Greg.

"Not exactly," he explained. "In Jesus' day, *Hades* was seen as the place where those who die await final judgment."

"But that's not Scriptural, is it?" asked Joseph.

"If you've heard of *Sheol* in the Old Testament," said Father Greg, "that's basically the same concept."

"The doctrine of purgatory is based on *Sheol*?" I asked.

---

17 See Matthew 5:25-26.

"Not entirely," admitted Father Greg, "there's a passage in the book of Maccabees that teaches the doctrine."

"We Protestants don't accept Maccabees as Scripture," said Joseph.

"What does the passage say?" I asked.

"Judas Maccabeus was a Jewish hero who lived a couple of centuries before Christ," explained Father Greg. "Some of his soldiers died in battle because of their idolatry, so he prayed for them and took up an offering to send to Jerusalem so they could be forgiven."

Joseph wagged his head,

"You don't really believe that forgiveness can be purchased, do you?" he asked.

"I didn't say that," replied Father Greg.

"I thought we were talking about purgatory," I interjected.

"We are," Father Greg continued, "the sinful soldiers in Maccabees were unprepared to enter heaven, so they had to await purification."

"They had to pay for it!" said Joseph.

"They couldn't pay, they were dead," said Father Greg.

"But a payment was made," I replied.

"An offering was given on their behalf by a righteous man, what's so bad about that?" said Father Greg, smiling.

"But *you* don't believe in purgatory, do you, Father Greg?" asked Cesar.

"No," admitted the priest, "but always be ready to argue your opponent's view!"

The Millennium

Another debate was stirring among several witnesses who had gathered around Mentor and were demanding to be heard on the subject of the thousand-year reign of Christ spoken of in Revelation 20. This was related to Cesar's question, and he knew a lot about it.

"There are two groups," he explained, "the *Chiliasts* believe in a literal, thousand-year reign of Christ on the earth, but the *Alexandrians* interpret the thousand years symbolically.[18] Mentor granted a hearing to the *Chiliasts* first, inviting Irenaeus of Lyon, who was respected by all, to represent their point of view.

"There are those among us," began Irenaeus, "who, though they seem to be true believers, are unaware of how we become equipped for eternity."

The Alexandrians murmured loudly at these words, and Mentor called for order.

"Ignoring the divine plan for the exaltation of the righteous," Irenaeus continued, "these men prefer to play around with certain heretical ideas. Like the heretics, they deny the salvation of the flesh and claim that immediately following death we shall pass directly through the heavens to the Father. In this way, they deny the resurrection of the body, and forget that our Lord Himself, after dying on the cross, did not rise until the third day. Indeed, during those days He dwelt in the place where the dead were, as the Prophet says concerning Him: 'And the Lord remembered His dead saints who

---

18 Chiliast is taken from *chiliasmos* which is the Greek number for 1000, and Alexandrians from the famous school of biblical interpretation in Alexandria, Egypt.

slept formerly in the land of the dead; and He descended to them, to rescue and save them.'"[19]

"What Prophet said that?" asked an Alexandrian witness.

"Isaiah," Irenaeus shot back.

"Show us the verse," he replied, and his fellow Alexandrians began to chant, "Show the verse!"

Mentor, aided by Irenaeus, searched for the passage.

"In any case," said Irenaeus when they could not find it, "all true believers affirm that our Lord descended to the dead."

"Why does he say that?" I asked.

"It's in the Apostles' Creed," said Father Greg, "where it says *He descended into hades.*"

"We always said *He descended into hell*," said Joseph.

"I know," said Father Greg, "but that's just wrong."[20]

"So, *He descended into Hades* is what the eastern Church says?" I asked.

"No," replied the priest, "we prefer the Nicene Creed which does not mention a descent into Hades at all."

Mentor, surrounded by witnesses arguing with him, was unable to restore order, so we moved nearer the lectern to listen in. Among the *Chiliasts*, a very elderly father called Papias prophesied to anyone who would listen, including Preacher who seemed to be in awe of him.

---

19 Irenaeus, *Against Heresies*, 5.31.1 (ANF 1.560).

20 *He descended to Hades*, the lower parts or underworld according to the creed's original language.

"The days are coming," announced Papias in a shrill voice, "when vines shall grow, each having ten thousand branches, and in each branch ten thousand twigs, and in each true twig ten thousand shoots, and in each one of the shoots ten thousand clusters, and on every one of the clusters ten thousand grapes!"

Two young men on either side of Papias steadied the witness as he spoke.

"And every grape when pressed will give five and twenty gallons of wine. And when any one of the saints shall lay hold of a cluster, another shall cry out, 'I am a better cluster, take me! Bless the Lord through me!'"[21]

"Dang," said Preacher, "that's a lot of wine!"

While this was taking place, the Alexandrians were loudly voicing their opposition to the Chiliasts' view. In the midst of this group stood Origen, condemning the view expressed by Papias in very harsh words. Some wanted to appoint him as spokesman, but other witnesses called Augustine, who was standing apart from the mob.

"I don't get it," I said to my friends.

"What?" asked Cesar.

"What's all the fuss about?"

"Millennialism," he replied, "Christ's thousand-year reign on earth."

"You remember the three views, don't you?" asked Joseph.

"Premillennial, postmillennial, and amillennial," I answered, recalling the terms of endless debates in our theology class.

---

21 Papias, Fragments (ANF 1,153) quoted in Irenaeus, *Against Heresies* 5.33.3 (ANF 1, 563).

"Many early Church Fathers held a view very much like premillennialism," explained Father Greg.

"But were they pre-trib or post-trib?" asked Preacher.

"Neither," replied Father Greg, "that idea only caught on when dispensationalism became popular in the late 1800s."[22]

"I remember my father's premill preaching," said Joseph, "most of his sermons were about how bad things will get before the Lord returns."

"What about all those grapes the elderly witness mentioned?" I asked.

"That happens after the second coming," explained Joseph, "when Christ reigns on the earth for a thousand years."

"What about postmillennialists," I asked, "what do they believe?"

"We believe this world is going to get a lot better before the Lord returns," said Cesar.

"You're postmillennial?" I asked.

"Of course," he replied, "we're building the kingdom now, but there's still a lot of work to do before the Lord returns."

At last Mentor had restored order in the Crux so we returned to our bench. Augustine, at the lectern, directed one of his scribes to read a lengthy passage from the book of Revelation (20:1-6).

---

22 Pre-trib, post-trib are short for pre-tribulation, post-tribulation. Those who in the 19th century developed Dispensational Theology debated whether believers would be snatched away by the Lord prior to (pre-trib), or following (post-trib), the great tribulation mentioned in Matthew 24:21, Mark 13:19, Revelation 7:14, and other passages.

> *Then I saw an angel coming down from heaven, holding in his hand the key to the abyss and a great chain. And he seized the dragon, that ancient serpent, who is the devil and Satan, and bound him for a thousand years, and threw him into the pit, and shut it and sealed it over him, so that he might not deceive the nations any longer, until the thousand years were ended. After that he must be released for a little while. Then I saw thrones, and seated on them were those to whom the authority to judge was committed. Also I saw the souls of those who had been beheaded for the testimony of Jesus and for the word of God, and those who had not worshiped the beast or its image and had not received its mark on their foreheads or their hands. They came to life and reigned with Christ for a thousand years. The rest of the dead did not come to life until the thousand years were ended. This is the first resurrection. Blessed and holy is the one who shares in the first resurrection! Over such the second death has no power, but they will be priests of God and of Christ, and they will reign with him for a thousand years.*

"As we have heard from the passage just read," began Augustine, "the evangelist John speaks of two resurrections, but some witnesses misunderstand the first resurrection, making the teaching into a fairy tale! This is because they believe that the first resurrection—which occurs at the beginning of the thousand years—is a resurrection of the body, while the resurrection at the end of the thousand years is the spiritual resurrection of the soul, when in fact the opposite is true."

"Did you hear a second resurrection mentioned in that passage?" I asked Joseph.

"Not in that way," said Joseph, "but it's implied, since the rest of the dead come to life after the thousand years."

"It *is* confusing," agreed Preacher, "because the theme of the passage is the first resurrection. But like Joseph says, it points to a second resurrection."

"Bishop Augustine," I asked, "how did the two resurrections become so confused?"

"Some of the brothers have been impressed by the number of a thousand years, during which time they believe the saints will rise again to enjoy a kind of Sabbath-rest," he said.

"Sabbath rest?" I asked.

"After laboring for six thousand years after being expelled from the garden, they get a holy rest," explained the Bishop. "Remember, Scripture says that with the Lord, one day is like a thousand years and a thousand years is like one day.[23] So, having worked hard for six days—meaning six thousand years—they get a sabbath rest, a sabbath that lasts for a thousand years!" [24]

"That makes sense," I agreed.

"Indeed," said Augustine, "I used to believe it myself, but a sabbath rest ought to be a spiritual rest, don't you think?"

"What do you mean?" I asked.

"Its delights are spiritual," explained Augustine "and made even more so by the Lord's presence."

"What else would they be," I asked.

"You heard the *Chiliasts*," replied Augustine, "they say those who rise in the millennium will enjoy a fabulous banquet with more food and drink than can be believed, and that exceeds all moderation."

---

23 2 Peter 3:8.

24 Augustine, *City of God*, XX.7 Bettenson, 906-907.

"I see," I said. "Is that why they call the first resurrection a resurrection of the body."

"Truly," agreed Augustine, "and it is the view of materialists."[25]

"What *I* want to know is, what exactly *is* the kingdom of God and when will it begin?" asked Cesar.

"Let us first answer the question of *when*," said Augustine, "and then we can proceed to the *what*." Cesar agreed.

"Here is my question for you," said the Bishop, "when did Christ bind the Strong Man?"[26]

"I believe he did that during his earthly ministry," replied Cesar.[27]

"Amen!" agreed Augustine, "therefore, the kingdom of God began with Christ's first coming."

"That's right!" said Cesar.

"What strong man?" I asked.

"The Lord Jesus Christ Himself says, *No one can enter a strong man's house and plunder his goods, unless he first binds the strong man*," explained the Bishop.[28] "By *strong man* he means the devil because he had power to take humanity captive. And by *plundering his goods* he means to deliver those held captive by the devil in various sins, who would come to believe in Him."

---

25 Materialists are those concerned with the fleshly and not the spiritual dimension of humanity.

26 The following dialogue is based on Augustine, *City of God*, XX.5-7 (NPNF 1.2, 423-427).

27 See Matthew 12:29.

28 Matthew 12:29.

Augustine paused while Joseph showed me the passage in Matthew's Gospel.

"Now then," he continued, "it was for the binding of this Strong One that John, in Revelation, had the vision we read about—the vision of *an angel coming down from heaven with the key of the abyss and a chain, and laying hold of the dragon, that old serpent, which is called the devil and Satan, and bound him a thousand years*,—that is, he bridled and restrained his power so that he could not seduce and gain possession of those who were to be freed."[29]

"The kingdom hasn't come in fullness yet, has it?" I asked.

"No indeed," said Augustine, "but we must not disregard what has already come to pass."

"What *has* come to pass?" I asked.

"So much has come to pass!" said Augustine, and my friends all laughed. I guess he meant the resurrection, the giving of the Holy Spirit, and all that, only I had not been thinking in those terms. Augustine silenced the laughter, and continued explaining.

"It is true," he said, "that when Christ returns he will say *Come, you who are blessed of my Father and take possession of the kingdom prepared for you.*[30] But even now, though in a lesser way, his saints are reigning with him. Are you not reigning with him even now?"

"Amen!" declared Preacher.

"Do you recall these words of our Lord?" the Bishop asked me. "*Have you understood all these things? And*

---

29 The following dialogue is based on Augustine, *City of God*, XX.5-7 (NPNF 1.2, 423-427).

30 Matthew 25:34.

they said to him, 'Yes.' And he said to them, 'Therefore every scribe who has been trained for the kingdom of heaven is like a master of a house, who brings out of his treasure what is new and what is old'"[31]

"I remember," I said.

"And to whom was our Lord speaking at that time?" asked Augustine.

"His disciples, I guess."

"Truly," he agreed, "and so the kingdom *has* come, for this is *when* His scribes are trained for the kingdom."

"That makes sense," I agreed.

"Of course," said the Bishop, "how else could the Church be called the kingdom of God if the kingdom had not already come?"

Augustine "proved" his point by equating the Church with the kingdom of God, but that raised another question for me.

"We were taught that the Church and the kingdom are not the same, right?" I asked Father Greg, who nodded in agreement.

"What are they teaching at your school?" asked Augustine.

"Our theology text says that the Church points to the kingdom," explained Father Greg, "but is not identical with it."

"Do you recall the parables of the weeds?" Augustine asked me.[32]

---

31 Matthew 13:51-52.

32 Matthew 13:24-30, 36-43.

"Yes," I said, "the weeds, or unbelievers, grow up alongside the wheat—the true believers."

"Well said!" he replied, "and what takes place at the consummation of the age?"

"At the end of the world?" I asked, and he nodded.

"God sends his angels to gather the weeds and separate them from the wheat," I said.

"And where does he find these stumbling blocks?" asked Augustine.

"You mean the weeds?" I asked, uncertain why he mentioned *stumbling blocks*.

Augustine nodded, and I answered,

"I suppose he finds them in the Church."

"Sadly, it is just as you say," he replied. Then to Joseph, who was following all this in his Bible, Augustine asked,

"What do the Scriptures say about this, pastor?"

Joseph read aloud from Matthew's Gospel.

"*The Son of Man will send his angels and they will gather out of his kingdom all causes of sin and all law-breakers.*"[33]

"What do you make of that?" asked Augustine.

"The parable seems to say that the kingdom and the Church are one and the same," I admitted.

We all expressed our thanks to the Bishop as he returned to his place. Listening to his insights, I realized that I did not know my Bible very well. Augustine knew every detail of every passage we had discussed, and he must have had much of the Bible memorized.

33 Matthew 13:41.

"The Bishop's main point," explained Father Greg, "was that, with the advent of the Church, the millennium is already unfolding, it's not something far in the future. His view has become what we now call amillennialism, where the thousand years are understood symbolically, and everything Christ taught about the end times is now coming to pass."

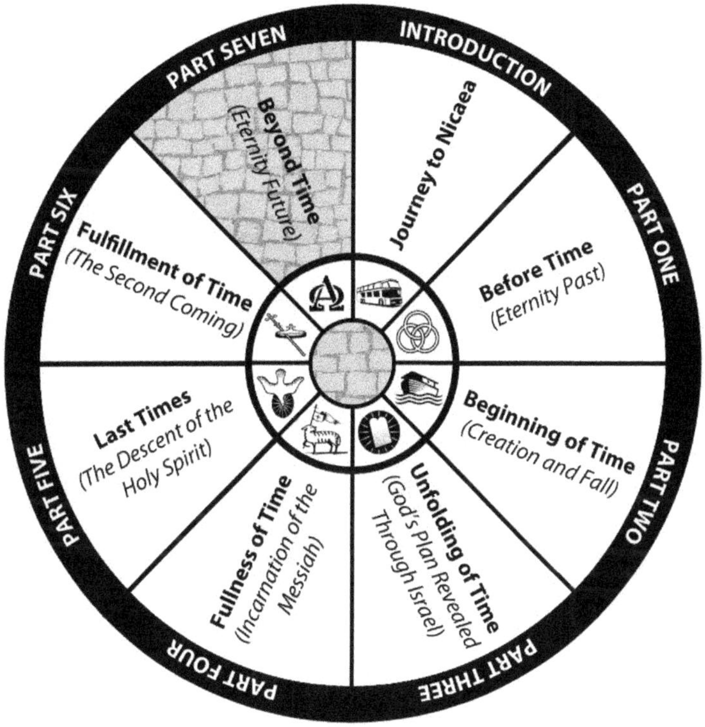
INTRODUCTION
Journey to Nicaea
PART ONE
Before Time
(Eternity Past)
PART TWO
Beginning of Time
(Creation and Fall)
PART THREE
Unfolding of Time
(God's Plan Revealed Through Israel)
PART FOUR
Fullness of Time
(Incarnation of the Messiah)
PART FIVE
Last Times
(The Descent of the Holy Spirit)
PART SIX
Fulfillment of Time
(The Second Coming)
PART SEVEN
Beyond Time
(Eternity Future)

Chapter 9: Beyond Time

"So, what comes next?" asked Preacher.

"Heaven!" said Joseph.

Having followed the Story of God through its various episodes, we had arrived at the consummation—the time God the Father would 'gather together in one all things in Christ, things in heaven and things on earth,' as Paul wrote to the Ephesians. Of course, no one, not even the ancient witnesses, could say exactly what that time would be like.

Earlier, Mentor had hinted there might be time for one of the witnesses to share his insights on the closing passages of Revelation. But now he quickly gathered up his books and rushed us toward the reading room. It looked as if our time had run out.

All the questions I meant to ask now flooded my mind, as Mentor explained that the witnesses were "overdue" to return to their respective times and places. We would have to find our own way back through the walls of Nicaea; then, time as we knew it would begin again. We would rejoin our fellow students and class and our lives as they were before, keeping forever the memory and secret of our unrepeatable experience. That much, anyway, is what I understood from Mentor's hurried farewell speech. One piece of the puzzle, however, did not fit: everyone we had met at the Athenaeum was an identifiable historical figure, except Mentor. Who was he and where would he go after this?

I could see by the look on Cesar's face that he was struggling with the idea of having to leave the Athenaeum behind. He quietly besieged Mentor with questions as we helped him reshelf his books. When the reading room was in order, Mentor hurried us through the same door we had entered when we first discovered the library.

"Come on Cesar," called Preacher, as we moved into the passageway.

"I'm not going," said Cesar, from the reading room.

Mentor, always peaceful and confident, now appeared anxious as Cesar revealed to us what he had learned about our guide.

His name was Cornelius Witherspoon and he was born in Scotland in the late 1700s. He had accidently discovered the Athenaeum while on antique buying trip to the Ottoman Empire. Captivated by all the ancient books, he remained within the walls of Nicaea to learn as much as he could from the man who was hosting visitors to the Athenaeum at that time. The host, who was known as Mentor, never explained how he had come to be there. Then one day he simply disappeared, leaving behind a note that read,

> My tenure is now completed.
> Please stay until a mature replacement arrives.
> Otherwise, the door to our ancient witnesses will be forever shut.
> You, sir, are now the Mentor.

We realized at once what Cesar had in mind.

"No way," said Joseph, "we're not leaving you behind."

"But I *want* to stay," said Cesar, "I *have* to stay or the door will close!"

"Don't make me have to carry you out of here!" said Preacher.

"I regret that you cannot stay," said the man we knew as Mentor.

"But what about the note?" asked Cesar.

"I have waited many years," replied Mentor, but my replacement must be a mature man. You are too young, Cesar, and since there is no one to replace me, the door must close.

"I will stay," said Father Greg.

Epilogue: Life after Nicaea

Father Greg is not the only professor ever to have left a faculty position while leading a study abroad course. But, as far as I know, he is the first to have done so in order to accept a position at the Athenaeum! Before we left him in the reading room that night, he assured us that all would be well: he was single man with no living family members; he was adjunct faculty at the seminary living in a campus apartment, whose contract ended when the summer was over. He deputized the four of us to help our fellow students finish the course, and gave us a note of permission as the professor of record.

"How can we teach a class we have not taken?" asked Joseph.

"You've seen *Ancient Christianity* in the flesh!" declared Father Greg, finally accepting the miracle of our discovery. This inspired me to share what we had learned. But how could I hope to motivate students who knew nothing about the fathers and mothers of the ancient Church, including at what cost they had purchased historic Christian doctrine? When it comes to our Christian forebears, the ministers of my generation are like those who never bothered to attend their own family reunion.

This challenge became a career passion for me, so after graduation I founded the Sacred Roots Institute, dedicated to introducing the next generation of Christian ministers to their ancestors in the faith.

Joseph, Cesar, and Preacher—my companions on our own journey to discover our sacred roots—became active supporters of the Institute. Joseph is now senior pastor of a growing church; Preacher has become a popular Christian speaker, combining styles he learned from Chrysostom, Ambrose, and especially Tertullian.

Cesar—the "Indiana Jones" of our Institute—now leads the *Ancient Christianity* tours to Nicaea, visiting the Athenaeum as often as possible. Thankfully, we have a man on the inside who stays in touch with the ancient witnesses.

Bibliography of Patristic Sources

Ancient Christianity, Patrology (Study of the Church Fathers)

Chadwick, Henry. *The Church in Ancient Society: from Galilee to Gregory the Great*. Oxford: Oxford University Press, 2001.

Davis, Don L. *Sacred Roots: A Primer on Retrieving the Great Tradition*. The Urban Ministry Institute, 2010.

Dietrich, Suzanne de. *God's Unfolding Purpose; a Guide to the Study of the Bible*. Philadelphia: Westminster Press, 1960.

Di Berardino, Angelo. *Encyclopedia of Ancient Christianity. 3 vols*. Downers Grove, Ill: IVP Academic, 2014.

Drobner, Hubertus R. *The Fathers of the Church*. Peabody, MA: Hendrickson, 2007.

Fitzgerald, Allan D. *Augustine through the Ages, an Encyclopedia*. Grand Rapids: Eerdmans, 1999.

Hall, Christopher A. *Reading Scripture with the Church Fathers*. Downers Grove: InterVarsity Press, 1998.

Haykin, Michael A.G. *Rediscovering the Church fathers: who they were and how they shaped the Church.* Wheaton, Ill: Crossway, 2011.

Kannengiesser, Charles. *Handbook of patristic exegesis the Bible in ancient Christianity*. Leiden: Brill, 2006.

Kelly, J.N.D. *Early Christian Creeds, 3rd* ed. London: Longman, 1972.

________. *Early Christian Doctrines, Revised*. Harper San Francisco, 1978.

Pelikan, Jaroslav. *The Christian tradition; a history of the development of doctrine*. Five volumes. Chicago: University of Chicago Press, 1971.

Quasten, Johannes. *Patrology*, 3 vols. Westminster, Md: Newman Press, 1950.

Stump, Eleonore, and Norman Kretzmann. *The Cambridge companion to Augustine*. Cambridge, UK: Cambridge University Press, 2001.

Ancient Geography and Architecture

Evers, Alexander. *Church, Cities, and People: A Study of the plebs in the Church and Cities of Roman Africa in Late Antiquity*. Leuvan: Peeters, 2010.

Herrin, Judith. *Byzantium, the Surprising Life of a Medieval Empire*. Princeton: Princeton University Press, 2007.

Grant, Michael. *A guide to the ancient world: a dictionary of classical place names*. Bronx, NY: H.W. Wilson, 1986.

McEvedy, Colin. *Cities of the classical world: an atlas and gazetteer of 120 centres of ancient civilization*. London: Allen Lane, 2011.

Möllers, Sabine. *Die Hagia Sophia in Iznik/Nikaia*. Verlag und Datenbank für Geisteswissenschaften, 1994.

Schmit, Theodor. *Die Koimesis-Kirche Von Nikaia, Das Bauwerk und die Mosaiken*. Berlin und Leipzig: Walter De Gruyter & Co, 1927.

Taylor, Jane. *Imperial Istanbul, A Traveller's Guide*. London: Tauris Parke Paperbacks, 2007.

The Nicene Creed (annotated)

Anatolios, Khaled. *Retrieving Nicaea, the Development and Meaning of Trinitarian Doctrine*. Grand Rapids: Baker Academic, 2011.

Ayres, Lewis. *Nicaea and Its Legacy*. New York: Oxford University Press, 2004.

Bray, Gerald Lewis. *Creeds, councils, and Christ*. Leicester, England: Inter-Varsity Press, 1984. [An independent scholar, evangelical in theology, treats the Nicene Creed thematically, not line by line. Chapters include *Modern theology and Christian Doctrine*, *The canon of Scripture and Christian doctrine*, *The spread of the Gospel*, *The rule of Faith*, *The City of God*, etc.

Forell, George Wolfgang. *Understanding the Nicene Creed*. Philadelphia: Fortress Press, 1965. [A popular lecture on the three articles of the Nicene Creed (Father, Son, Holy Spirit) from a Lutheran perspective]

George, Timothy. 2011. *Evangelicals and Nicene faith: reclaiming the Apostolic witness*. Grand Rapids, Mich: Baker Academic, 2007. [Anthology of articles on the "Identity, History, and Practice" of the Nicene Creed by Thomas Oden, G. Bray, Timothy George (Dean of Beeson Divinity School), and others]

Jackson, L. Charles. *Faith of our fathers: a popular study of the Nicene Creed*. Moscow, Idaho: Canon Press, 2007. [A thematic treatment of the Nicene Creed by a Covenant Presbyterian pastor-theologian, including "No Creed but Christ?" Almighty Creator, God of God, For us and for our salvation, filioque, etc. Each chapter concludes with a set of study questions.]

Johnson, Luke Timothy. *The creed: what Christians believe and why it matters*. New York: Doubleday, 2003. [A former Benedictine monk, now Prof of NT at Candler School of the Theology, Emory University, treats the Nicene Creed traditionally: Origins & development, What the Creed is and does," We believe in One God…" etc.

MacGregor, Geddes. *The Nicene creed, illumined by modern thought*. Grand Rapids: Eerdmans, 1980. [Former USC professor of religion opens his book with the Greek text of the Nicene Creed followed by chapters that treat the creed historically-contextually, with special emphasis on how modernity has transformed the modern reader's understanding of key term in the creed. Chapters include "On Faith," "Ground of Process," "Nature and God," "Uniqueness of Jesus Christ," etc.

Marthaler, Berard L. *The creed: the apostolic faith in contemporary theology*. Mystic, Conn: Twenty-Third Publications, 1993. ["One volume compendium of the Catholic theology" by a Franciscan Priest-educator. Included here since it is occasionally cited by other authors in this bibliography.]

Seitz, Christopher R. *Nicene Christianity: the future for a new ecumenism*. Grand Rapids, Michigan: Brazos Press, 2001. [An anthology of well-written articles on select lines from the Nicene Creed, e.g. "And in One Lord Jesus Christ," together with thematic articles such as "The reality of the resurrection," by an ecumenical selection of moderate-evangelical theologians.]

Timiadis, Emilianos. *The Nicene Creed: our common faith*. Philadelphia: Fortress Press, 1983. [The author is an Orthodox Metropolitan. His treatment of course includes standard Greek Orthodox themes ("Theosis—Deification; "Problems behind the Filioque", etc.) Otherwise the treatment is thematic and not exegetical: "God as creator and man as steward of creation," "God's action in time beyond space and time," "The oneness of the Church."

Williams, Donald T. *Credo: meditations on the Nicene Creed*. St. Louis, Mo: Chalice Press, 2007. [An excellent and informative set of meditations on the Creed from an EV-Free minister and Professor of English at Toccoa Falls College. After citing the creed in Latin and English translation, each chapter addresses the four articles in detail, The Father, The Son, The Holy Spirit, The Church. The Father, for example, treats of *Credo*, then *Credo in Unum Deum,* and so forth, treating the entire creed line by line.

Willis, David. *Clues to the Nicene Creed: a brief outline of the faith*. Grand Rapids, Mich: William B. Eerdmans, 2005. [Reformed theologian at Princeton University treats the Nicene Creed broadly *and* thematically. Chapters include "The earthiness of the creed," "what believing means," "The point of creation," "The person of Christ," etc.]

Patristic Literature and Theology

Allert, Craig D. *Revelation, truth, canon, and interpretation: studies in Justin Martyr's Dialogue with Trypho*. Leiden: Brill, 2002.

Allison, Gregg R. *Historical Theology An Introduction to Christian Doctrine*, 2011.

Aróztegui Esnaola, Manuel. *La Amistad del Verbo con Abraham Según San Ireneo de Lyon*. Roma: Editrice Pontificia Università Gregoriana, 2005.

Barnes, Timothy D. *Constantine and Eusebius*. Cambridge, MA.: Harvard University Press, 1981.

Behr, John. *Irenaeus of Lyons: identifying Christianity*. Crestwood, N.Y.: St. Vladimir's Seminary Press, 2013.

_______. *The mystery of Christ: life in death*. Crestwood, N.Y.: St. Vladimir's Seminary Press, 2006.

Blackburn, B. Lee, Jr. *The Mystery of the Synagogue: Cyril of Alexandria on the Law of Moses*. PhD Dissertation. Notre Dame, 2009.

Blosser, Benjamin P. *Become Like Angels, Origen's Doctrine of the Soul*. Washington, D.C.: Catholic University of America Press, 2012.

Blowers, Paul M. *Drama of the Divine Economy*. Oxford University Press, 2012.

Broadhurst, Laurence. "Melito of Sardis, the Second Sophistic, and 'Israel'" chapter 3 of Willi Braun (ed) *Rhetoric and Reality in Early Christianities* (Ontario: Laurier University Press, 2005.

Brock, Sebastian. *The Luminous Eye, The Spiritual World Vision of Saint Ephrem*. Kalamazoo, MI: Cistercian Publications, 1985.

Cohick, Lynn H. *The Peri Pascha Attributed to Melito of Sardis: Setting, Purpose, and Sources*. Brown Judaic Studies, #327. Providence: Brown University, 2000.

Colish, Marcia. *Ambrose's Patriarchs*. Notre Dame, Indiana: University of Notre Dame Press, 2005.

Daniel-Hughes, Carly. *The Salvation of the Flesh in Tertullian of Carthage*. New York: Palgrave McMillan, 2011.

Dulles, Avery Cardinal. *A History of Apologetics*. Eugene, Oregon: Wipf and Stock, 1991.

Dunn, Geoffrey D. *Tertullian's Adversus Iudaeos: A Rhetorical Analysis*. Washington, D.C.: Catholic University of America Press, 2008.

Edwards, Mark Julian. *Origen Against Plato*. Aldershot: Ashgate, 2002.

Giles, Kevin. *The Eternal Generation of the Son. Maintaining Orthodoxy in Trinitarian Theology.* Downers Grove: IVP Academic, 2012.

Greer, Rowan A. *Broken Lights and Mended Lives: Theology and Common Life in the Early Church*. Pennsylvania State University Press, 1986.

Griffith, Sidney H. *Faith Adoring the Mystery: Reading the Bible with St. Ephraem the Syrian*. Milwaukee, WI: Marquette University Press, 1997.

Hill, Charles E. *Regnum Caelorum: Patterns of Millennial Thought in Early Christianity, 2nd ed.* Grand Rapids, MI.: Eerdmans, 2001.

Hill, Robert C. *Cyril of Alexandria, Commentary on Isaiah*, in two volumes. Brookline, M A.: Holy Cross Orthodox Press, 2008.

Horner, Timothy J. *Listening to Trypho, Justin Martyr's Dialogue Reconsidered*. Sterling, Virginia: Peeters, 2001.

Howell, Kenneth J. *Ignatius of Antioch. A New Translation and Theological Commentary*. Zanesville, Ohio: Coming Home Network International, 2008.

Kannengiesser, Charles. *Arius and Athanasius, Two Alexandrian Theologians*. Hampshire: Variorum, 1991.

Keating, Daniel A. *The Appropriation of Divine Life in Cyril of Alexandria*. Oxford University Press, 2004.

Kiraz, George Anton. *The New Syriac Primer.* Piscataway, NJ.: Gorgias Press, 2007.

Lampe, G.W.H. *A Patristic Greek Lexicon*. Oxford: Oxford University Press, 1961.

Lashier, Jackson. *Irenaeus on the Trinity*. Boston: Brill, 2014.

Leemans, Johan, Brian J. Matz, and Johan Verstraeten (eds). *Reading Patristic Texts on Social Ethics*. Washington, D.C.: The Catholic University Press of America, 2011.

Lienhard, Joseph T. *The Bible, the Church, and authority: the canon of the Christian Bible in history and theology*. Collegeville, Minn: Liturgical Press, 1995.

Lotz, John-Paul. *Ignatius and Concord. The Background and Use of the Language of Concord in the Letters of Ignatius of Antioch.* New York: Peter Lang, 2007.

Malcolm, Lois. *God: The Sources of Christian Theology*. Louisville, Ky: Westminster John Knox Press, 2012.

Martens, Peter W. *Origen and Scripture, The Contours of the Exegetical Life*. Oxford University Press, 2012.

Mateo-Seco, Lucas Francisco and Giulio Maspero. *The Brill Dictionary of Gregory of Nyssa* (Seth Cherney, trans.) in Supplements to *Vigiliae Christianae*. Boston: Brill, 2010.

Moreschini, Claudio and Enrico Norelli. *Early Christian Greek and Latin Literature: A Literary History* in two volumes (Matthew J. O'Connell, trans.) Peabody, MA: Henrickson, 2005.

Muraoka, T. (ed). *A Greek-English Lexicon of the Septuagint*. Walpole, MA: Peeters, 2009.

Narinskaya, Elena. *Ephrem, a 'Jewish' sage: A Comparison of the Exegetical Writings of St. Ephrem the Syrian and Jewish Traditions*. In Studia Traditionis Theologiae, Explorations in Early and Medieval Theology #7. Turnhout, Belgium: Brepols, 2010.

Neil, Bronwen. *Leo the Great*. New York: Routledge, 2009.

Norris, Richard A. "Hypostasis," in Everett Ferguson, *Encyclopedia of Early Christianity, Second Edition*. New York: Garland, 1997.

Orbe, Antonio, S.J. *Teología de San Ireneo Comentario al Libro V del Adversus Haereses*, three volumes, in *Biblioteca de Autores Cristianos*. Madrid-Toledo: Estudio Teologico de San Ildefonso de Toledo, 1988.

Parvis, Sara, and Paul Foster. *Justin Martyr and his worlds*. Minneapolis: Fortress Press, 2007.

_____. *Irenaeus: Life, Scripture, Legacy*. Minneapolis: Fortress Press, 2012.

Ramsey, Boniface. *Ambrose*. London: Routledge, 1997.

Rokéah, David. *Justin Martyr and the Jews*. Jewish and Christian Perspectives Series. Leiden: Brill, 2002.

Roukema, Reimer. "The veil over Moses' face in patristic interpretation." *In The Interpretation of Exodus: Studies in Honor of Cornelius Houtman*. Dudley, MA.: Peeters, 2006.

Shepardson, Christine. *Anti-Judaism and Christian Orthodoxy: Ephrem's Hymns in Fourth-Century Syria*.

Washington, DC.: Catholic University of America Press, 2008.

Shotwell, Willis A. *The Biblical Exegesis of Justin Martyr*. London: S.P.C.K, 1965.

Sider, Robert D. (ed). *Christian and Pagan in the Roman Empire: The Witness of Tertullian*. Washington, DC.: Catholic University of America Press, 2001.

Stewart-Sikes, Alistair. *The Lamb's High Feast: Melito, Peri Pascha and the Quartodeciman Paschal Liturgy at Sardis*. Boston: Brill, 1998.

Wagner, Siegfried. 'āmar ("The Creative Word") in G. Johannes Botterweck & Helmer Ringgren, *Theological Dictionary of the Old Testament*. Grand Rapids: Eerdmans, Vol. 1, 1977.

Walsh, Milton. *Witness of the Saints, Patristic Readings in the Liturgy of the Hours*. San Francisco: Ignatius Press, 2012.

Wandel, Lee Palmer. *Reading Catechisms, Teaching Religion*. Boston: Brill, 2016.

Wilkins, Robert Louis. *Judaism and the Early Christian Mind, A Study of Cyril of Alexandria's Exegesis and Theology*. New Haven: Yale University Press, 1971.

________. *John Chrysostom and the Jews*. Los Angeles: University of California Press, 1983.

Williams, Rowan. *Arius: heresy and tradition*. Grand Rapids, Mich: W.B. Eerdmans, 2002.

Texts & Translations

Ambrose, and Tomkinson, T. *On Abraham*. Etna, CA: Center for Traditionalist Orthodox Studies, 2000.

Arator, and Richard J. Schrader. *Arator's On the acts of the Apostles (De actibus apostolorum)*. Atlanta, Ga: Scholars Press, 1987.

Behr, John. *St. Irenaeus of Lyons On the Apostolic Preaching*. Crestwood, NY: St. Vladimir's Seminary Press, 1997.

Brock, Sebastian. *Hymns on Paradise, St. Ephrem*. Crestwood, NY: St. Vladimir's Seminary Press, 1998.

Brock, Sebastian P. and George A. Kiraz. *Ephrem the Syrian, Select Poems* in the Eastern Christian Texts series, vol.2. Provo, Utah: Brigham Young University Press, 2006.

Chrysologus, Peter and William B. Palardy. *St. Peter Chrysologus: selected sermons, volume* 3. Washington, D.C.: Catholic University of America Press, 2005.

Cyril, and R. Payne Smith. *Commentary upon the Gospel according to St. Luke, now first translated into English from an ancient Syriac version*. Oxford: Univ. Press, 1859.

Ephraim the Syrian and Bishop Theophan the Recluse. *A Spiritual Psalter or Reflections on God*. Liberty, TN: St. John of Kronstadt Press, 1997.

Eusebius of Caesarea, with G.A. Williamson (translator) and Andrew Louth (ed.). *Eusebius, the History of the Church*. Suffolk: Penguin Classics, 1989.

_______, W.J. Ferrar (translator-editor). 1981. *The Proof of the Gospel*. Two volumes, Grand Rapids: Baker, 1981.

Hall, Stuart George. *Melito of Sardis On Pascha and Fragments*. Oxford: Clarendon Press, 1979.

Heine, Ronald E. *Origen, Commentary on the Gospel of John*, in *The Fathers of the Church*, volume 80. Washington, D.C.: Catholic University Press, 1989.

Jurgens, William A. *The Faith of the Fathers, A source-book of theological and historical passages from the Christian writings of the Post-Nicene and Constantinople eras through St. Jerome, selected and translated by W.A. Jurgens, 3 vols.* Collegeville, Minnesota: The Liturgical Press, 1979.

Kellerman, James A. and Thomas C. Oden. *Incomplete Commentary on Matthew (Opus Imperfectum)*, in two volumes, Ancient Christian Texts. Downers Grove: IVP Academic, 2010.

Kenyon, Frederic G., and Alfred Chester Beatty. *The Chester Beatty Biblical papyri; descriptions and texts of twelve manuscripts on papyrus of the Greek Bible.* London: E. Walker, 1933.

Lienhard, Joseph. *Homilies on Luke; Fragments on Luke*, in *The Fathers of the Church*, volume 94. Washington, D.C.: Catholic University Press, 1989.

McCarthy, Carmel. *Saint Ephrem's Commentary on Tatian's Diatessaron, an English Translation of Chester Beatty Syriac MS 709 with Introduction and Notes.* Oxford University Press, 1993.

MacKenzie, Iain M. *Irenaeus's Demonstration of the Apostolic Preaching.* Burlington, VT.: Ashgate, 2002.

McVey, Kathleen E. *St. Ephrem the Syrian: Selected Prose Works* in *The Fathers of the Church, vol.91.* Washington, D.C.: The Catholic University of America Press, 1994.

_______. *Ephrem the Syrian: hymns.* New York: Paulist Press, 1989.

Martyr, St. Justin. *Dialogue with Trypho*. Translated by Thomas B. Falls. Washington, D.C.: The Catholic University of America Press, 2003.

Schoedel, William R. *Athenagorus, Legatio and De Resurrectione*. Oxford, 1972.

Stewart-Sikes, Alistair. *Melito of Sardis On Pascha, with the Fragments of Melito and other Material Related to the Quartodecimans*. Crestwood, NY: St Vladimir's Press, 2001.

Testuz, Michel. *Papyrus Bodmer XIII: Méliton de Sardes Homélie sur la Pâque, Manuscrit du IIIe siècle*. Cologny-Genève: Bibliotheca Bodmeriana, 1960.

Tzalmalikos, P. *Origen: Cosmology and Ontology of Time*. Supplements to Vigiliae Christianae, vol. LXXVII. Boston: Brill, 2006.

Tertullian, and J. H. Waszink. *Quinti Septimi Florentis Tertulliani, De anima*. Leiden: Brill, 2010.

_____ and Earnest Evans. *Tertullian, Adversus Marcionem*, two volumes. Oxford University Press, 1972.

Weinrich, William C. *Latin Commentaries on Revelation: Victorinus of Petrovium, Apringius of Beja, Caesarius of Arles and Bede the Venerable*. In Thomas C. Oden and Gerald L. Bray (eds.) *Ancient Christian Texts*. Downers Grove: InterVarsity Press, 2011.

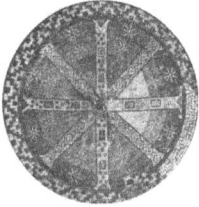

Index

About the Author

"Dr. Bob," as he is known by students and colleagues, serves as the Dean of The Urban Ministry Institute of Los Angeles (TUMI-L.A.) and as a Field Representative for TUMI-National. He earned a Doctorate in Practical Theology from Union Presbyterian Seminary in Richmond, VA., and Masters degrees from Gordon Conwell Theological Seminary (Magna Cum Laude, Old Testament Studies) and the University of North Carolina at Charlotte (M.Ed.). He has served as Director of Christian Education for St. Giles Presbyterian Church (EPC) of Charlotte (1980-1986); Assistant Professor of Religion at Northwestern College of Iowa (1990-1995); and as Professor of Christian Educational Ministries at Taylor University in Indiana (1995-2010). Dr. Bob has published *Readings in Historical Theology: Primary Sources of the Christian Faith* (Kregel Press, 2009), *Lessons of Infinite Advantage: William Taylor's California Experiences* (Scarecrow Press, 2010), and scholarly articles in American religious history, some of which appear in the *Encyclopedia of Religion in America* (CQ Press, 2011) and the *Encyclopedia of Christian Civilization* (Wiley-Blackwell, 2011). In 2010 Dr. Bob resigned his faculty post to join the staff of World Impact. He and his wife Chris now serve in Los Angeles as licensed ministers of the Gospel. They have a daughter, Rebekah, whose husband Jorge Veitia is founder and Executive Director of The Life of Freedom Center of Miami, serving the victims of human trafficking. Bob and Chris are the proud grandparents of Isaac (b.2012) and Benaiah (b.2014)